Consultancy in the United Kingdom

Education and Alienation Series

Series Editor: Neville Jones, Principal Educational Psychologist, Oxfordshire

Consultancy in the United Kingdom:

Its Role and Contribution to Educational Change

Edited by

Carol Aubrey

The Falmer Press

(A member of the Taylor & Francis Group)
London • New York • Philadelphia

UK   The Falmer Press, Rankine Road, Basingstoke, Hants RG24 0PR

USA   The Falmer Press, Taylor & Francis Inc., 1900 Frost Road, Suite 101, Bristol, PA 19007

© Selection and editorial material copyright C. Aubrey 1990

First published 1990

British Library Cataloguing in Publication Data
Consultancy in the United Kingdom: its role and contribution to
  educational change — (Education and alienation series)
  1. Great Britain. Schools. Education consultants
  I. Aubrey, Carol II. Series
  371.2'07

  ISBN 1–85000–434–X
  ISBN 1–85000–435–8 pbk

Library of Congress Cataloging-in-Publication Data
Consultancy in the United Kingdom: its role and contribution to
  educational change/edited by Carol Aubrey.
      p.   cm.––(Education and alienation series)
  Includes bibliographical references.
  ISBN 1–85000–434–X. –– ISBN 1–85000–435–8 (pbk.)
  1. Educational consultants––Great Britain. 2. School
  improvement programs––Great Britain––Case studies. 3.
  Oxfordshire Disaffected Pupil Programme. I. Aubrey, Carol. II.
  Series.
  LB2799.3.G7C66   1990
  371.2'07––dc20

Jacket design by Caroline Archer

Typeset in 10/12 Garamond by
Chapterhouse, The Cloisters, Formby L37 3PX

Printed in Great Britain by
Redwood Burn Limited, Trowbridge, Wiltshire

Contents

Preface

As schools have entered a new era of in-service training they have drawn increasingly on a wider range of professional skills — both from within schools and without. Large numbers of new professionals are being invited to train teachers on short, half-day or day courses or for more extended periods in the role of consultant. Whilst schools and the educational system do not have a history of using a professional consultancy, there exists already a well-developed tradition and a professional literature in this area, which is available to those seeking information, guidance or extension of existing professional skills. The writers in this book have both formal knowledge and a considerable practical experience and expertise in educational consultancy. It is hoped, therefore, that the book will serve as both an introduction to those interested in gaining professional knowledge of this area and as a guide to those already providing such a service to schools, who wish to reflect on their own existing skills and practice.

Neville Jones
Director
Oxfordshire Disaffected Pupil Programme

Editor's Introduction

Many definitions of consultation and of its application to educational problems exist. A number of characteristics can be isolated. Among those generally agreed can be identified the provision of an independent and objective professional service in identifying organizational problems, analyzing situations, recommending action and solutions, and, if required, helping in the implementation of such solutions. Practical assistance or advice on the content, processes or structure of tasks or procedures may be given to the client organization.

Traditionally consultancy has been used in commerce and industry. From its origins in private business, consultancy has spread to the public sector. In fact, it can be used in all sectors of society and in all sorts and sizes of organization. It may involve introducing new techniques or expertise. It may provide for gaps in technical or managerial knowledge or may help in the planning and coordinating of new policy.

Current organizations, even those with strong and successful practice may call on consultants in order to fine-tune or enhance existing managerial and staff skills. This has led to the identification of different types of problem situation. The consultant may be asked to remedy or rectify a deteriorated situation. This is the *corrective problem*, the commonest and best known, which calls for immediate attention to troubleshoot or track down the cause or reason for reduced performance and, hopefully to restore, if not improve, the previous condition. Taking an existing situation and improving it will involve the consultant with a *progressive problem*. Here the task will be to identify means of improving procedures — technological, procedural, financial or personnel — in order to realize higher, yet still realistic targets, in one or more areas. *Creative problems* may be generated more from a desire for change or a fresh and novel approach than from any identifiable existing shortcoming. Often consultancy on such assignments will carry elements of all three types of problem. Successful tackling of a corrective problem may stimulate the addressing of a progressive or creative one; a progressive problem, on the other hand, may reveal the need for corrective measures.

Whilst consultancy developed originally as an external service where the consultant is administratively and legally independent of the client organization, some organizations in the public and private sector use internal and external consultants. Internal consultants have the advantage of detailed knowledge of the organization's politics, procedures and relationships though this may be at the expense of some degree of impartiality and objectivity. In some cases, too, the internal consultant may lack the necessary technical skills.

Thus two dimensions of the consulting approach can be seen: the technical and the human. In practice these two dimensions cannot be separated and by bringing about organizational change in dealing with a specific technical problem, the consultant deals, too, with human problems and human responses to change.

In summary, the consultant's job starts with a perceived need for help in problem-solving a situation which needs improvement and, ideally, leads to change and development in efficiency and performance. If diverse consultation services share any common characteristics it is the agreed objective to plan and implement organizational change.

This is set against a background of unprecendented rates of general economic, social and technological change during the 1980s. In education specifically this has been reflected in changing demands in the labour market, developments in information technology and adaptations to a fully multicultural society. It has been an era of increased accountability and performance indicators, with the development of school self-evaluation and changes in funding and forms of in-service provision, not to mention the new GCSE examination. Now the Education Reform Act 1988 will increase this still further with vast investment in in-service training over the next five years for the National Curriculum and associated assessment and testing, together with substantial training generated by the introduction of local management in schools. Over the same period will come the introduction of records of achievement and increased demands for the induction of new, licensed teachers. Whilst there is little tradition in the British educational system for the practice of bringing in expert help — an outside, objective view of a specific problem — potentially there will be a climate for increasing use in education of various kinds of consultant.

Part 1
Nature and Scope of Consultancy

1
An Overview of Consultation

Carol Aubrey

Consultation is an indirect service which takes place between equal professionals of coordinate status. It is initiated by the client, who has total freedom to accept or reject the services at any point. It involves the consultant and client in a confidential, collaborative relationship which is shaped by consultant goals to:

1 offer an objective point of view;
2 help to increase problem-solving skills;
3 help to extend the client's freedom of choice in action;
4 support the client in choices made;
5 increase the client's awareness of the resources available to deal with persistent problems.

The Consultant's Roles

The consultant will assume two mutually supportive roles. The consultant's assignment will probably arise from a specialist knowledge or expertise in a particular area but beyond the purely technical the consultant must know about the relationship between technology and management and the complexity of the social and psychological aspects of change in organizations. Without knowledge of the social sciences and their methodologies the consultant could not operate as an effective change agent. Therefore the consultant will adopt two basic roles — the resource consultant and the process consultant.

The resource consultant provides expert knowledge and information or recommends a particular course of action to improve the performance of the organization. This will depend upon accurate diagnosis of needs, provision of the appropriate knowledge or assistance and the successful implementation of the recommended changes by the client. It depends, too, upon effective communication between consultant and client and successful change in attitudes and behaviour of individuals and groups and subsequently change in organizational performance.

The process consultant's skills are contrasted with those of the resource consultant which aim to provide technical skills with regard to a specific problem but do not aim to change the organizational skills or relationships of organizational members. The process consultant will attempt to pass on methods, approaches and values so the organization can diagnose and remedy its own problems. The consultant may collaborate with the school, or sub-group within the school, to improve organizational functioning by concentrating on procedural problems through examination of communications, interaction patterns, roles and norms, decision-making or style of leadership which is affecting task performance and morale.

Consultant Skills

Whilst the two roles are separated for discussion in the context of consulting practice the human and technological dimension cannot be separated and an appreciation of this will be central to the consultant's effectiveness. Consultation thus has the ultimate goal of increasing managerial competence and organizational performance and as such carries a strong training element. Central to the success of this is the quality of the collaborative relationship established between consultant and client and the consulting modes which require active involvement from the client. At one level this involves the consultant's relationship-building and interpersonal skills of warmth, empathy and genuineness, at another it utilizes group training exercises and simulations to improve communication skills, negotiation of goals, identification and resolution of conflict and practice in conducting effective meetings.

At both individual and group level, skills of effective communication are crucial. Training procedures may include: techniques of active listening — acknowledging, paraphrasing and summarizing; the use of questions to clarify and elaborate; and giving and receiving positive and negative feedback in a tentative and non-judgmental way, which serves both to highlight possible inaccuracies and inconsistencies in the client's or consultant's perception and to describe behaviour which appears to be impeding the consultancy process.

Training may also take place as an intervention technique to assist the change proposed by the assignment. This may involve developing skills in action planning, such as searching for solutions or evaluating alternatives. Training services offered to client organizations will vary and workshops focusing on methodology, for instance problem-solving and other skills, can be effective provided they are based on practical experience and focus on an agreed, priority problem.

It must be appreciated, however, that while training may be effective in transmitting new ideas and in teaching some new skills, this will not be sufficient training for clients to start applying what has been learned in new situations. Training and consultation are so close that it is more accurate to say that consultant assistance will consist of providing professional help in mastering and applying a broad range of intervention methods.

Kubr (1983) has suggested that the following intellectual and personal qualities are the key attributes for a would-be consultant:

1 *Intellectual ability:*
   — ability to learn quicky and easily;
   — ability to observe, gather, select and evaluate facts;
   — good judgments;
   — inductive and deductive reasoning;
   — ability to synthesize and generalize;
   — creative imagination;
   — original thinking.

2 *Ability to understand people and work with them:*
   — respect for other people, tolerance;
   — ability to anticipate and evaluate human reaction;
   — easy human contacts;
   — ability to gain trust and respect;
   — courtesy and good manners.

3 *Ability to communicate, persuade and motivate:*
   — stability of behaviour and action;
   — facility in oral and written communication;
   — ability to teach and train people;
   — ability to persuade and motivate.

4 *Intellectual and emotional maturity:*
   — stability of behaviour and action;
   — independence in drawing unbiased conclusions;
   — ability to withstand pressures and live with frustrations and uncertainty;
   — ability to act with poise and in a calm objective manner;
   — self-control in all situations;
   — flexibility and adaptability to changed conditions.

5 *Personal drive and initiative:*
   — right degree of self-confidence;
   — healthy ambition;
   — entrepreneurial spirits;
   — courage, initiative and perseverance in action.

6 *Ethics and integrity:*
   — genuine desire to help others;
   — extreme honesty;
   — ability to recognize the limitations of one's competence;
   — ability to admit mistakes and learn from failure.

7 *Physical and mental health:*
   — ability to sustain the specific working and living conditions of the consultant's work.

Further, as Kubr (1983) noted, the consultant must be extremely flexible in his leadership role, which can be best described along a directive and non-directive continuum. In the purely non-directive role the consultant may encourage the client to make decisions by asking reflective questions to help clarify, modify or change a situation. He may act as process specialist in helping the client develop interpersonal and group skills, and to initiate relevant tasks and activities for organizational development. He may influence the client in choice of data gathering and presentation techniques and generally propose criteria for assessing identified alternative courses of action. Thus, in the problem-solving processes the consultant will offer collaboration and assistance to the client whilst at the same time maintaining objectivity and balance. This will contrast with a more directive role towards the client in the choice of methods and techniques to be employed for problem-solving or in delivering technical expertise, and in the designing of appropriate training exercises and experiences.

The Consultant–Client Relationship

The first step is to clarify the problem for which the consultant's services have been solicited. This entails ensuring the consultant can concur with the client's definition of the problem situation. Next the client and consultant must establish the exact nature of the consultancy assignment, what it should achieve and how this will be measured. Respective roles and commitment at various stages of the assignment must be agreed, at the same time leaving enough flexibility to allow for any necessary modifications to the original plan. A direct contract between the consultant and person or persons acting on behalf of the organization is essential. In the case of school consultation the consultant must know:

1 who holds the real power for making decisions relating to the assignment at all stages (whether the head teacher, governors or local authority);
2 who has the main interest in the success or failure of the assignment (depending on the nature of the assignment, this might be the head teacher, deputies, faculty or departmental heads);
3 whose direct collaboration is essential.

If it is taken for granted that the head teacher is the main client, this may upset the senior management team who will have ultimate responsibility for implementing the change. This means the consultant must seek continually to refine his or her understanding of the roles played by various people.

The Consulting Process

In the sense that all models of consultation aim to generate the best possible solution to a presenting problem, all models of consultation are problem-solving models. Common to all are the following stages:

1 problem identification;
2 problem analysis;
3 plan implementation;
4 problem evaluation.

Definitions and analyses of presenting problems, intervention strategies and methods of follow-up, with corrective feedback, vary from model to model. A simple five-stage model can be used which incorporates the role of the consultant from the first contact with the client to the withdrawal: entry, diagnosis, action planning, implementation and termination.

Entry

This stage includes making initial contacts with the client, undertaking a preliminary problem diagnosis, drawing up an assignment plan, making a proposal to the client which leads to a consulting contract being signed, if both parties are in agreement to continue. It is the time when the consultant must convince the client that she or he possesses the relevant technical skills and expertise but, perhaps more importantly, it is the time when the basis for a successful relationship is being established. The consultant must determine how the client can be assisted with the organization, clarify respective roles and begin planning and preparation.

During the initial contacts the consultant must make sure she or he is dealing with the key person in the organization, who has both the power to make available the relevant facts for this preliminary investigation, and who has an interest and understanding in the consultation assignment.

If the consultant and client decide they can work together profitably, then the client will signal agreement to a preliminary diagnosis taking place. Terms of reference will need to be agreed, a decision reached on the scope of the preliminary diagnosis and the mode of presentation of the proposals, together with discussion regarding the fee to be paid. Agreement must be reached on the information and records to be made available to the consultant, which staff shall be seen and when, which further data should be made available and what techniques are approved for data collection.

The scope of the preliminary diagnosis will depend on the type of problem. A very specific problem of a technical nature may not require a very detailed and wide-ranging survey, though the consultant will, nevertheless, beware of accepting a narrow, prescribed problem definition. If the problem is broad and general in nature, then a longer and more comprehensive survey will be essential. In practice, it is unlikely that the consultant will have reached a clear decision on the nature of the problem. It will need to be viewed from different staff perspectives within the organization. Human dimensions of technical issues will need to be borne in mind. Relationships between major issues surrounding the presenting problem will need to be examined in the hope of teasing out cause and effect.

The consultant will take a comprehensive view of the organization. Maher (1982) has suggested the school organization as client can be conceptualized as a programme consisting of four kinds of resources: human, technological, informational and financial. Human resources are the staff, management team and related personnel. Technological resources will comprise methods and materials utilized to deal with the instrumental needs of the wide range of pupils catered for. Informational resources provide the policies, procedures and performance data to assist in making decisions about programmes. Informational resources give structure to the human resources and provide evaluation data regarding the effective use of technological resources. Financial resources refer to individual school, local authority or central government funds allocated to provide effective education to children.

The consultant will examine relationships between major functions and activities. This may involve looking at the four related resource areas to provide an organizational framework and may include complementing this functional approach with a more detailed examination of individual or group level practice. If the identified problem lies in a specific, technical area it is likely the survey will be more focused in scope. A useful tool of analysis is comparison. The consultant may wish to examine the trend of the organization's performance by studying previous performance or looking at present achievement in terms of the client's plans for the future. The consultant may draw for comparison on data from other similar school organizations and, likewise, his own case experience will provide yardsticks for comparison.

An alternative approach is to use this preliminary stage for staff training in problem identification. Here, workshops will be provided for groups to develop their own lists of problems requiring attention which are taken for discussion and comparison to the larger organization group, in order to agree a priority list. Futher group sessions are convened for more detailed analyses of the priority problem list which, as before, are referred back to the larger group for a final comparison. The desired goal is a collectively agreed definition of the problem and a plan of action acceptable to all groups represented.

Whatever the technique employed to make the preliminary problem diagnosis, the end-product will be an assignment plan. The conclusions are summarized and the consultant offers his/her analysis of the problem, set within the context of the consultant's investigations undertaken. The plan then describes the objectives to be achieved and actions to be taken. The stages of the problem-solving sequence, as outlined, offer a useful framework. Roles and responsibilities will need to be carefully defined and a time-scale agreed. Agreement will have to be reached about what activities and meetings will take place, what training will be involved and which groups convened. As mentioned by Gray (1988), in schools periods of examination and holidays get in the way of long-term planning and momentum may be difficult to maintain.

Normally the proposal will be presented in the context of a meeting in order that points can be raised, queries dealt with and comments made. Usually the agreement to go ahead will be in the form of a contract or letter of agreement.

Diagnosis

This is a detailed phase of fact finding, data collection and analysis in which it is hoped that client and consultant will agree the nature of the change that is required, whether technological, organizational, informational or behavioural, and the likely response to change of personnel involved. The very fact of exploring the problem may influence attitudes and lead to changes in work behaviour.

The problem will need to be described in observable and measurable terms, in terms of its location in the organization and its relative magnitude, in terms of organizational performance, its present duration and future implications, and in terms of its effect on key staff in the organization. Hypotheses will be established on possible causation of the problem and on the client's attidues to, and potential available for, solving the problem. This is a necessary preliminary to collecting data as it defines what facts are required, which processes need examination, whose views are obtained and what practices observed.

Data will be collected in three main forms:

— *records* — of people and performance, of materials and resources, of policies, processes and procedures;
— *events, activities and conditions* — in terms of frequency, duration, trends and context;
— *views, attitudes, recollections* — which include fact, opinion, prejudice and even insight.

Existing records can be supplemented with requests from particular groups for special reports on specific issues or aspects of the problem. Observation can be made of events, performances, groups processes or individual behaviours. In addition to questionnaires, interviews and data gathering meetings, the consultant will record impressions of the personal qualities, social behavioiur and styles of work of management and staff. Throughout the period of consultation a diary record will supplement other recorded information in providing further detail on the sequence and significance of events.

Before analyzing the data the consultant must be confident of their accuracy, completeness and reliability. Some attempt at classification of both qualititative and quantititative data will be essential in order to reveal relationships, to make comparisons and to determine trends. Evidence for causal relationships between conditions and events will be sought as this information is central to the planning and implementation of change. However, the difficulties should not be underestimated and even when an association has been established between variables, this does not argue for a cause–effect relationship. Similarly, just as multiple causes can lead to one effect, several effects may result from one cause. The goal of this stage is to form a synthesis of significant relationships, comparisions and trends in order to identify key dimensions of change, whether technological, organizational, informational or behavioural. Conclusions will be drawn from the problem diagnosis and the sort of change that is required will be emerging at the end of this phase.

Action planning

This phase concentrates on problem solution. It involves work on alternative solutions, evaluation of alternatives and the eventual presentation of a plan for implementing change. It is essential that this phase has the complete commitment of the client. It provides an opportunity for harnessing staff expertise and creativity in examining alternatives, and this will both increase staff motivation and identification with the proposed change and offer further training opportunities in the search for ideas and information to obtain the best solution. Considerations will include the nature and complexity of the technical characteristics of the problem, whether new or novel solutions must be generated or whether an established solution is available with or without modification.

Once all the known facts have been obtained and the problems stated in alternative forms, creative thinking can be mobilized to generate a phase of idea production, which will later be subjected to a stage of idea evaluation to identify a best solution. Brain storming, attribute listing or synectics are just some of the many techniques available which can be used as a springboard to generate new ideas rapidly and uncritically, as a prelude to recombining and developing the ideas for others before a final stage of idea evaluation.

Whatever the circumstances or conditions employed to generate alternative solutions, the outcome will usually be a shortlist of two or three alternatives. In practice it is likely there will need to be a balance made of positive and negative consequences of each, according to some identified criteria. Some will not be directly quantifiable and others will not admit direct comparison. The best resolution to these difficulties may be the use of a panel of experts from the organization whose task it is to assign some value to the particular criteria.

Ultimately, it is the client's decision as to which solution will be adopted and the consultant's responsibility to present a detailed picture of solutions considered and an honest account of risks involved and the conditions which must be maintained to sustain the proposed change.

Implementation

The consultant may not be involved at all in the implementation phase. The problem may be relatively straightforward and the client may need no further assistance. There may be an agreement for further, planned visits to check progress and to offer advice where necessary. It is quite common for staff to need training for new methods or techniques which may, or may not, be provided by the consultant. Staff development may include seminars, workshops and discussion groups or very detailed and specific training programmes.

Original plans may need modifying and new problems may emerge which had not been foreseen. Resistance from staff may be stronger than was anticipated. For all these reasons it is desirable for the consultant to maintain involvement in the implementation phase. Sometimes, however, the client may wish to terminate the relationship at this point since what was wanted was a report, rather than a change.

Termination

The final stage of the consultation process involves the consultant's withdrawal. This will take place when the client and consultant agree that the assignment is completed, will proceed without further consultant assistance or the assignment will not proceed beyond the report stage.

The most important part of the termination stage is evaluation. As at previous stages this is a joint enterprise between client and consultant and involves evaluating both the assignment and the consultant's performance. Typically the benefits to the client will include the acquisition of new skills, for instance, problem-solving or managerial skills, or specific technical skills. New systems changes may be introduced at the policy or procedural level in the curriculum or appraisal areas and these will lead to outcomes in changed behaviour. New performances can be expected from changes in the examination system or methods of recording and profiling which can be observed at the individual level, departmental or faculty level or school level.

The evaluation of the consultation process will involve the design of the assignment, the range and quality of consultant inputs, the nature of the consulting mode or client–consultant relationship and the overall management of the assignment by the client and consultant. Whilst the outcomes of the change itself may be quantifiable, obtaining opinion from interview or questionnaire may be important in evaluating the consultant–client relationship and the consulting style.

The evaluation will be summarized in a short report or included in the final assignment report before termination. There may be an agreement to undertake a further, follow-up evaluation in six to twelve months time. Final reports are presented and the consultant–client relationship concluded. At this point the consultant withdraws, the assignment is terminated and contract completed.

References

GRAY, H. L. (1988) *Management Consultancy in Schools*, London, Cassell.

KUBR, M. (Ed.) (1983) *Management Consulting: A Guide to the Profession*, Geneva, International Labour Office.

MAHER, C. A. and ILLBACK, R. J. (1982) 'Organisational school psychology: issues and considerations', *Journal of School Psychology*, **20**, pp. 244–53.

2
Consultation and Change in Educational Settings

Carol Aubrey

Introduction

Three years ago I gave up working as an educational psychologist to organize a part-time Master's degree course in learning and behaviour problems in schools, delivered from a systems perspective. As the course had a traditional focus on institutional change I proposed that individual students as agents of change in their own institutions should have training in the role of internal consultant, using a problem-solving model of investigation to assist in identifying priority educational needs in their own schools. Aims were two-fold:

1 to obtain personal change in the individual student in terms of cognitive, behaviour and affective/interpersonal skills;
2 to obtain institutional change in the student's 'home' school organization, which would lead to the development of improved policies, procedures, programmes or practices for pupils with behaviour or learning difficulties.

The broad goal was to enhance the quality of education for these children. It would involve collaborating with school colleagues and close liaison with senior members of staff.

Course material was influenced by, and derived from, a range of knowledge bases: organizational psychology, social psychology and sociology, applied behavioural analysis, programme planning and evaluation, school organization development, management theory and educational research. Goals for student education (development of knowledge) and training (development of skills) to which particular methods of instruction were linked, were separated into three domains: cognitive goals, behavioural goals and affective/interpersonal goals. Cognitive goals included:

(a) development of the knowledge of a school as a social, political and educational institution;

(b) development of the knowledge of the school as an open system utilizing areas of organizational development change;

(c) development of understanding of role theory and pupil/teacher interactions;

(d) development of understanding of relevant areas of social psychology;

(e) development of an understanding of the historical bases of movements in manpower shortages and service delivery in community, clinical and educational psychology;

(f) development of an understanding of the role of the consultant and indirect service delivery;

(g) development of increasing knowledge of classroom management and effective instruction;

(h) development of knowledge about programme planning and evaluation, data analysis and educational research methodology.

Behavioural goals included development in:

(a) organizational approaches to assessment;

(b) effective classroom organization and management;

(c) effective instructional strategies;

(d) effective behaviour management techniques.

Affective/interpersonal goals included development of an appreciation for more cooperative working relationships with colleagues and relevant personal skills in communication and interpersonal problem-solving.

Teaching methods included traditional lectures to present factual information, theories, principles and their applications, and to demonstrate strategies and skills. Group discussions provided an arena to examine the implications of reading and course material in students' own 'home' schools and tutorials offered a more detailed and individualized focus on the application of course work to the student's own work situation.

Practical experiences included the use of video, with follow-up individual, pair and group activities to address individual problem behaviours and to examine pastoral or counselling procedures. At the systems level, focusing on change in organizational procedures, students' practical experience included training exercises and simulations to explore interaction patterns, leadership and communication, decision-making and team-building, and procedures for conducting effective meetings, and confronting and managing conflict.

Assignments included work-type activities to develop practical interventions for dealing with individual pupil problem behaviour and two school-based studies, the first an in-school review and the second adopting a problem-solving approach to instigate some institutional change in the student's own school.

This became for me, as well as the students, a valuable learning experience on the nature of individual and institutional change. Change is the purpose of all consultation and can take place at many levels, with the consultant working with individual teachers, or at the sub-group level or up to the school organizational level. Organizational factors which may affect the consultant's successful implementation of change will be both internal and external. This was true both for me as a university lecturer working in a particular context and for the students. The school, as Gallessich (1973) suggested, is itself caught up under complex and continually changing environmental pressures. The values and decisions of central government, for instance, over the last ten or so years have exerted the most profound influence in schools. At the local educational authority level, the consultant needs to know if his school is regarded by the advisory staff or local inspectorate as, for example, high status, marginal, maverick or declining, and whether this results in special favours, trust, autonomy, surveillance or plain ignoring. The key variable, here, will be the competence and status of the head teacher. Governors, parents and community groups or the local training institution, however, will all exert other environmental pressures.

Internal forces acting on the institution will be both the formal and informal structure of the organization, its leadership, framework of roles and responsibilities and, less visible, the informal norms, powerful informal leaders, the strengths, biases and coping patterns of sub-groups, alliances based on historical conflict and emergent alliances.

In terms of the particular course in question, under the pressures of external forces, its original goals became transformed out of all recognition in the second year of my leadership, under the twin exigencies of course amalgamation resulting from the collapse of full-time funding for practising teachers, and the university reorganization of the pattern of delivery for higher degree courses to conform to a modular structure. All the original impetus to develop institutional change strategies was lost under the pressure to provide short, focused courses in identifiable and non-overlapping curriculum areas.

With respect to internal forces on student attempts at impact and innovation in their own schools, the scope for institutional interventions — with the exception of those of two head teachers and a deputy head (who sent two year-heads on the course the following year) — was limited to the area of their work specialism or responsibility, and without reference to the overall system organizational development or restructuring. As Medway (1975) noted with regard to external consultants:

> Presently there is no recognition or overt acceptance of persons concerned predominantly with facilitating change in schools, nor is there reward, incentive, or acknowledgement contingent upon the initiation and communication of . . . educational alternatives. Whatever impetus for modifying school procedure exists is diffused (as opposed to shared) among administrative, teaching, and special service groups. Each group institutes changes only within its own designated speciality without regard to ultimate system effects. This has resulted in an unsystematic, atheoretical, and reactive pre-occupation with symptoms (e.g. absenteeism, misconduct, poor achievement, etc.) rather than causes of psycho-educational malfunctioning . . . (p. 20)

Over a two-year period, twenty out of twenty-seven students successfully carried out behavioural interventions with individual children in schools, and fourteen out of twenty-seven carried out some intervention or improvement to a policy, practice or procedure within the area of their responsibility. Six students attending the course over the two years, were not in a position to carry out interventions, being overseas students on leave or indigenous students 'between jobs'. Interventions included provision of more preventive approaches to truancy, modifications to homework systems, the introduction of counselling, modifications to classroom management and extension of staff support, increases in parental involvement, the introduction of a token economy system in a special-school setting, a review of a special needs department curricula for less-able 15–16-year-olds.

Most students within an appropriate work context were able to introduce effective intervention with individual pupils and, on a post-course questionnaire, claimed the factors which hindered them most in the success of these interventions, were lack of time or lack of opportunity in terms of rate of contact with target pupils.

In terms of the broader policy or procedural intervention, again, adjusting for those students unable to undertake an innovation, 70 per cent of the students reported the introduction of some successful school change. Whilst lack of time, again, figured as a factor hindering change, the main factor reported was staff resistance. One student fairly commented on the need for further staff training in order the extend the use of behavioural approaches but still noted that staff willingness, as well as ability, would affect success. Some individual comments were made about recommendations being blocked or head teachers feeling 'threatened', others reasonably reported being 'new' in the institution, 'not in a position' to guide staff or recognized that staff might genuinely not share the same educational philosophy or have confidence in the innovation. Most comments related to the staffs' lack of openness to change, either in attitude or behaviour. Reluctance to cooperate, suspicion of the consultant's motives, dismissal as someone else's problem, failure to recognize the issue as a whole school problem, and taking a negative view of pupils, all were cited as reasons for staff's lack of involvement. Whilst some staff were willing to discuss the merits of a new procedure, on the whole they were less willing to try it out in the classroom situation.

Three main conclusions may be drawn from this experience of training internal consultants. Firstly, unless the change agent is in a position of formal leadership or authority, it may be difficult to effect change beyond the sub-group or sub-system of work specialism and responsibility and thus to influence organizational change. Moreover there may be a tendency for the internal consultant to focus on the symptom rather than to take an overview and examine underlying causes. In terms of organizational factors, the school effectiveness literature is clear in identifying the leader as focal point for innovation but less clear on what constitutes effective leadership (see Bickel and Bickel, 1986). Purkey and Smith (1983) review of the literature shows leadership as one of a set of organizational factors supported and driven by process variables. These process variables have been elaborated by Fullan (1985) as: (i) a feel for the improvement process by the leadership, something akin to Schon's (1983) 'reflection in action'; (ii) an explicit value system, shared goals and a sense of community; and (iii) collaborative planning, whether internally generated or with the assistance of external agents of change.

The second conclusion that may be drawn from the experience of training internal consultants is that successful consultation — and hence change — takes a considerable amount of time. School organizations have a tendency to look for short answers and organization development takes a long time. Fullan, Miles and Taylor, (1980) in their review of organization development in schools as a change strategy for organization self-development and renewal, agree that limited interventions which address only part of the organization or problem are not valid:

> Since OD (organization development) not only has to address, but to balance a number of complex factors — individual and organisation, content and process, task and structure, and so forth — over a long period of time, it is understandable that OD has had uneven success, especially since most definitions of OD do not stress the problem of balance.

They conclude:

> knowledge about OD cumulates slowly. Any given project takes at least 2 to 3 years... The complexity of organisations and change processes, and the diverse state of present organisation theory, retards the development of good OD theory.

The third conclusion to be drawn from the course training relates to the second: the fundamental dimension of organization change is human. People must be willing and able to undertake the intervention and this involves acquiring new knowledge and information, learning new skills, but above all, changing attitudes and values. Lewin (1947) has likened change in people to a three-stage sequence of 'unfreezing', 'changing' and 'refreezing'. Unfreezing describes an unsettled condition which recognizes the need for change, changing involves the effort to try out the new changes and the gradual acceptance of an internalization of the new practice, followed by a refreezing, when the new behaviour has been internalized and is maintained.

Adjusting to new conditions or procedures reasonably causes a certain amount of stress or discomfort, individuals may fear failure or inadequacy, or simply fear the unknown, some may particularly dislike imposed change or surprises, some may not trust or respect the change agent, some may genuinely feel the change is unneccessary. In the case of innovation generated by the group of students discussed above, although there had been a problem in the identification stage, change might well have been perceived by staff as motivated by the students' own course assessment needs rather than the needs of the institution. That said, as Gallesich (1973) noted, a key variable in successful consultation is the consultant's skill in assessing the organization in which she or he is working. His or her values, motives, competencies and vulnerabilities in interaction with organizational factors are central to his/her assessment and decision-making. A successful intervention presupposes an accurate assessment of the need for change *and* a readiness for change.

Sarason (1967) suggested that some of the most interesting and important aspects of the processes of change are revealed before the point of implementation of proposals for change is reached, not only in the way they affect implementation but in the degree to which they result in no implementation at all. It was his contention that the fate of any single proposal for change will be determined in part by the number of previous changes which have been proposed but never implemented. This is because those involved react not only to the proposal in hand but in the light of their previous knowledge of other proposals, implemented or otherwise, and particularly in terms of the satisfaction or dissatisfaction these previous proposals generated.

Reilly (1978) took a more cynical view. He suggested even successfully implemented innovative programmes have a 'half life of 1–3 years and most will be externally funded'. Most clear-cut changes that have taken place in our society and schools have been the result of unanticipated spin-offs from various developments, technological and otherwise. First, he suggested a definition of system is needed to examine the adoption process. There are at least two types of change: first-order and second-order. First-order change is that change which occurs within a given system which itself remains unchanged (i.e. function change). This was the level of change initiated by most of the students. Second-order change is one whose occurrence changes the system itself (i.e. structural change). Reilly has suggested that a school system itself, by and large, cannot generate from within itself the conditions for its own change; it cannot produce the rules for the change of its own rules. School system change generally comes from the environment rather than the system itself. Thus, for Reilly, a third aspect of change is that system change must be introduced from outside the system. From this he concludes that a systems need assessment and action proposal of first-order change will more likely be accepted by school personnel, but not result in significantly altering the situation. Recommendations of second-order change, calling for system change, will most likely not be accepted, nor diffused throughout the whole system!

Resistance to Change

Resistance to treatment is regarded as a central problem in psycho-dynamic theory and more recently behavioural psychologists as well as clinical therapists have looked for similar explanations for clients' resistance to the process of behaviour change (Jahn and Lichstein, 1980). Piersel and Gutkin (1983) have suggested that clients' reluctance to engage in the problem-solving sequence may be conceptualized in terms of social learning theory (Bandura, 1969) or cognitive behavioural modification (Meichenbaum, 1977). It has already been noted that change causes anxiety and discomfort. In behavioural terms the client's resistance is seen as avoidance of consultation, which is regarded as potentially punishing and negative, or at the very least, inadequate in reinforcement.

Effective consultation requires considerable investment in time and effort on the part of the client before any long-term benefits accrue. From the point of view of a busy teacher the best solution may well be the one which involves least involvement. Further consultation sessions must take place at lunch times or after school and thus intrude work-problems further into preparation or relaxation time. Since consultation involves collaborative problem-solving, teachers may be unsettled by role ambiguity and anxious at the possibility of their being observed in the classroom, at meetings or in other interpersonal contexts. Consultation models, which assume the actual implementation is the client's responsibility, similarly lead the client to feel inadequate should the intervention prove unsuccessful. In spite of a primary aim of consultation being the improvement of client skills, in the short term teachers may feel the consultation process aversive and non-rewarding. From a social pyschological perspective, the best strategy for the consultant in minimizing feelings of client conflict will be to clarify as far as possible the scope of each professional's responsibilities and functions, how roles may overlap and the best means to resolve conflict which could reduce efficiency.

Recently, the social psychological theory of reactance has been explored as a means of dealing with client resistance, (Brehm, 1966). Brehm postulated that 'people have the subjective experience of freedom to do what they want, to do it in the way they want, and to do it when they want in regard to limited and specifiable areas of behaviour'. When people experience threats to their freedom they experience psychological reactance, which is a motivational state directed towards restoring the threatened freedom (similar to resistance to consultation, as described above). In order to minimize reactance the consultant will use verbal persuasion, which, to be effective, will have to exceed the client's perceived threat to his/her freedom to choose other behaviours.

The concepts of persuasion, power and influence can be applied to the consultation process and may provide a framework for enhancing the competence and maximizing the personal influence of the consultant. French and Raven (1959) provided a classification of forms of social power which lead to social change: reward power, coercive power, legitimate power, expert power and referent power. Influence is regarded as the successful application of that power. The consultant as 'boundary role' professional carries out his/her roles and functions in a range of organizational contexts or work units and has little formal authority over the clients encountered. Thus, as noted by Illback and Maher (1984) the consultant must rely on sources of personal power and expertise to gain influence. Expert power is gained from professional standing or status, while referent power is achieved from credibility acquired through effective interpersonal skills. Martin (1978) has suggested that the most influential persons are those who have more than one source of power, though accentuation of expert power should be tempered by an emphasis on commonalities between the consultant and client, in case identification becomes difficult and consultant attractiveness declines.

Implementing Organizational Change

The resistance to change section has focused on individual responses but as noted by Katz and Kahn (1967) a major error in dealing with problems of organizational change at the practical and theoretical level has been the tendency to disregard the systemic properties of the organization and to confuse individual change with modifications in organizational variables.

In terms of educational change Dalin and Rust (1983) have identified the individual school as the organizational unit of formal education and the prime force for genuine change. During the 1960s numerous attempts were made across the US, western Europe and Scandinavia to 'develop' schools. Research and development centres were established to supply applied research, and often local teams were provided to adapt and diffuse the reforms in curriculum classroom management or teaching materials. In practice, the educational consumers were resistant to these innovations from external sources, as they had not been actively involved in defining their own needs, setting goals and participating in programme development.

Havelock's (1971) review of the literature on change and development suggested three different models: the Research, Development and Diffusion model; the Social Interaction model; and the Problem-solving model. His description of the Research, Development and Diffusion model aptly defines features of the research and development centres that many nations established at this time, whatever individual modifications were made in response to particular socio-cultural circumstances. It was assumed the evaluation and application of a large-scale, empirically-grounded innovation would follow a rational sequence, with costly and lengthy planning, by division and coordination of labour, delivered to a rational, educational practitioner, who was a more or less passive consumer and who would accept the presumed long-term benefits of the innovation, if it were offered in the right place at the right time. This model, named the 'centre-periphery'model, was used for many Nuffield and early Schools Council projects.

Later Schools Council projects bore more resemblance to Havelock's 'periphery–periphery' Social Interaction model, which moves from a central team to intermediate agencies, such as teachers' centres, which were being developed at this time. This model proposes an individual user who belongs to a network of social relationships which influence his or her acceptance of the new ideas. Group membership and identification are good predictors of potential individual adoption, and the rate of diffusion follows an S-shaped pattern: very slow at first, followed by a rapid phase, and a final long, late adoption period. Like the Research, Development and Diffusion model, this model is suited better to a subject-based innovation, rather than a systems-based change.

If a whole-school approach is to be adopted then Havelock's third, Problem-Solving, 'periphery–centre' model is more suitable. This assumes self-initiated innovation will have the best chance of survival and user need is of paramount importance. The outside change agent, in this case, is non-directive and internal resources are fully utilized in needs diagnosis which is integrated in the change process. The outside consultant may offer training in group processes and support in developing problem-solving skills. The collaborative and interactive nature of this model with its emphasis on the process of problem-solving bears resemblance to the consultation model advocated in Chapter 1, and its focus on institutional growth and development is precisely the strategy used for organization development (Schmuck *et al.*, 1977).

The models offer little in the way of description of the agent of change, though later, Havelock (1973) described 'psychological wholeness' in attitudes, knowledge and skills, as an essential characteristic of the change agent. A later model, the *Linkage* model, attempted to develop the facilitating role of linking agent to establish communication networks between sources of innovation and the consumer. Rutherford *et al.* (1983) suggested the key task of the link agent was to help the users to adopt the new ideas, programmes or activities.

A review of four major US federally-funded innovations, the Rand Change Agent Study designed to develop educational innovation, concluded: 'the net return to the federal investment was the adoption of many innovations, the successful implementation of few, and the long-term continuation of still fewer' (Berman and McLaughlin, 1978).

Successful implementation strategies developed at local level promoted mutual adaptation by the project staff on the one hand, and the teachers and school management on the other. This ensured that:

— concrete, teacher specific and extended training was provided;
— classroom assistance from project staff was given;
— opportunity was provided for teacher observation of similar projects in other schools;
— regular project meetings on focused problems were held;
— teachers participated in project decisions;
— local materials were developed;
— the head (principal) participated in training.

Fullan (1985) has suggested, like Sarason (1982), that our knowledge about effective change processes is far from complete. His phrase 'change is a process, not an event' captures something of the complexity of implementation of innovation in individuals and institutions. He suggested at the individual level it is a process of developing new skills, which involves thinking and doing and thereby creating new meanings and new satisfactions. The following factors associated with change can be identified:

1 it takes place over time;

2 the initial stages always involve anxiety and uncertainty;

3 ongoing assistance and psychological support are crucial;

4 it involves learning new skills through practice and uncertainty;

5 the most fundamental breakthrough occurs when the underlying concept and rationale is understood cognitively;

6 success depends upon organizational conditions in the school — peer norms, leadership;

7 success involves pressure — through interaction with other peers and leaders.

The implications of this for the consultant are that change must be planned and participative, that training requires good demonstrations, materials and awareness, and as much assistance as possible in the early stages, with provision of training for assisters and clarity about who does what, at which stages. Learning to be proficient involves initial anxiety, a variety of assistance, small experiences of success, incremental skills development and eventual conceptual clarity and ownership.

Well before, Fullan *et al.* (1972) and Hall and Ford (1972) first coined the phrase 'change is a process not an event'. For them, understanding change depends on understanding teacher attitudes and skills so that support activities, such as staff development, coaching or provision of materials, can be based on teachers' own needs. This will be undertaken by a change facilitator adopting their concerns-based approach. According to Hall and Ford (1984), change facilitators have access to a resource system, including not only library facilities, but staff developers, curriculum coordinators and other personnel utilized according to an on-going concerns-diagnosis.

In Hall and Ford's CBAM model, the needs of individuals and groups are identified through a diagnosis of (i) stages of concern, (ii) levels of use, and (iii) innovation configurations, which together represent key aspects of the change process as perceived by teachers. Seven stages of concern range from early teacher-focused or self-type concerns, through task-centred concerns related to the use of the innovation, to impact concerns which explore and evaluate the effectiveness of the innovation. At different stages of the change process, different concerns will be more powerful. Similarly, the second dimension, levels of use, includes three levels of non-use (no action, orientation to the innovation and preparation for use), and five levels of use. The latter five levels include: mechanical use, where the teacher relies closely on the use of a manual or instructions; routine use, which leads to refinement; integration with colleagues to increase the impact; and finally, renewal, where the user re-evaluates, modifies or seeks alternatives. The third dimension, innovation configurations, focuses on the innovation itself. As noted by Fullan (1985) teachers adapt innovations. Through the innovation configuration adaptations or modifications are identified and appropriate interventions planned according to accurate operational use of the innovation. The CBAM model provides professionals with a means of describing the change process, of taking action to facilitate change and a means of predicting the effect of change. Without effective users new technologies and procedures are worthless. The key to effective change is the human participation.

In conclusion, returning to the introduction of this chapter, a distinction was made in the students' interventions between first-order change, which takes place within the institution, and second-order change, which takes place at the system level. Clearly we know considerably less about effective school-wide strategies than about first-order, innovation-focused change. In the latter, strategies closely resemble the process advocated in chapter one of plan, action and evaluation, or from the perspective of staff involved, a process of identification and adaptation (with development and technical assistance), and review. School-wide strategies will share many of the same principles, but in the view of the investment involved, in terms of time and resources, the chances of success must be considerably less. The benefits of innovation-focused change will be its cost-effectiveness, the knowledge available about suitable strategies to use and hence, the likelihood of successful implementation. The disadvantage is the narrowness of its focus and its potential lack of relationship to the school's overall goals.

References

BANDURA, A. (1969) *Principles of Behaviour Modification*, New York, Holt, Rinehart and Winston.

BERMAN, P. and MCLAUGHLIN, M. W. (1978) Rand Change Agent Study Federal Programs Supporting Educational Change: Vol. VIII, *Implementing and sustaining innovations*. R–158918–HEW.

BICKEL, W. E. and BICKEL, D. D. (1986) 'Effective schools, classrooms and instruction: implications for special education', *Exceptional Children*, 52, pp. 489–500.

BREHM, S. S. (1966) *A Theory of Psychological Reactance*, New York, Academic Press.

DALIN, P. and RUST, V. D. (1983) *Can Schools Learn?* Windsor, NFER/Nelson.

FRENCH, R. J. and RAVEN, B. (1959) 'The bases of social power'. In: Cartwright, D. (Ed.) *Studies in Social Power*, Ann Arbor, University of Michigan Institute of Social Research.

FULLAN, M. (1985) 'Change processes and strategies at the local level', *The Elementary School Journal*, 3, pp. 391–421.

FULLAN, M., HALL, G. E. and FORD, S. M. (1972) 'Change is a process not an event' cited in Hall, G. E. and Ford, S. M. (1984) *Change in Schools. Facilitating the Process*, New York, State University of New York Press.

FULLAN, M., MILES, M. B. and TAYLOR, G. (1980) 'Organizational development in schools: the state of the art'. *Review of Educational Research*, 50, pp. 121–83.

GALLESICH, J. (1973) 'Consultation in schools', *Journal of School Psychology*, 11, pp. 57–65.

HALL, G. E. and FORD, S. M. (1984) *Change in Schools. Facilitating the Process*, New York. State University of New York Press.

HAVELOCK, R. G. (1971) *Planning for Innovation through Dissemination and Utilization of Knowledge*, Ann Arbor, University of Michigan, Institute for Social Research.

HAVELOCK, R. G. (1973) *Training for Change Agents*, Ann Arbor, University of Michigan, Institute for Social Research.

ILLBACK, R. J. and MAHER, C. A. (1984) 'The school psychologist as an organizational boundary role professional', *Journal of School Psychology*, 22, pp. 63–72.

JAHN, D. L. and LICHSTEIN, K. L. (1980) 'The resistive client', *Behaviour Modification*, 4, pp. 303–20.

KATZ, D. and KAHN, R. L. (1967) *The Social Psychology of Organizations*, New York. John Wiley.

LEWIN, K. (1947) 'Group decision and social change'. In: Newcomb, T. and Hartley, E. (Eds.) *Readings in Social Psychology*, New York, Holt, Rinehart and Winston.

MARTIN, R. (1978) 'Expert and referent power: a framework for understanding and maximising consultative effectiveness', *Journal of School Psychology*, 16, pp. 49–55.

MEDWAY, F. J. (1975) 'A social psychological approach to internally based change in the schools', *Journal of School Psychology*, 13, pp. 19–27.

MEICHENBAUM, D. H. (1977) *Cognitive Behaviour Modification: an Integrative Approach*, New York, Plenum.

PIERSEL, W. C. and GUTKIN, T. C. (1983) 'Resistance to school-based consultation: a behavioural approach to the problem'. *Psychology in the Schools*, 20, 311–20.

PURKEY, S. and SMITH, M. (1983) 'Effective schools: a review', *Elementary School Journal*, 83, pp. 427–52.

REILLY, D. (1978) Program evaluation of system change: some issues and considerations. *Journal of School Psychology*, 16, pp. 368–74.

RUTHERFORD, W. L., HORD, S. M., HULING, L. L. and HALL, G. E. (1983) *Change Facilitators: In Search of Understanding their Role*, (Report No. 3159), Austin, The University of Texas at Austin, Research and Development Centre for Teacher Education. (ERIC Document Reproduction Service No. ED 250 801).

SARASON, S. B. (1967) 'Towards a psychology of change and innovation'. *American Psychologist*, 22, pp. 227–33.

SARASON, S. B. (1982) *The Culture of the School and the Problem of Change*, Boston, Allyn and Bacon.

SCHON, D. A. (1983) *The Reflective Practitioner. How Professionals Think in Action*, London, Temple Smith.

SCHMUCK, R. A., RUNKEL, P. J., ARENDS, J. H. and ARENDS, R. I. (1977) *The Second Handbook of Organizational Development in Schools*, Eugene, OR, Center for Educational Policy and Management.

Part 2
Consultancy in Action

3
Research, Consultancy and Staff Development in Schools

Les Bell

Consultancy and Research

The practice of inviting specialists into schools in order to benefit from expert advice on a wide range of educational issues has been evident to a greater or lesser degree in the education system of England and Wales for many years. Areas such as the assessment and testing of children's performance, the design of school buildings, the development of materials and equipment are just some of the aspects of education that have benefited from the collaboration between teachers and consultants. With the growth of LEA (Local Education Authority) advisory services this type of relationship became one of a number of strategies commonly used to support the work of schools and to generate change within them. At the same time the staffs of teacher training institutions were gradually developing this type of cooperative activity with their colleagues in schools. More recently specialist bodies such as the National Development Centre for School Management Training, The Regional Staff College at Dudley and the Centre for Adviser and Inspector Development have been established in order to help groups of teachers acquire specific skills by providing courses and through working alongside teachers in schools.

In March 1983 the Department of Education and Science (DES) issued Circular 3/83, *The In-Service Training Grant Scheme*. Few people at the time, especially among in-service providers, recognised how seminal a document this was to be. Within four years the provision of in-service training for teachers was to be radically reorganized and the nature of its funding changed significantly. Traditionally in-service training was the province of institutions of higher education who provided an annual programme of long and short courses both nationally and within their own regions, usually in consultation with LEAs. Successful courses, those that were well attended, were repeated. Others were dropped or changed. Circular 3/83 was the first part of a process that was to change all this. By 1986 the nature, but not the extent, of the impending changes was becoming clearer. Circular 6/86, *Local Authority Training Grants Scheme*, asked LEAs to give details of planned expenditure on in-service training for 1987/88 in respect of both national and local priority areas. Training under the first heading attracted grant support at 70 per cent and under the second at only 50 per cent. Furthermore all the course fees and travel costs for all full- and part-time courses had to be met out of LEAs' own resources as from April 1987. The effect of this was to cut the number of full-time secondments from LEAs by 74 per cent (Poster and Day, 1988). One section in the circular was to bring home to in-service providers just how far-reaching the changes in in-service work were to be since it redefined what might, legitimately, be regarded as appropriate forms of in-service training.

> Eligible training may include any activity directed to the development, expertise or effectiveness of one or more of the specified types of trainees; this may include school or college-based training, training courses, secondments to industry and commerce, and secondments of teacher trainers to schools (para. 10, quoted in Poster and Day, 1988, pp. 20–1).

At the same time schools were being provided with funds with which to organize at least some of their school-based in-service training. With the establishment of training days as part of the School Teacher's Pay and Conditions of Service Order (DES, 1987), schools also have some limited time available to implement their own plans for staff development. As a result of these changes in-service providers find themselves existing in a marketplace that consists of institutions of higher education, industrial trainers, specialist units and independent consultants, not to mention the LEAs and their own advisory services. All of these groups are seeking to convince clients that they are able to meet client needs and that they offer the most effective form of in-service training. These changes required in-service providers to begin to operate in significantly different ways because the concept of a course conducted through lectures had less credibility with potential clients than more action-based seminars and workshops. Thus in-service training providers have had to become facilitators, advisers, trainers and consultants working in a variety of settings including school itself. These activities are unfamiliar to many providers of in-service training and extremely time-consuming because they require much more careful and detailed negotiation with the client about agreed objectives, processes and forms of evaluation. Furthermore these activities do not fit easily within the accepted paradigms of educational research as it is usually defined with universities and colleges.

Approaches to research

Research is one of the three main areas of activity in any institution of higher education, along with teaching and administration. It is argued that commitment to research and the ability to attract considerable sums of money for externally-funded research is what distinguishes a university from any other higher education establishment. Following the Report of the Jarratt Committee (1985) the University Grants Committee has embarked upon a public process of evaluating universities and departments within them on the basis of the amount of money they have attracted in externally-funded research as well as on the number and type of publications produced by members of departments. Research activities have become crucial as performance indicators in the university sector. The performance of individuals within universities is judged in a similar way. This system may contain inherent inflexibilities but the criteria by which judgments are made are public, commonly applied and known in advance. They do, however, assume an agreement about the nature and purpose of research.

Research can often be thought to be conducted by interested individuals in semi-private situations, such is the mystique that can surround it. Research will, almost certainly, consist of some form of investigation of a defined problem or issue with the intention of achieving an outcome that may well have no practical application but which can eventually be made public in a written form. Even within this extremely broad formulation consultancy, even consultancy grounded in research, tends to become marginalized as an activity within the broad range of research activity. This is less likely to be the case where the tradition of in-service training is not restricted to courses and lectures. The current emphasis on research as a performance indicator and the associated debate about the nature of research within universities as a whole may still have a significantly marginalizing effect on consultancy activities. This may be especially true where approaches are made to a limited number of individuals within a particular department of education by schools or LEAs to become involved in work which is not entirely within the public domain and is not firmly rooted in established research traditions.

It is a mistake, however, to assume that research is, in fact, a unified or a unifiable set of activities using an agreed methodology and leading to identifiable findings that can be made public. Research might best be understood as a series of choices, the first of which will be about the nature of the research itself and how it is initiated. Ziman (1988), for example, has argued that research might be either 'curiosity-directed' or 'results-oriented'. The first of these involves the pursuit of ideas for their own sake. Goals or outcomes, if they exist, belong only to the researcher and there is no pressure to produce instant results or direct applications. The second approach to research takes the form of the pursuit of answers to sponsor-defined problems where the sponsor may identify the parameters within which the research takes place and in terms of which the answers or solutions may be formulated.

If we take Ziman's typology as further extended it can be seen that we do not have mutually exclusive alternative approaches to research only one of which falls within an acceptable tradition. In fact Ziman identifies two approaches to research each with its own traditions and expectations and each having its own place in the totality of research activity. This is what I have termed the Dual Economy Paradigm of Educational Research (see Table 3.1). Curiosity-directed research emphasizes ideas and problems, is concerned with methodology and originality and is not concerned with 'real-world' applications. Results-oriented research emphasizes ideas and problems, is concerned with methodology and originality and is not concerned with 'real-world' applications. Results-oriented research emphasizes outcomes and solutions and is concerned with results and applications rather than with abstract ideas and theoretical issues. The former may well be researcher inspired and focused, while the latter will be sponsoring-agency focused and controlled.

Table 3.1   The dual-economy paradigm of research

Curiosity-directed Research	Results-oriented Research
Emphasis on:	Emphasis on:
ideas	outcomes
problems	solutions
issues	practical applications
Concerned with:	Concerned with:
quality	applications
originality	relevance
accessibility	cost effectiveness
methodological soundness	financial returns
	results
Not concerned with:	Not concerned with:
results	ideas
deadlines	problems
financial returns	issues
'real-world' applications	
Researcher inspired and focused	Market or sponsoring agency directed and focused

Managing and organizing the competing claims and demands within this dual economy presents major difficulties for any university department. This is especially true in education where, only in exceptional circumstances is there a tradition of results-orientated research unless this has been action research in schools. Action research, although offering a challenge to other more traditional paradigms of research, is easier to encompass within that tradition since it is less client- or sponsor-directed than, say, research based on evaluation or consultancy.

Even curiosity-based research has two main, often competing strands, the positive and the interpretive. The former, as Ribbins (1986) argues, is based on conjecture and refutation and moves by deduction from the general to the particular. The latter is based on conjecture and explanation and moves by induction from the particular to the general. As presented in Table 3.2 these approaches share one characteristic in common. They both appear to be made up of a series of discrete and linear stages. This may not be an entirely accurate depiction for, as Sanders and Pinney (1983) point out, the process of data collection and data interpretation are closely interrelated in interpretive studies. They also tend to concentrate to a far greater extent than positivistic work on attempting to understand and explain how schools actually work and how they are perceived by those within them. As I have argued elsewhere, however, these studies have concentrated on the less powerful or influential groups in schools such as pupils and, as a result, they still tell us very little about how schools are managed and about how decisions are actually made (Bell, 1980). It may be that results-orientated research offers a more fruitful, although less direct, way of exploring the organization and management of schools.

Table 3.2   Curiosity-based research approaches

Positivistic	Interpretive
Theory construction	Observation and data collection
Hypotheses	Analysis and generalization
Observation and data collection	Theory construction
Refutation, revision or confirmation of theory	Theory testing
Deductive	**Inductive**
No immediate application	Solutions implied in prevention of problem or policy
Not rooted in 'real' or 'live' issues	Only certain outcomes acceptable

Here again, however, we find that there are a number of distinctive strands within a general research perspective (see Table 3.3). Shipman (1985) has suggested that there are three possible relationships between research and policy. The first is where research develops a substantive theory which then becomes espoused in policy. The second is where research is undertaken with the express intention of providing data on which policy formulation can be based or existing policy influenced or challenged. The third is what Shipman terms 'just doing research' where research influences policy indirectly. Accurate data collection is fundamental to all three of Shipman's positions. In the first and third positions the agenda for research tends to be set by the researcher while in the second the agenda is more likely to be set by the policymaker. Decisions about the organizing and carrying out of the research will, in all cases, be those of the researcher.

With evaluation-based research the agenda for the research may be a product of the pre-existing context and will be determined by what is to be evaluated and for whom the evaluation is being conducted. Evaluation itself, where it is funded by external bodies, takes the form of intensive and planned data collection on which informed judgments about policy implementation can be based. The client may wish to have some influence over the choice of evaluation methodology although this is likely to be identified, at least initially, by the evaluator. As Fox (1980) points out, the significant feature of evaluative work is that it is not objective in the sense that it is more centrally located in the political, social and ideological arenas than most other forms of research. In fact it takes us ' . . . deep into the areas in which policy, practice and research collide' (Bell, 1986, p. 75). To the extent that the evaluation is formative rather than summative it can also involve the researcher in providing support for implementing the recommen-

Table 3.3 *Results-oriented research approaches*

Policy	Evaluation	Consultancy
Theoretical and policy framework	Predetermined objectives and possibly predetermined processes	Consultant theoretical and professional stance
Data collection and observation	Data collection and observation	Client framework and objectives
Analysis	Evaluation	Data collection and analysis
Recommendations	Recommendations	Recommendations
Policy implementation	Implementation	Implementation of client centred outcomes
Theory revision or confirmation	Theory revision or confirmation	Theory revision or confirmation
Solutions implied in presentation of problem or policy	Nature of activity determines outcomes	Tends to be client led. Leads to 'facilitator' role
Only certain outcomes accepted	Outcomes expressed in terms of objectives which evaluator may not accept	Tends to respond to market needs and demands

dations that are made as a result of the evaluation (see, for example, Bell and Merson, 1985). The evaluator thus becomes part of the situation being evaluated rather than apart from it. The boundary between research and evaluation becomes blurred and the ownership of the outcomes may be unclear.

Such issues also emerge in the third category of results-oriented research, that of consultancy. Here it is the client who creates the initial frame of reference, often independently of the consultant. The agenda will be a product of the client's analysis of the situation and of what the consultant can bring to it. Thus client expectations and knowledge are central to the process. The ownership of the consultancy process may remain with the consultant but the client may well wish to influence its precise application in the particular setting. In any case the setting will influence the application of the process. The ownership of the outcomes will usually remain with the client although, again, there may be an obligation on the part of the consultant to implement at least some of the recommendations.

Consultancy thus moves into an area where issues of definition and ownership can present significant problems yet, as has already been suggested, it can also take the researcher into areas which other forms of research cannot reach, especially in terms of how schools are managed and how important decisions are taken. Much depends on the shared expectations about the nature of consultancy which exists between consultant and client at school and LEA level. Central to this is the extent to which it is possible to identify a set common understanding about the consultancy process itself. These may be expressed in terms of a series of stages through which a consultancy might pass.

Consultants in Schools

There are a variety of different models of the consultancy process which identify a range of different stages through which each consultancy might progress. Awareness of all these possible stages will aid the selection of the most appropriate route for any particular consultancy.

Morris (1988), for example, suggests that the key stages in any consultancy are analysis, feedback, preparation for action, problem-solving and follow-up (see Table 3.4). Morris here misses out what most consultants would identify as the single most important phase, that of negotiating entry. He also links together analysis and diagnosis which can be seen as separate activities. Boud and McDonald (1981) highlight the need to define the relationship and clarify the processes for reporting back to the client towards the end of the consultancy while Elliott-Kemp (1988) focuses on the exploration and sharing of meaning within the process. In the final column of Table 3.4 is a series of eight stages which have been identified as common to many school-based and other forms of consultancy (Bell, 1979).

Table 3.4 Stages in the consultancy process

Morris (1988)	Boud and McDonald (1981)	Elliott-Kemp (1988)	Bell (1979)
Analysis	Initial contact	Awareness	Entry
Feedback	Defining the relationship	Data collection and analysis	Analysis
Recommended actions	Identifications of working methods	Exploration of meanings	Diagnosis
Preparations	Reporting	Hypothesis testing	Objectives
Problem-solving	Further action	Action planning	Resources
Follow-up	Completion	Implementation	Implementation
		Evaluation	Evaluation
			Exit

These headings are derived from a detailed analysis of the literature on consultancy in schools including the work of Bolam *et al.* (1978), Campbell (1985), Havelock (1969), Eraut (1977) and Lockwood (1988). They have been refined through a series of consultancies in a range of different schools and through a detailed evaluation of some of the current forms of consultancy activity associated with curriculum initiatives such as the Training and Vocational Educational Initiative (TVEI) (Bell, 1986). It is recognized that current developments in education will extend the opportunities for such forms of consultancy (Bell, 1988). The headings in the final column of Table 3.4, therefore, are the product of analysis and practical experience. They provide a coherent framework which can and did guide the work of the writer as consultant in schools. These headings will be used in this section to examine the work of two consultants working in a group of secondary schools within one LEA. The process began when the consultants were invited, as a result of other work they were doing in the LEA, to become involved in school-based work, the objective of which was to facilitate staff development within the schools.

Entry

The invitation to carry out a consultancy will normally come from the headteacher, some other senior member of staff or a representative of the LEA. In each case it is vital to negotiate the terms of entry with the headteacher or another senior member of the staff who can act for the headteacher. In the case of the consultancy described in this chapter, the invitation to act as a consultant came from a senior officer within the LEA who wanted developmental work carried out in a number of schools, each of which was deemed by the LEA to be 'ready' for such activities. Two consultants were involved. Their initial contact with the LEA was through two concurrent series of management training courses for primary and secondary headteachers throughout the authority. As a result of these courses, discussions about other forms of involvement in the work of the LEA and its schools took place with the Chief Inspector and, subsequently, with the Deputy Director of Education. The first approach to the schools was made by the officer responsible for Grant Related In-Service Training (GRIST). Two schools rejected the opportunity to be involved in the programme; one because the head felt that the situation in the school was not sufficiently stable owing to recent changes in senior staff and a possible threat to closure through falling roles; the other because the head himself announced his resignation. The remaining three schools were interestingly different.

School A was a small mixed comprehensive school that had previously been a single-sex grammar school. It had a head who had been in post two years and a strong senior management team that included a long established deputy who had been appointed to the grammar school, a senior teacher who soon expected to become a deputy (which he did in the second year of the consultancy) and another deputy with responsibility for staff development who had an authority-wide reputation for his work. The school was on a small restricted site near the centre of a medium sized industrial and mining town.

School B was a larger school, previously a high school but now a mixed comprehensive with a staff of almost fifty. The head had been in post for some time and wanted to prepare the school to meet the challenges of GCSE and other changes that would soon face the school. The senior management team were all well-established but none were, at that time, seriously considering further promotion. The school was on the outskirts of the same town as School A and the two schools have previously cooperated on providing in-service courses for their two sets of staff.

School C was a high school in a market town where children still took the 11 +. The school was in direct competition for pupils with two single-sex grammar schools. Its head had been in post for a considerable period of time and its senior management team consisted of one deputy who had been at the school for almost twenty years, another who had been in post for six years but who hoped for promotion, and a senior teacher with responsibility for staff development.

There were two major problems associated with negotiating entry into these schools. The first was to explore with the heads what they wanted to achieve from the consultancy. The second was to involve the whole staff in the consultancy process so that, at the very least, they were all informed about what was going on since they would all be affected directly or indirectly. In Schools A and B discussions took place with the two headteachers and their deputies who had staff development responsibility. This group of four met the two consultants in a neutral setting to discuss what might be done. The LEA was providing the financial resources for this work so the first entry problem, agreeing on fees and deciding who pays, was easily overcome. It was agreed that the main task for the consultants should be to help both schools to identify their own staff development needs for the next three years and to enable them to use this information to prepare a three-year rolling programme for staff development as required by the LEA if a school was to have its GRIST bid accepted. It was also agreed that the initial contact with the whole staff of each school was to be through making a major contribution to the in-service residential weekends which each school had already planned.

The prior existence of these residential weekends was fortuitous. The third school had no such weekend planned but it did have an in-service day for which the programme had already been agreed and announced. Here the negotiations over entry took place at the school with the senior teacher with responsibility for staff development acting on behalf of the headteacher who was involved in the discussions briefly and intermittently. This proved to be a less effective form of entry as did the brief presentation to the staff of the school that took place as part of an already full in-service programme held after school. It was agreed that the consultancy would concentrate on the senior staff of the school.

Gray (1988) reminds us that most schools do not have a tradition of working with consultants and that, 'only when heads acknowledge that employing consultants is a positive and enriching process that will support their headship, rather than challenging it, will consultancy become a functionally integrated aspect of school development' (Gray, 1988, p. 2). The first two heads had some appreciation of this but the third saw the consultants as having a role with his senior staff but not with him as headteacher. Two of the three heads found some difficulty in committing themselves and their schools to a particular course of action for a sustained period of time, although the possible use of GRIST funding was seen as a way of overcoming this. At the same time the degree to which the senior staff of the school were able to work together as a team was a significant factor in making effective use of the external consultants. The three teams differed in this regard. One group was extremely coherent with a clear set of school-wide policies already agreed with the staff. Significantly the head was an integral part of the group, rather than apart from it. The implementation of some policies had already started. In the second school the senior management team was moving towards this situation but was experiencing some difficulty in bringing the whole of the staff with them. In the third school the head carried out most of the key administrative and managerial functions within the school, leaving his senior staff to cope with day-to-day issues and with their considerable pastoral responsibilities.

Analysis

Such insights as those indicated above form part of the process of analysis which begins for both clients and the consultant from the moment that the negotiating of entry begins. The analysis in this case took place at three levels. The first level was concerned with the organization of the schools themselves. Here particular attention was paid to the extent to which there was general agreement on the aims and purposes of the schools, how clear teachers were about their duties and responsibilities, and how knowledgeable they were about those of their colleagues. At the same time, at the second level, attention was paid to how effectively the internal communication system worked since this might be crucial to making subsequent arrangements. In the event the consultancy in one school almost floundered on the failure of one senior member of staff to communicate with his colleagues in the senior management team in advance of making arrangements with the consultants. The third level of analysis concerned individual members of staff and how they saw their own roles both now and in the future. This was a prelude to the identification of staff development needs in a structured and formal way.

This analysis was relatively informal but did require the consultants to spend some considerable time talking or, more appropriately, listening to members of the staff of the three schools. Both consultants already had a well established network of contacts within the LEA. This included staff already in post in the three schools and others who were familiar with each school. Information was collected from these contacts as part of the analysis but it was all cross-checked by the consultants with each other and against available hard evidence or evidence gleaned from observations within the schools. Evidence from outside the school which formed part of the analysis was only significant to the extent that it drew attention to some aspect of the school that might need to be considered. The consultants based their substantive analysis on evidence which they obtained from the school itself. In many instances matters would be discussed with senior members of the staff, including the head, for clarification and confirmation. Thus the analysis stage tended to run into the diagnosis stage.

Diagnosis

This stage of the consultancy inevitably overlapped with the previous phase since diagnosis involves data collection and analysis. Interviews, observation, surveys and the collection of quantitative data are all part of the diagnosis stage in many consultancies since this phase is a form of problem-solving. The consultants here were seeking to establish what, if anything, was wrong; what needed changing or developing within the schools and which members of staff needed to be included in the process. Much of this had to be based on some understanding of where the schools were in terms of their development, where they were wanting to go and, within this overall plan, what were the immediate priorities. At the same time the consultants were trying to identify possible barriers to achieving the changes which the schools wished to bring about.

Some of this information emerged during the early discussions with the heads and senior staff. Some emerged during the initial analysis. The focus in all three schools was developmental, rather than coping with specific professional or organizational problems, although it soon became clear that one of the schools had to face some fundamental organizational changes if it was to move in the direction that it was claimed the staff wanted to go. The diagnosis consisted in all schools of group activities designed to identify individual, department, and school-wide professional development needs. At the same time staff were consulted about the most appropriate ways of meeting those needs, timing, venues and composition of possible groups. In two cases this part of the diagnosis involved all teachers and took place in meetings after school with one or, more usually, both consultants. In the third school the work was carried out with senior staff and heads of departments during school time.

As a result of these meetings and subsequent follow-up interviews with a random sample of staff, the consultants drew up a report which identified a range of professional development needs for each school. These were presented under six headings: personal management skills; personal professional and curriculum skills; departmental curriculum and professional skills; staff or departmental management skills; school-wide organizational and administrative skills; school-wide curriculum and professional skills. At the same time these needs were prioritized based on the information collected from the staff. Recommendations were also made about possible ways of meeting those needs. Each report was discussed with the same group with which the initial entry had been negotiated. The time which elapsed between the group activities and the discussion of the report was never more than two weeks.

This discussion sought to do three things. Firstly it was an information giving session in which the consultants clarified and explained any points in their written report that was not sufficiently clear. Secondly the school representatives were encouraged by the consultants to organize the perceived staff priorities in terms of the overall priorities for the school in order that some view could emerge about which areas of need were to be met first, which were to be part of a later staff development programme and which had to be met from individual or departmental resources. This information was to be fed back to the staff. In two schools this was done indirectly by the consultants who produced a revised version of their report for distribution to all staff, and in the other school it was done by placing a summary of the report, produced by the senior teacher, on the staff room notice board. The third part of the discussion looked at how best to meet the priority needs and at what role the consultants might play in this.

Up to this stage the consultants had used their expertise as facilitators to bring staff together in order that professional development needs could be identified. This also meant that ways had to be devised of carrying out and recording information from this process of identification. Here the consultants modified a process which they had used with other teachers. To this extent they were acting as experts since they were using technical skills in need identification. They were also acting as facilitators since the process was highly participative and required open discussion and sharing of perceptions. During the discussion of the report the consultants also played both facilitating and expert roles by encouraging the identification of priorities and conducting the meeting so that this happened, and by bringing their expertise to bear in order to express those priorities in terms of objectives.

Objectives

The identification of priorities and the setting of objectives are closely related activities. The priorities expressed what it was that the schools wished to achieve and the objectives were statements about how this was going to happen. Thus the objectives became, for each school, a set of statements about precisely what actions were to be carried out, by whom, for whom and by when. The inclusion of a specific time-scale was not restricted to those objectives which related to the immediate priorities. Some indication was also given of approximate time-scales for meeting other needs over a three-year period in two schools. The third school found itself in an extremely turbulent environment and did not, therefore, wish to commit its resources for more than one year.

Taken together these objectives provided the schools with a coherent framework within which could be located future discussions about professional development needs at school, departmental or individual levels. Any such discussions could now focus on key aspects of that framework since it gave a clear indication of where the immediate priorities were and how they might be achieved. Thus, those within the school who found that they disagreed with the priorities as formulated could engage in informed debate about the nature of those priorities and possible alternatives. In creating such a situation the schools had taken the first step towards establishing a structured and credible programme of staff development.

Resources

Any programme of professional development within a school only has credibility if its priorities are shared by the staff and if its objectives are achievable and achieved. The process of establishing the priorities used by the consultants within the three schools was concerned to achieve agreement about priorities. The discussion of the report with the senior staff of those schools helped set up structures and identify resources for implementing the programme. These programmes of professional development required, for successful implementation, three main types of resources. These were time, money and people with the appropriate expertise. It has to be remembered, however, that the objective for any programme of development will tend to be tailored to the means available for implementing that programme and not the other way round. Thus a realistic notion of the available resources is crucial and it is the consultant's responsibility to ensure that such realism exists. The funding for much of the work was to come either from GRIST or from other headings within the school budget. Finance played a major role in restricting what could be done in the schools in those areas where outside expertise was required. Such areas formed a relatively small part of the needs which had been identified. Two of the three schools contained among their staff the expertise to meet many of their own priorities. The consultants had sought to identify these skills as part of their diagnosis stage to provide the schools with a full picture of the expertise available within their own staff and within the LEA. Time also had to be found for this necessary developmental work. Here the smallest school was most imaginative in the way it coped with the problem by using its GRIST money carefully and by targeting specific groups of teachers at particular times to be involved in staff development activies. In all the schools possible strategies were suggested by the consultants and discussed as part of the consideration of their report. Helping the schools to identify available times for staff to work together was a major facilitative exercise. When all three school invited the consultants to play a significant part in the implementaiton of their professional development programmes it became even more important.

Implementation

From the outset those who were most likely to be involved in the implementation were part of the consultancy process. In one school the senior staff and heads of departments, in the other schools all staff were part of the process. Implementation took three main forms. In two schools curriculum needs were identified which the schools set out to meet from within their own resources. These were in new technology and pupil assessment techniques. Team building and similar forms of staff cooperation were a priority for one school. These were met, in part, by using an outside specialist who had not been involved in the consultancy but who worked with many schools on team building and development. In two schools the consultants, in conjunction with the deputy head responsible for staff development, planned a programme of training in management skills. In both schools this led to more detailed cooperation over a period of time in key areas, namely staff appraisal and communication in the school. This programme was open to all staff although it was designed for senior and middle management, and in both cases the head attended most sessions. It was felt that nobody should be excluded from this work. In the third school these sessions were restricted to the senior management group. The head attended reluctantly and, at first, infrequently. This led to an open discussion between the consultants and the head which resulted in the head being at all subsequent sessions except the last one.

Staff in all schools could recognize the benefits of these programmes because they had been involved in identifying the need for them. Nevertheless barriers to implementation did arise. Some of the areas identified did impinge on teachers' classroom autonomy. As long ago as 1975 Stenhouse was warning of the difficulties that the appeal to professional autonomy could create for consultants and curriculum developers in schools. He went on to argue that there were several factors which made such a highly individualist conception of teacher autonomy inappropriate. These included the extent to which cross-school cooperation was necessary in order to maximize educational benefits for pupils; the extent to which it is necessary to avoid radically divergent teaching methods for the benefit of pupils who could encounter too wide a range of teaching styles; and the need to break down the privacy of the classroom for the benefit of teachers themselves. Such arguments as these had to be deployed during the implementation of the programme in order to convince some colleagues that the benefits of the proposed changes outweighed their disadvantages.

In so doing it was necessary for the consultants to remember Fullan's strictures about 'brute sanity'. He pointed out that there is a natural tendency for all of those seeking to bring about change to do so through sheer argument alone (Fullan, 1986). This is not a very effective strategy since it tends to reinforce entrenched positions rather than change them. Thus attention to both the process of implementation as well as to the content of the programme was vital. In order to implement the programme successfully support was required to encourage colleagues to apply the skills they were seeking to learn. Peer group pressure, as Fullan (1986) points out, can also be effective here if this can be mobilized in an effective and supportive way. Implementing any programme of staff development has to take into account how adults learn.

In order to facilitate this more widely within the three schools, the two consultants went back to the LEA to argue that each school should be given extra resources in order that key staff could be trained to work as staff development consultants and trainers. This was forthcoming for two of the schools but not for a third whose head had recently attended a similar industrially-based training programme. Training staff within the school to facilitate staff learning and development was one strategy which the consultants adopted to ensure that the exit left the schools self-reliant and non-dependent. It also helped to confront other difficulties with these consultancies which emerged as the consultants evaluated their own work.

Evaluation

The evaluation of these consultancies took place at three levels. The consultants themselves were constantly evaluating what they were doing in the light of their entry discussions with senior staff. They recognized that, while some of the changes being achieved were quite fundamental, others were marginal. They also acknowledged that more lasting change in some areas could best be brought about by successive approximation, that is a whole cycle of small changes over a period of time. They also saw the need to avoid the marginalization of some activities and some groups within the schools and the need to make other activities more central. This was especially true in the management and decision-making structures of one school. Thus steps were taken, as outlined above, to ensure that some staff were trained to facilitate developmental work within the school. In one case the consultants helped to conduct a dialogue between the head and one of his senior deputies about the possible changes which needed to be made in the management structure of the school, if the maximum benefit were to be obtained from the staff development programme which had been implemented. All of this resulted from the consultants' own evaluation of their work.

The consultancy was also evaluated by the staff of the school both as a process and as a series of individual and skill-specific staff training sessions. Since all of the schools sought to incorporate the consultants' reports into their GRIST bids, the work was deemed to have been successfully carried out. Two of the schools obtained more than the average funding for their proposals and received considerable LEA support for the implementation of their future plans. In one school, however, the consultancy was less successful in this regard since the GRIST bid was only partially successful. The reasons for this are partly to be found in the failure to involve all staff in the process and partly in the extent to which the head had been involved in the early discussions about the consultancy and his subsequent ambivalent position towards it. Negotiation of entry and continued support must come from the highest levels in any organization.

The consultants' work was also evaluated by the LEA who had funded it in the first place. This was done by the officer responsible for GRIST, an ex-secondary school head. He did his evaluation by reading the reports which were produced and by discussing the work with staff in the participating schools and with the consultants. The information obtained was then shared with the pastoral inspectors of the three schools who undertook to monitor subsequent developments in the three schools. The consultants have now started to work in two more schools and are in the process of setting up a complete training programme for school-based staff development coordinators.

Each of these three levels of evaluation contained sets of problems. The evaluation of their own work by the consultants required them continually to pose eight questions to themselves and to the senior management teams of the participating schools. These were:

1 Are we still moving in the agreed direction?
2 Is this still the direction in which we wish to move?
3 Are the priorities still the same?
4 What else do we need to know?
5 Why?
6 What will we accept as evidence?
7 Is that evidence worth the time and effort to collect?
8 What will we do with it when we have collected it?

Even with questions such as these it was not possible in any of the schools to identify clear and precise evidence about those changes which, in the longer term, the consultants and clients wished to generate. These were the changes in teacher performance, school organization and management that would have a direct effect on the education provided for the pupils in the school. Evaluation at that level was for the school and the LEA to carry out over a longer period of time following the consultancy.

Evaluation at the second and third levels had to take account of the strictures of Olsen and Olsen (1981) about effective evaluation. This must identify the extent to which:

1 information and specific proposals contained within a consultant's report are a natural outgrowth of the perceived needs of the teachers in the schools;
2 teachers play a significant role in determining and implementing the action programmes that arise from a consultancy;
3 sufficient time has been allowed for a thorough exploration of the ways in which external ideas can be adapted to the needs of particular schools.

By producing written reports for the schools and the LEA which stated exactly how the data had been collected and interpreted, by including a clear statement of objectives for the present and future staff development programmes, and by indicating who was to do what, by when, and with what resources, the consultants tried to ensure that all these conditions were met. Schools have to be sufficiently disciplined to follow through such plans and the LEA has to be committed to resourcing its own follow-up to the consultancy to ensure that the school plays its part. Negotiating a set of conditions for this to happen and enabling the schools to be as self-sufficient as possible in formulating and implementing their future plans were major parts of the final stage of the consultancy.

Exit

Consultancy has often been described as a dependency relationship where a client comes to rely on the consultant for help in difficult situations and, therefore, neither owns the problems nor becomes able to cope with them. Effective exit from or termination of a consultancy should ensure that these two situations do not arise or, if they have arisen, that they are addressed and removed. The very nature of this consultancy and the extent to which it contained the objective of making the schools self-reliant in planning and implementing their own professional development programmes, helped to minimize the risks of such dependency relationships developing. The dilemma here is between helping others and helping others to help themselves.

Where a consultant is using a particular form of expertise then there is a danger of providing sets of interpretation that confirm the consultant's expectations and require the application of the specific expertise processed by that consultant. This risk decreases as the consultant shares the definition of the problem with the client. The client must then be encouraged and helped by the consultant to acquire the skills of the consultant. In the case studies under discussion the consultants helped the client schools to train key staff in facilitating staff development and in implementing professional development programmes. They ensured that staff had access to necessary skills and they used what Havelock (1969) called 'linkage skills', that is the skills of identifying and bringing together the best resources and the correctly identified needs.

At the same time great care was taken with the senior staff and, as far as possible with all staff, in the participating schools to check that the work of the consultants had met the expectations of the clients. Opportunities were provided for group, individual and whole school feedback. This could be confidential where required and some of it took the form of anonymous summative evaluatory comments on the management training sessions provided by the consultants. The main contribution that the consultants could make at this stage was to raise issues appropriately and to ensure that these were fully discussed even to the extent of drawing attention to what had not been done during the consultancy so that the client could begin to address these issues immediately if they were in priority areas. Thus, in these ways the consultants tried to ensure, from the very point of negotiating entry to the consultancy, that the client schools were not left with any unfullfilled expectations. They also tried to ensure that colleagues in the three schools could play an active, independent role within their schools to follow-up and extend the consultancy work. In this way dependence was avoided and self reliance was reinforced. As Boud and McDonald remind us: 'Attention in the termination stage needs to be focused on how consultants can withdraw in a planned way without overstaying their welcome, finishing abruptly, or being seduced into a (sometimes) unhealthy long-term dependent relationship' (Boud and McDonald, 1981, p. 36).

Conclusions

At the exit stage, as in all the other stages of the consultancy, the expectations of the client and the consultant and the values exposed by them are instrumental in shaping the client–consultant relationship. As was argued above, every consultancy is shaped by the values of the parties involved in it even where these are not made explicit. Davies (1977) points to some of the value issues involved in using consultants in schools when he reminds us that ' . . . Jesuits have God . . . , clinicals have Freud, accountants have profitability, and so on. The theory-that-can-be-translated-into-practice in the educational organization . . . is still a highly infant growth' (Davies, 1977, p. 115).

The complexities involved here were explored in the third section of this chapter when differing value positions of the consultant as expert and the consultant as facilitator were considered in some detail. It was shown subsequently that these positions are not mutually exclusive, nor entirely distinct even within the same consultancy. Underpinning all the activities of the consultants in this case were a set of values which are closely related to those implied by Havelock (1969) in his definition of consultancy and made explicit by Filley (1975) when he argues that certain value positions, when adopted by external consultants, tend to lead to independence at the end of a consultant–client relationship rather than interdependence or dependence. He suggests that developing and maintaining such a relationship depends on trust. This is difficult to establish, takes a considerable period of time, and can easily be damaged or destroyed. Consultants must therefore, be seen by the client to be behaving in a way which is consistent, predictable to a large extent and beneficial to the client. Filley (1975) suggests that such behaviours will be based on a set of beliefs:

1 a belief in the availability of a mutually acceptable solution or appropriate development;
2 a belief in the desirability of a mutually acceptable solution;
3 a belief in the benefits of cooperation rather than competition;
4 a belief that everyone is of equal worth;
5 a belief that the views of others are a legitimate statement of their position;
6 a belief that differences of opinion can be helpful;
7 a belief in the trustworthiness of colleagues.

Based on these sets of beliefs the consultants sought to understand the positions of the teachers in the participating schools and to create and sustain sets of relationships that were beneficial and mutually advantageous. This was done, in part, by creating and sustaining a forum for exchanges of views, in part by providing specific skills, and in part by helping key staff to have access to skills that would help them to sustain and develop such beneficial relationships.

In this consultancy certain values about staff development were also significant. The consultants espoused a professional development model of staff development. This is based on the view that teachers can and will take a significant responsibility for their own professional development. This is especially true where it is seen to be relevant to their current or future professional roles and where it equips them with skills to cope with changing situations. Such a position is different from the deficit model of teacher development which rests on the assumption that problems in school, or their failure to change, are a result of a lack of skill or knowledge on the part of teachers. If these skills can be learned then all will be well. The deficit model is a 'top down' model where the experts in the senior management team or LEA transmit the skills to the teacher who then applies them. In all three schools in this case study the consultants adopted a 'whole school' approach to professional development in which the school itself, not individual teachers, was the significant unit for change. Thus all staff in two of the schools were involved in determining the process and the content of the professional development. In the third the consultants made every attempt to ensure that all staff were involved and did ensure that every teacher was informed at all stages. This was not a satisfactory situation in terms of ensuring maximum benefit for all concerned with the school. As I have pointed out elsewhere (Bell 1988) the essence of such professional development is that:

1 it should be conducted on the basis of a genuine exchange of views;
2 it should produce negotiated and agreed actions;
3 it should be directly related to the roles played by teachers in their schools;
4 it should be implemented through a structure that is understood by and open to all staff.

Contained within such perceptions are a set of notions about how schools change and develop. It was argued above that the consultant as expert appeals to rational forces to generate organizational change while the consultant as facilitator relies on developing appropriate group dynamics. These two positions bear some similarity to the rational–empirical and normative re-educative strategies identified by Bennis *et al.* (1970). Their third change strategy, power–coercive, which depends on the direct application of political power, would until recently have been thought entirely inappropriate in schools. Recent political initiatives, however, have been implemented in this way. Nevertheless such strategies remain inappropriate for consultants working in schools. In this case study the two consultants tended to adopt a combination of approaches although they relied heavily on demonstrating that certain skills were relevent to and would work in the particular circumstances in which the schools found themselves. They also devoted considerable effort to enabling teachers to share ideas, exchange and debate different views, and establish patterns of relationships that might support and facilitate change both at that time and in the future. They were mindful of Pettigrew's (1985) comment that change often does not conform to the theories produced by behavioural scientists.

In schools top-down change may not always work, especially if colleagues have not been involved in its planning and do not support its intention. It has to be recognized, however, that the head is a significant figure in most schools. Developments initiated inside the school are unlikely to succeed if they do not have (as a basic minimum) the tacit support of the head. This is partly because schools have very diffuse goals. Heads play the major role in the setting of those goals. Heads also have a significant part to play in the interpretation of those goals both inside and outside the school. At the same time they are responsible for the organization of the school. Thus, at one and the same time, heads set goals and structure the school and administer its resources in order to achieve those goals. This, together with the traditional high degree of authority still enjoyed by heads places most of them in an extremely influential position within the school. This central feature of school organization has to be taken into acocunt by consultants throughout the whole of any consultancy in schools.

At the same time consultants have to recognize that teachers tend to operate in very private settings. They are isolated from colleagues by the way in which teaching is organized, by the fragmentation caused by the timetable, and by the very building itself in many cases. Not surprisingly, therefore, there is frequently a very low degree of integration among any group of teachers. Many will be unused to cooperating and collaborating on professional matters. They will also have been socialized into the norms and values that come from a strong belief on the right to professional autonomy. This position is the subject of debate at the present time and it is not the intention to rehearse the arguments on either side here. The point is that consultants have recognized that the lack of professional integration among teachers reinforced by a strong belief system is a factor which has to be taken into account during any consultancy if there are to be successful outcomes in terms of appropriate developments as defined by those working within the particular school. It was necessary to involve staff at all stages in this consultancy to attempt to forestall any barriers that could have been created to effective professional development by such cultural factors.

There are, as Holly (1986) has argued, two fundamentally different interpretations of the role of school cultures in facilitating or inhibiting change and, therefore in responding to the consultancy process which is about a specific form of change. One view, conservative yet provocative, argues that schools with strong social cohesion tend to undermine efforts to bring about change. From the second perspective, more radical but reactive almost to the point of inactivity, it can be deduced that schools will resist much top-down change because such change is imposed and therefore unacceptable. Alternatively change that can be accepted or accommodated through a process of adaptation to the cultural norms of the school is more likely to be successfully implemented. Thus consultants need to be aware of the culture of the schools within which they are working.

Such awareness, together with the steps that any consultant will need to take in order to cope with the situation and to help the staff within the school to facilitate change, constitutes a significant learning process. Theories are tested against reality. Empirical evidence about how schools change and respond to change is collected. It is not simply that the consultant working within schools can and will learn from experience. Indeed it is possible, as Steele (1975) has argued, for individuals and groups not to learn from experience at all. Rather they will re-create the very situations that had previously caused them difficulties, pain and anguish. Learning within consultancy is a process of testing theory against practice and of re-testing successful practice, rooted in theory, in new situations. It involves accepting feedback and evaluation from clients as well as monitoring the effectiveness of the consultancy process itself. It can develop new conceptual views of the world of schools and schooling and lead to a deeper understanding of schools and the people within them. In this very real sense an effective consultant can make a significant contribution to educational research.

References

BELL, L. A. (1979) *The Management of Organisational change*, *Unpublished MSc Thesis*, Department of Educational Management, Sheffield City Polytechnic.

BELL, L. A. (1980) 'The evaluation of an in-service course: The planning', *British Journal of In-service Education*, 7, 1, pp. 38–48.

BELL, L. A. (1986) 'An investigation of a new role in schools: the case of the TVEI co-ordinator', In: Simpkins, T. (Ed.) *Research in the Management of Secondary Education*, Sheffield City Polytechnic.

BELL, L. A. (Ed.) (1988) *Appraising Teachers in Schools*, London, Routledge.

BELL, L. A. and MERSON, M. (1985) 'Technical and Vocational Educational Initiative'. *Metropolitan Borough of Solihull Evaluator's Report*, Department of Education, University of Warwick.

BOLAM, R., SMITH, G. and CANTER, H. (1978) *The LEA Adviser and Educational Innovation*, NFER, University of Bristol.

BOUD, D. and MCDONALD, R. (1981) 'Educational development through consultancy', *Monograph 42*, Society for Research in Higher Education.

CAMPBELL, R. J. (1985) *Developing the Primary Curriculum*, New York, Holt, Rinehart and Winston.

DAVIES, W. B. (1977) 'Consultancy — some of the Issues', *British Journal of In-Service Education*, 3, pp. 112–16.

DES (1987) *The Education (School Teacher's Pay and Condition of Employment) Order*, London, HMSO.

ELLIOTT-KEMP, J. (1988) 'The international consultant: some principles, problems and pitfalls'. In: Gray, H. L. (Ed.) *Management consultancy in Schools*, London, Cassell, pp. 183–94.

ERAUT, M. (1977) 'Some perspectives on consultancy in in-service education', *British Journal of In-Service Education*, 4, pp. 45–99.

FILLEY, A. C. (1975) *Interpersonal conflict Resolution*, Glenview, Il., Scott, Foresman and Company.

FOX, T. (1980) *Reflecting upon Education*, London, OECD/CERI.

FULLAN, M. (1986) 'Improving the implementation of education change', *School Organisation*, 6, pp. 314–20.

GRAY, H. L. (Ed.) (1988) *Management Consultancy in Schools*, London, Cassell.

HAVELOCK, R. G. (1969) *Planning for Innovation through Dissemination and Utilisation of Knowledge*, Centre for the Utilization of Scientific Knowledge, University of Michigan.

HOLLY, P. (1986) 'Soaring like Turkeys — the impossible dream', *School Organisation*, 5, pp. 346–64.

JARRATT (1985) *The Report of the Steering Committee for Efficiency Studies in Universities*, London, UGC.

LOCKWOOD, B. (1988) 'The Management of the GRIST Initiative', *Unpublished M.Ed. Dissertation*, The Department of Education, University of Warwick.

MORRIS, G. (1988) 'Applying business consultancy in schools'. In: Gray, H. L. (Ed.) *Management Consultancy in Schools*, London, Cassell, pp. 93–104.

OLSEN, E. and OLSEN, G. (1981) 'The use of consultants for school development: a Norwegian case study', *School Organisation*, 1, pp. 11–19.

PETTIGREW, A. (1985) *The Awakening Giant. Continuity and Change in ICI*, Oxford, Blackwell.

POSTER, C. and DAY, C. (Eds.) (1988) *Partnership in Educational Management*, London, Routledge.

RIBBINS, P. (1986) 'Qualitative perspectives in research in secondary education: the management of pastoral care'. In: Simkins, T. (Ed.) *Researching in the Management of Secondary Education*, Sheffield City Polytechnic, pp. 3–54.

SANDERS, W. and PINNEY, T. (1983) *The Conduct of Social Research*, New York, Holt, Rinehart and Winston.

SHIPMAN, M. D. (1985) 'Ethnography and educational policy-making'. In: Burgess, R. G. (Ed.) *Field Methods in Study of Education*, Lewes, The Falmer Press, pp. 273–82.

STEELE, F. (1975) *Consulting for Organisational Change*, Reading, Mass., Addison-Wesley.

STENHOUSE, L. (1975) *An Introduction to Curriculum Development*, London, Heinemann.

ZIMAN, J. (1988) 'Science in a Steady State', *The Guardian*, 5 April, p. 4.

4
In-service as Consultancy:
The Evaluation of a Management Programme for
Primary School Curriculum Leaders

Chris Day

The chapter will describe the way in which, through initial contracting, negotiation, and a mix of off- and on-site peer-assisted work over a period of nine months, forty primary school curriculum leaders from a number of different LEAs engaged in processes of professional learning and change which affected themselves and their schools. It raises issues of professional intervention through consultancy and provides evidence through independent evaluation, observation and personal testimony which supports the notion of effective professional and institutional development through a mixed economy of in-service opportunities for teachers.

The chapter is organized into three parts. The first briefly presents the purposes, structures and processes of the course itself, the second presents a summary of the course participants' reflections on the course, together with extracts from the independently conducted evaluation, and the third part discusses intervention theory on the context of teacher learning and change.

The Course

The course which will be described was collaboratively planned, and based upon principles of contracting, ownership and a recognition that the most important teaching and learning resource is the teacher him/herself. It extended over a period of ten working days between June and March, and was divided in six related phases:

June	*Phase 1*	Contracting (half-day attended by heads and curriculum leaders)
June–September	*Phase 2*	School based peer-supported classroom observation task (half-day)
September	*Phase 3*	First residential phase (three days)

September–February	*Phase 4*	School-based peer-supported negotiated curriculum development (two-and-a-half days)
March	*Phase 5*	Second residential phase (three days)
June	*Phase 6*	Networking continued (locally negotiated meetings)

The need for the course had been identified initially through a primary phase regional consultative committee on which the teaching profession, higher education and local education authority advisory and inspection services were represented. A half-day seminar was then held to which curriculum leaders (defined as teachers in schools with designated responsibility for the development of one or more aspects of the curriculum) from each participating LEA were invited. Here, specific needs and preferred learning models were identified. A planning team of LEA inspectors/advisers and teachers chaired by a higher education colleague was then formed and detailed course design began. At these meetings — six during the year preceding the launch of the course — the philosophy, structures, practices and resources for the course were determined. Continuity was assured by the teachers on the planning group who also acted as small group leaders, individual counsellors, and facilitators of locally based network meetings during the course. All attended a training course in preparation for this. Essentially, they provided moral and intellectual support to the course participants.

In a sense, planning group meetings themselves are a form of collaborative professsional development, since all members do not know each other, have different viewpoints and experiences (e.g. in large or small schools, urban or rural) and have not all been involved in course design before. It is crucial, therefore, that the course director/convener is able to play a variety of leadership roles himself. His/her considerations will be to ensure that the group becomes cohesive and coherent as soon as possible. Just as important, the course planning enterprise must be established as a corporate responsibility in practice. There are those who would wish to criticize planning groups on the basis that they will produce courses which are a 'compromise' of ideas and opinions. The experience of this writer suggests that effective planning decisions are those which illustrate a consensus which will be far more than the sum of individual ideas and opinion. In a sense, the planning itself represents a mutually supportive consultancy exercise in which the model of learning matches that intended for the course itself.

The course was marketed through an explanatory leaflet which was sent to all schools in the region and applications were sifted by the LEAs according to agreed selection criteria. The course aimed, according to the publicity, to help its members 'become more effective curriculum leaders, have improved knowledge and skills of leadership, and be better able to lead and be part of a team; to become more aware of current educational thinking, and be able to plan, support and evaluate curriculum development in conjunction with their headteacher and colleagues'.

The central theme of the course was the role of the curriculum leader and from this arose three related topics:

(a) leadership: helping qualities and skills;
(b) working alongside colleagues in professional and curriculum development in the classroom and in the staffroom;
(c) observing teachers and children in the classroom

In addition to the course content work, members were required to undertake pre-course and interphase tasks which, would 'be of practical relevance to their roles as curriculum leaders and their work in their own schools'.

The residential phases and their contents were built around the school-based work, and the initial contracting that had taken place. The dominant mode of organization was cross-authority small group work in which participants shared experiences and opinions critically; and 'pairings' of participants in order to provide 'close' support for school-based work. These were complemented by 'expert' input on issues related to the management of curriculum and professional development, which the planning group regarded as inseparable (Stenhouse, 1975), and local authority group networking. This reflected the planners desire to minimize or avoid problems of knowledge transfer and ownership which are often associated with the more traditional patterns of in-service, while at the same time avoiding the problem of parochialism which is associated with school-based work. The course was, in effect, an extended exercise in consultant supported school-focused development. It was designed specifically to enable teachers to reflect systematically on their thinking and practices and to confront these; and to provide active support for them both in their learning processes and in the planning, implementation and evaluation of changes which arose through the school-based curriculum developments which, with the learning networks, formed the central core of the course. The course members held responsibilities in a variety of curriculum areas and had a wide range of experience. Most had taken a leadership role in curriculum development prior to attending the course.

Expectations

Acceptance on the course was signalled by a letter which spelt out the level of commitment required, and indicated the emphasis upon school-based work and the value placed upon the teachers' own 'practical knowledge' (Elbaz, 1983). Below is an extract from the letter:

I am pleased you have been accepted on the above course which starts in September. The structure of the course will be:

1 Course task 1 (see below) to be completed before the pre-course meeting (NB This involved thinking about current responsibilities and roles).

2 A half-day pre-course contracting meeting in June which you and your headteacher will attend.

3 Course task 2 (paired classroom observation) to be completed before the first residential phase ($\frac{1}{2}$ day release).

4 First 3-day residential phase.

5 Course task 3 (school-based development task) to be completed between the first and second residential phases ($2\frac{1}{2}$ days release).

6 Second 3-day residential phase.

7 Post course meeting ($\frac{1}{2}$ day).

The planning team are fully aware that you, as a curriculum leader, can only develop your role successfully with the support of your headteacher. With this in mind we have built in a half-day element which both the course members and their headteachers attend, supply cover being given for both, at which there will be a discussion of:

(a) the types of support required from the headteacher both during and after the course.

(b) the need to ensure feedback into the school during and after the course.

(c) the need for task negotiation, contracting and confidentiality.

(d) observing and being observed in Course task 2.

At this meeting you will have the opportunity of meeting other members of the course from your own and other education authorities as well as your county group leader and adviser.

Contract building, contract making

The contracting meeting, which was attended by headteachers and their curriculum leaders, provided opportunities for heads to meet and discuss expectations, needs and practices with their peers, and for the curriculum leaders to do the same (Task 1 had been to prepare thinking on their current roles outside the classroom but inside the school, and how they saw the school themselves as benefiting from their attendance on the course). It also provided preparation for the first school-based task which involved classroom observations. More important, however, was that it introduced and actively encouraged the notion of contract making:

1 *with self*: to undertake to give the commitment, time and resources in order to fulfil obligations as a professional;

2 *with schools*: to ensure that colleagues in school benefit from my attendance on the course through regular feedback;

3 *with course members*: to agree with colleagues on the course to build trust through willingness to share and receive feedback; and to provide moral, intellectual and practical support as appropriate;

4 *with course organizers*: to attend all sessions; to fulfil written work requirements and to share these within negotiated frameworks of confidentiality; to contribute expertise and experience in small and whole group work;

5 *with LEA*: to ensure that the LEA benefits from my attendance on the course through affirmation/enhancement of my current management practices in school; and to be prepared to contribute to LEA in-service work where appropriate and through negotiation.

In particular, heads and curriculum leaders were encouraged to establish written contracts in consultation with other colleagues, concerning their responsibilities and answerabilities for the duration of the course. A proforma was provided in order to help participants focus upon issues of collaboration, communication and role before, during and after the course. Zaltman *et al.* (1977) are in no doubt that commitment through involvement will increase the likelihood of successful implementation: 'Implementation is possible when there is a feeling of ownership and commitment among the organizational membership'. There was no expectation that contracts or agreements would be completed immediately — indeed, quite the reverse, since in many cases staff would have to be consulted. It was recognized also that for many the idea of written agreements is alien, since the predominant primary school culture is that of informality, trust and collaboration. However, although there was no compulsion, most did make a written agreement. The comments below, elicited after the course express the range of response to the task:

> I came away feeling bewildered . . . when it came to writing the contract we both found it very difficult . . . I don't think my head and I really needed a contract as I know she would support me wherever possible . . . it must be left to the teacher and head to work out for themselves if they need a contract . . .

> I've never made a written contract before but can really see the value of them. They are:
> good for setting targets;
> good for negotiating time for task;
> good for ensuring commitment;

> The rock on which the whole thing (task) has been built has been the contract made first with Head and then with colleagues in my own school. We would have gone nowhere slowly without these.

Below is an example of one such contract:

Agreement reached between Headteacher and Curriculum Leader with reference to the curriculum leadership course June 1987–March 1988

Needs of Curriculum Leader
— to have ongoing review of curriculum through GRIDS (Guidelines for Review and Internal Development of Schools);

— to look at topic work throughout the school, i.e. aims, objectives, methods and evaluation;
— to involve staff in discussion;
— to develop professionally in order to fulfil role of curriculum leader.

Needs of Headteacher
— to provide on-going stimulus throughout the school as a back-up to basic fundamentals;
— to give staff and post holders opportunity to engender enthusiasm and interest in different curricular areas;
— to enable curriculum leaders to act as leaders and resource persons in these areas;
— to ensure use of all school resources.

Expectations of Curriculum Leader
— to implement course skills within the framework of the school;
— to be responsible for a specific area within a topic;
— to have specific times each week for curriculum development to take place;
— to provide feedback regularly to both head and staff;
— to liaise with relevant staff.

Expectations of Headteacher
— to provide opportunities for curriculum leaders to be responsible for different areas of the curriculum, to recognize the particular strengths of individual members of staff and to use them for the benefit of both children and staff;
— to emphasize the value of the stimulus created by topic work and a variety of approaches;
— to help the staff as a team to evaluate their work and the effectiveness of their teaching.

Support of Curriculum Leader
— to gain support and confidence of head and staff;
— to maintain a degree of confidentiality with head;
— to offer ongoing support in role as curriculum leader after the course.

Support of Headteacher
— to ensure that opportunity to use the course experience for the benefit of children and other staff is provided;
— to ensure that a positive attitude to the benefits of the course is engendered at staff meetings;
— to provide opportunities for curriculum leader to work in other areas in the school.

Responsibility of Curriculum Leader
— to the head, staff and children;
— according to the needs of the school, and the task set on the course.

Responsibility of Headteacher
— to the governors so that they will understand the purpose of the course;
— to the Authority that has financed it;
— to the children and staff who hopefully reap the benefits.

Constraints on Curriculum Leader
— lack of clarity about precisely what authority has been delegated;
— a lack of time in which to carry out responsibilities;
— a need for first-hand experience and knowledge of work being done in other areas of the school;

— an awareness of high expectations of other members of staff.

Constraints on Headteacher
— a need for an awareness of the effects on other members of staff who have not had the same opportunity;
— a need to avoid possible conflict by falling in with other people's ideas, if relevant;
— a need to recognize that an invitation to another teacher's classroom is necessary in order to work with any degree of ease;
— a need to show sensitivity in staff relationships.

Staff
— to adopt a positive attitude to members of the course;
— to show courtesy and a helpful attitude which will produce lasting benefits.

Headteacher
— to organize for unexpected emergencies, e.g. if time allotted to Curriculum Leader unable to be given;
— to view any criticism as constructive criticism from which benefit will be derived;
— to strive to be just and fair to all parties.

The residential phases

The course planners wanted to maximize motivation, commitment and learning, and the residential phases of the course were intended to build on the contracting by providing opportunities for teachers to distance themselves from the classroom in order to reflect on and plan for action in a variety of ways. The curriculum of these phases was in part prescribed (in relation to the advertised content of the course), in part self-generated (through school-based issues) and in part negotiated (through the peer group challenge and support groups which acted as reference points and met throughout the year). Reflection on the learning process was legitimized through the provision of timetabled time for this purpose; and the phases made active use of participants' knowledge and experiences and provided inputs which helped in planning and implementing the school-based tasks.

Peer supported school-based research and development

One course member described a school-based task as follows:

> I feel much relieved after spending half a day with Linda hammering out practicalities of the task. I am very thankful that course organizers have built this kind of 'moral support' in. We now approach the task with a greater degree of confidence ... We found the time we spent pooling our thoughts really helpful and, we thought, satisfying.
> One of the most useful aspects of the course has been the

opportunity of working with each other and having another person to bounce ideas off and to give moral support.

The task was to, 'plan and implement or evaluate/monitor a small-scale piece of curriculum development with one or more colleagues in your own school, including classroom observation. This should take account of the developmental context of your school, but not be dictated by it'. The task was documented and shared with colleagues during the second residential phase.

The emphasis upon school-based work is important, since it underlined the planners' subscription to the 'practicality ethic' of teachers. They believed that course members would value the work if they perceived it as having direct and tangible practical benefits for themselves and their schools. It was recognized, also, that moral and practical support would be necessary, and so this was built into the work through pairing with peers and through network support groups which met regularly.

Summary

It will be clear, then, that the course was designed specifically to enable teachers to reflect systematically on and confront their thinking and practices; and to provide active support for them both in their learning processes and in the planning,

Figure 4.1 An in-Service professional development process (based on Day, 1987)

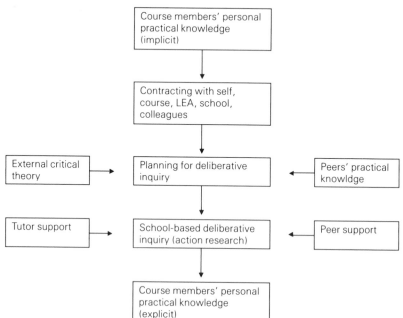

implementation and evaluation of curriculum development in school. This arose through the school-based action research which, with the learning networks, formed the central core of the course. The processes by which this was achieved are represented in Figure 4.1. Deliberative reflection and inquiry, contracting (with self and others), self- and peer-confrontation, and the sharing of insights gained from this are posited as essential ingredients in professional learning.

The Course Evaluation

This section of the chapter summarizes the reflective responses of the course members, documented in course diaries to which only the writer had access, and presents extracts from the independently conducted evaluation report. This was written as a result of collecting course members expectations prior to the course through questionnaires, questionnaire returns from all participants on completion of each residential phase, interviews with a sample of course members and non-participant observation of elements of the course:

> The majority of members had selected to come on this course because they had been looking for a means to improve their skills in curriculum leadership and perceived the course to be a stimulating and challenging opportunity . . .' (Banks, 1988).

Course members were asked what they hoped to gain from the course, and indicated that they hoped to:

(a) *improve skills* — in leadership, observation, management (group, team, of change of time, of conflict), running staff meetings, communication, 'handling' colleagues and innovation;

(b) *review attitudes* — towards colleagues, improve confidence, positive attitudes towards team work and curriculum innovation, create a positive attitude in overcoming difficulties encountered, tolerance, patience, more positive attitude in relation to own abilities and promotion prospects;

(c) *develop relationships* — improve working relationships with colleagues, influence other members of staff, ways of dealing with older 'set-in-their-ways' colleagues, and improve credibility with staff;

(d) *improve promotion prospects* — many but not all course members hoped to improve their promotion prospects as a result of participating on the course. (Banks, 1988)

Essentially, it seemed that members wanted to gain self-confidence and credibility with colleagues, to gain a broader perspective through temporarily but systematically distancing themselves from their own situation and evaluating it. Crucially, all felt themselves to be 'at a critical point' in their teaching careers:

> I felt if I did attend a curriculum leaders' course I might gain some

credibility, give them something to think about and even a little more confidence in me when I sit up and say 'I think we ought to do this'. I am also at a critical point in my teaching career. I need either a new challenge — like a new job outside of teaching, or something different within teaching — like responsibility for environmental studies which is my area — the one I'm trained in and have most interest in. I thought having attended a course for curriculum leaders it might actually help me to become just that — a proper curriculum leader in a 'proper subject', or one that I would enjoy.

Also if I'm honest, at the time, the idea of being away from my 35 second- and third-year juniors in my shoebox classroom appealed. I miss the intellectual side of my college sometimes too and also looked forward to meeting staff from other areas. We all tend to know each other very well and rarely get outside it. So with several misgivings and worries I agreed to go on the course.

Most members found that the classroom observation task (Phase 2) was 'for their own benefit' but 'had led to a general interest amongst staff in observations'. Although 'there was some criticism that the task was too open-ended', many 'commented on the value of visiting another school and sharing observations with a critical friend' (Banks, 1988). Diary extracts support these evaluations:

> . . . I found it an interesting and valuable experience, especially as I was observing middle infants, an age range in which I've had no experience at all. I also encountered many of the problems that arise in observation (deciding exactly what a child is doing, are they working or playing, is their talk task-related or not, what to do when your stop clock stops etc.), all experiences which will make my next set of observations hopefully more successful. I also then felt I had something concrete to take to Nottingham — I felt I'd achieved something and gained experience from it.

> I felt somewhat clumsy and was feeling in the dark.

> I am amazed at how much can be learnt about individual children when observation is properly planned and something specific is being looked at. I have resolved to try and set aside some time each week for this kind of observation in my own classroom.

Although some found it, 'difficult to adjust to these very stationary days after the demands of school', responses to the residential phases revealed 'general appreciation of the opportunity to have "time out" to reflect on your own practice and a chance to focus on the curriculum for three days' (Banks, 1988). Again, diary extracts support this:

> I enjoyed having the time to concentrate on just one thing. Although I found it difficult to switch off from school at first, I found in the three days that I could see my role more clearly. I could see what I was trying

to achieve and had just settled into lectures and thinking when it was time to go home.

Several times it occurred to me just how much you should be doing to become an effective curriculum leader and several times I felt 'I don't want to be a curriculum leader if I've got to put that much effort in'. So I suppose I panicked several times. I think my confidence, however, increased.

I began to feel that I was just as good as the others and maybe what I thought was just as relevant as anyone else, and that maybe I could be an effective curriculum leader. I also began to look foward to the piece of curriculum development that I was to do in my own school.

I was now more aware of the skills, I needed to develop in order to interact with my colleagues, to chair meetings in a more professional manner, to plan and assess innovations in specified areas of the curriculum . . . I returned to school feeling that I had taken a few steps in the right direction down a long and winding road.

I returned to school feeling more equipped to motivate my colleagues towards helping me seek ways in which curriculum development could be more effectively implemented in my own situation.

I was able to reflect upon last year in a more detached way and see the need for a change of priorities. Talking to colleagues on the course also helped, and made me realise that I was not alone in grappling with the demands of a post of responsibility.

School-based work

Banks (1988) reported that:

Course members seemed to find this task of benefit to themselves and also to their schools. Many indicated that they had learned or developed generalised skills such as co-operation with colleagues, how to gain access to colleagues' classrooms, the value of staff meetings and how to lead. There was also a sense that people felt more valued for their leadership qualities and that colleagues did take them more seriously. The awareness of the needs of colleagues also appeared to be heightend by the task including the value of listening to others, using their suggestions and a realisation that staff do welcome help. Other comments referred to the time-scale involved in curriculum development and the need to 'start small but think big' and 'to make haste slowly'.

The effect of this task on participants' schools varied considerably and many suggested that the effect was on-going and that they would be more likely to see the benefits in the coming months. In general the task seemed to have generated discussion amongst staff and made people

> aware that we need to evaluate what we are doing. In some cases the task had generated liaison between departments and schools. Further comments referred to the advantages of having an outside stimulus and that staff had realised the need to make the best of all their abilities. (Banks, 1988).

All the diaries reflected this valuing of the opportunity to engage in an extended piece of curriculum and professional development that had been 'legitimized' through course and contracts:

> I found it a real opportunity to think, to write, to find out what was going on. As a teacher I think we spend so long trapped in our classrooms with a group of children we forget what goes on outside the classroom. I found it a really valuable experience to be in school but out of the classroom and away from the children. To be able to sit in the staff room at break and not feel harassed or rushed, or exhausted was wonderful and I felt I'd been far more part of the school somehow. I feel through doing this study that I have changed enormously. I found myself getting really enthusiastic, looking for where I could go next and seeing where I could be of help.

> Immediately back at school I found myself using the strategies we had seen developed and discussed. Staff relationships have never been my strong point, but I find myself making suggestions to a member of staff about how to inform another member over the presentation of her children's books.

> Other members of staff are beginning to take an interest in the work we are doing . . . Teachers are beginning to stop me and ask advice on an informal basis . . . I am beginning to appreciate the skills of the other members of staff I am working with. I think I am at long last beginning to appreciate the meaning of tact.

Changes

The evaluator had asked course members to comment on how the course had affected: (a) their competence and effectivess as curriculum leaders; (b) their knowledge and skills for leadership; (c) their ability to lead and be part of a team; (d) their general awareness of current educational thinking; and (e) their ability to plan, support and evaluate curriculum development with their headteacher and colleagues. All of these areas had figured in the 'purposes' and 'intended outcomes' sections of the course publicity. The evaluation report stated that:

> From the responses it was evident that everyone felt that they had increased their competence and confidence in most, if not all of these

areas. The sense of improvement in self-esteem and confidence was particularly striking.

Responses concerned:

(a) *specific knowledge and skill acquisitions*, e.g. 'I will be able to organise a meeting more effectively'; 'I feel more able to handle people — to be aware that they may feel threatened — to make sure everyone has an opportunity to contribute'; 'I feel more confident in leading a team, feel more able to share experience and responsibility'; and 'It has given me a theoretical background to complement my practical experience in school'.

(b) *general gains*, e.g. 'I'm amazed at how the course has changed and clarified my thinking and practice. It has given me many new skills; 'It has changed my thoughts of how I see myself. Now I feel I have the confidence and powers to be a leader'; 'It has made me more positive, more aware of others' feelings, it has given me confidence in myself and my own abilities'; 'I am really grateful for what the course has done for me in restoring my self-image. This must reflect in an advantageous way what I'm going back to do in school'; and 'I am glad I was forced to ''action plan'' so all this won't fizzle out or grind to a halt'.

(Banks, 1988)

The diaries of the participants elaborated on these themes:

At the end of the course I was beginning to see the role of curriculum leader differently and to revise my opinions. The emphasis that the course had given to teaching styles, interpersonal skills, observation and assessment, as well as the general discussion with other course members was leading me away from regarding a curriculum leader as an 'expert' in a subject area who wrote schemes and organised resources. (He or she is) . . . an experienced, interested and professional teacher who considers wider issues and cross curriculum matters . . . just writing and organising them is not enough. The curriculum leader must know how to implement the ideas, to involve all the staff.

My ideas began to develop as to what was actually meant by curriculum leader . . . Time is needed to sit back and think of your own classroom practices and methods of improvement.

The idea of someone being a definitive authority I now found rather arrogant . . . Curriculum leadership, as I now perceive it, involves drawing on the collective skills of all one's colleagues rather than being totally dependent upon one's own assimilated knowledge.

Below is an extract from one diary which provides apt illustration of the psychological and practical results for one course member:

Before the course, I very much saw myself as an ideas person for Art and Craft, and waited for other staff members to come to me if they wanted help or advice. It was very much on an individual basis. I now see that role differently, with regard to bringing the staff together more as a team, involving every member of staff and valuing their involvement in developing the Art and Craft curriculum.

The course has given me the confidence to do this, and the feeling of credibility. Beforehand, I found approaching other members of staff with ideas very difficult, but the course has taught me how to deal with this through very different approaches which I hadn't thought of before.

The best example of this for me is the idea of ownership. I had never really realized before how much more willing people are to participate in something if they have played a part in it's initiation. I have put this into practice as part of my interphase task with very pleasing results.

Before the course, I probably would have approached the staff about the interphase task by stating that it might be a good idea to look at 'x' area of Art and Craft because people weren't doing it, or because there seemed to be a gap there etc.

Using the knowledge gained from the course, I opened it out to all the staff, to tell me which area they would like me to look at and work on, and the response was really pleasing, which gave me the confidence to carry it out. They wanted me to look at the area of technology because they all felt that it was their main weakness. They asked for simple ideas that they could use in the classroom, and to do this they wanted me to do a workshop after school.

I did this, using the knowledge and skills I had learned from the course about handling meetings. The workshop, and the previous meeting called to discuss what the staff wanted me to do, where the first meetings I had ever led. The workshop was extremely successful, everyone enjoyed it and gained confidence to try technology themselves in their classrooms, which they did that week.

Before the course, I would not have had the know-how or skills needed, to make those meetings successful. Previously I was afraid of meetings, but now my confidence has been boosted.

To conclude, the course has given me a renewed enthusiasm for teaching — 'recharged my batteries' so to speak — and enabled me to look at my teaching, and my relationships with a new perspective.

At times parts of the course were very daunting, and made me feel quite inadequate, but at least it created an awareness of issues in the curriculum.

If I had to choose one phrase to describe this course, so far, I think an apt one for me would be 'an eye-opener', as it has really raised my level of awareness, both as a classroom teacher and curriculum leader.

External Interventions in Teacher Learning: Support for Change

Teachers attending professional development activities will be in different 'states of readiness' to engage in learning — even where they themselves have participated in the planning. They will have different specific needs since they are likely to be at different stages in their own personal and professional development. Moreover, there can be no assumption that all the participants will be operating with equal effectiveness in their different school contexts. Planners of professional development activities must take these factors into account.

The structures and processes of the course had been in part dictated by available finance, but principally by assumptions concerning the conditions most likely to provide stimulus and support for teachers' learning and, where appropriate, commitment to change. The next part of this chapter makes these implicit assumptions explicit. The assumption both in the planning and processes of the course was that professional development cannot be forced. Teachers cannot be developed (passively), but can best develop (actively). Teachers gain new perspectives, increase their knowledge and skills as a natural part of their working lives. The problem is that although much teacher learning occurs naturally, gradually and by a variety of means, for years teaching has been an activity in which work has been planned, carried out and assessed for the most part privately. So much of this growth is unnoticed (by those outside the school), many changes are slow and unperceived (often even by the teacher); and growth in learning is not linear. With this in mind, the planners attempted through course structures and processes to:

1 support and extend teachers' capacities to be self-critical;
2 ensure participation in, and ownership of, the learning;
3 support self and peer confrontation of problems and issues.

Supporting and extending teachers' capacity to be self-critical

> The best way to improve practice lies not so much in trying to control peoples' behaviour as in helping them control their own by becoming more aware of what they are doing. (Elliott, 1977)

If we begin from the premise that '. . . the ultimate arbiter of whether some finding has implications for practice is the person engaged in practice . . . (Fenstermacher, 1983) then it follows that teachers have the capacity to be self-critical. Many, hopefully most, teachers will be 'connoisseurs' or potential connoisseurs who are able not only to distinguish between what is significant about one set of teaching and learning practices and another, and to recognize and appreciate different facets of their teaching and colleagues or pupils' learning, but also, as critics, to 'disclose the qualities of events or objects that connoisseurship perceives' (Eisner, 1979). In-service events should recognize and capitalize upon teachers' capacity to be self-critical. They are, in effect, external interventions in teachers' and schools' professional learning lives. Although most teachers are capable of reflecting on their thinking and practice, few have the time or energy to do this systematically or deliberatively. Most engage in what Elliott (1983), writing in the context of self-evaluation and professional development, calls 'unreflective self-evaluation based on tacit practical knowledge'. He defines practical knowledge as that which 'is derived from their own and others past experience' (Elliott, 1983). Elliott goes on to argue that for teachers to be truly autonomous, responsible, and answerable they must have opportunities to engage in 'deliberative inquiry' on past, current and future practice (see also Schwab, 1969, and Reid, 1978). Thus there was recognition that the quality of the teacher's reflective framework is a decisive factor in his or her development and that opportunities for the growth of clarity and awareness of one's own thinking and behaviour must therefore be built in as essential items to this course. The teachers themselves, then, acted as researchers (Stenhouse, 1975) within an action research model which involved *conscious reflection* and *'consciousness raising'* through dialogue provided by course tutors, peers and invited lecturers/workshop leaders.

In his survey of research in this area, Smyth (1984) reports that adults learn when they are provided with opportunities for continuous guided reflection, based on 'lived experience'. He suggests that adults and teachers learn by doing, and benefit most from those situations which combine action and reflection. Elliott (1984) comments upon the 'lack of a rich stock of self-generated professional knowledge', seeing the cause of this as being the traditional isolation of teachers' practice. An ILEA Report (1984) notes that 'a well intentioned respect for professional autonomy can lead some teachers to become prisoners within their classrooms'. Clearly, in-service courses should present opportunities for less teacher isolation and more time for reflection upon action, outside as well as inside the classroom.

Most, if not all teachers, often engage in what Schon describes as 'reflection-in-action . . . a reflective conversation with the situation' (Schon, 1983). Indeed, this is a significant means of generating new knowledge (e.g. of children's learning processes), skills (e.g. in responding to children) and concepts (e.g. of the communication of knowledge). In fact, 'reflection-in-action' and 'reflection-on-action' are both necessary parts of professional growth. However, capacities to reflect 'on' the action are often limited by social, psychological and practical factors such as isolation, time, energy and lack of opportunity. In addition, our explicit actions are often based upon implicit, unstated knowledge of the nature of practice in any given setting (Polyani, 1967).

Teachers very quickly develop what Yinger (1979) has labelled as 'routines' or decision habits which serve to keep mental effort at a reasonable level. Since it is rare for these to be made explicit or tested, the possibilities for evaluating those values, expectations and assumptions which underpin teaching are minimal. This evolution and internalization of a self-perpetuating theory of action has been characterized by Argyris and Schon (1976) as 'single-loop'. While single-loop learning is necessary as a means of maintaining continuity in the highly predictable activities that make up the bulk of our lives, it also limits the possibilities of change. It is argued that if we allow our theory of action to remain unexamined indefinitely, our minds will thus be closed to much valid information and the possibilities for change will be minimal. In effect, if we only maintain our field of constancy we become 'prisoners of our programs' and only see what we want to see. Thus planned professional development activities must provide structured opportunities for engaging from time to time in what Argyris and Schon (1976) call 'double-loop' learning. This involves allowing things which have previously been taken for granted to be seen as problematic, and opening oneself to new perspectives and new sources of evidence. Essentially, one has to be prepared to see oneself as others see one in order to understand better one's behavioural world, and one's effect upon it (Eraut, 1977a).

In effect, the course gave participants the opportunity to move from a normal mode of 'insider activity' (Ebbutt, 1982) in which they worked in isolation in their own classrooms and schools, reflected on their own practice from time to time, incorporated the results of their reflections into their practice sometimes, but did not collect data systematically nor produce written reports, towards a teacher researcher 'classic' action mode. Here the teachers worked in isolation in their own (and sometimes other) classrooms as part of a coherent pair and group which met regularly. They systematically collected and analyzed data concerning their own and colleagues' practice, generated hypotheses and wrote reports open to public critique. In addition research and development were concurrent interactive activities in which course members worked towards improvement by testing hypotheses at individual and institutional levels. In this very real sense they were involved in innovation and change, promoting confrontation of thinking and practice at both personal and institutional levels.

Ensuring participation and ownership

Most teachers share needs of:

— affiliation — the need for a sense of belonging (to a team);
— achievement — the need for a sense of 'getting somewhere' in what is done;
— appreciation — the need for a sense of being appreciated for the efforts one makes;
— influence — the need for a sense of having some influence over what happens within the work setting;
— ownership — the need for a sense of personal investment in the process of curriculum development and its outcomes.

Alongside this, there is much accumulated evidence to suggest that teachers learn best when they are actively involved in determining the focus of the learning. Participation for teachers, as for children, provides opportunities, 'for the development of decision-making skills, enlarges their perspectives and helps them become better informed about their own roles, responsibilities and problems of their colleagues' (Simons, 1982). Although writing in the context of whole school evaluation, the claims for participation that Simons outlines would apply equally to in-service work. However, there can be no assumption that all teachers wish to be self-directing. Some, like children, may wish to be 'told' things, or may have an expectation that they should be told. Indeed, where teachers are participants in their own learning, problems may arise because their inquiry skills are under or undeveloped. Indeed for some teachers who, for example, may be 'currently encountering conditions of decisional equilibrium or saturation, increasing participation may actually prove to be highly dysfunctional' (Aluth and Belasco, 1972). Similarly, attempts to change one's practice may involve a temporary 'de-skilling' or felt 'burden of incompetence' (MacDonald, 1973).

Although there is research which indicates that not all teachers wish to participate or indeed derive satisfaction from doing so (Duke *et al.*, 1980), this is more often than not the product of role expectation, personality factors or socialization. There are schools and LEAs in which teachers have long been treated as 'passive consumers within their own organizational structure' (House, 1974) and where 'time constraints and the control ethos of bureaucracy stand in the way of a teacher forging regular contacts with a range of different educators. This is not a situation which lends itself to obtaining and reflecting upon new ideas' (Morrison *et al.*, 1977).

Through participation, then, the traditional problems of assessing the significance of the impact of research on teachers' thinking and practice which have been identified by Eisner (1984), House (1974) and Phillips (1980) among others are avoided, as is the criticism that generalized research conclusions are not appropriate for all school and classroom circumstances. Furthermore, it was hypothesized that teachers would give serious consideration to findings which they themselves had made, and that in this way their understandings and perceptions of their work would be enhanced. Whilst not dismissing attempts to 'bolt on' to teachers' thinking, externally-generated knowledge, this model of learning asserts that connections between thinking, learning and actions are both acquired and made explicit through self-generated work, which is perceived as relevant and appropriate by each individual teacher.

Supporting self and peer confrontation of problems or issues

> ...effective change depends on the genuine commitment of those required to implement it, and that commitment can only be achieved if those involved feel that they have control of the process... Teachers will readily seek to improve their practice if they regard it as part of their professional accountability, whereas they are likely to resist change that is forced on them. (McCormick and James, 1983)

Essentially it was recognized by the course planners that the process of learning for change means that private assumptions and practices must be shared with, and opened up for questioning by self and scrutiny by others; and that, therefore, the process of development is unlikely always to be comfortable — even where extensive negotiations have taken place, contracts made and forms of confidentiality ensured. Consciously suspending judgment about one's own work will almost inevitably raise doubts about what under ordinary circumstances appears to be effective or wise practice. Yet the raising of doubts is only the first in what will be a number of potentially painful steps along the road to change — a road which can be littered with obstacles of time, energy, resources and, perhaps most important, self doubt.

Individual programmes of professional and curriculum development were, therefore, strengthened by peer support which was built into the course structure and processes. Teachers were thus enabled to confront their beliefs in the light of new personal and practical knowledge; reflection and confrontation were seen as a necessary prelude to transformation.

The Role of the External Consultant in Professional Development: a Partnership Model of In-service

The model of professional development which underpins the in-service work described in this chapter may be characterized as a 'partnership model' in which need is recognized as complex and not deriving from one source. The course does not, therefore, belong to any one individual or one interest group. It is jointly owned by each of the participants — the course member, school, LEA and planning group. It is an 'operational relationship in which people work together towards the achievement of their goal' (Bradley, 1988), a partnership between 'those who know how' and 'those who know what', in which no one individual or group claims a monopoly of wisdom.

The partnership model is similar to other client-centred models of in-service education in which the interventionist acts as a consultant. These are based on the assumption that professional development is a normal rather than an exceptional process, and that the function of the in-service educator should be to enhance this process. In-service education is viewed as a collaborative venture in which teachers and significant others are actively involved in negotiating processes and outcomes; and the power relationships of traditional in-service models are avoided.

Elliott (1976, 1978) views a teacher as an autonomous person who is responsible for his or her own learning and influenced by rational discussion. So for him, the role of the external agent is to promote and sustain an environment in which rational discussion may occur. Eraut's (1972) model of school-focused in-service education links success in helping schools solve problems to the quality of the relationship between the consultant(s) and the teacher(s). He suggests that the consultant's role cannot and should not always be non-directive. While emphasizing the importance of building a mutually supportive relationship with clients based on the commitment of the consultant to serving the client's needs, he develops a preliminary typology of consultants' roles which affect the complexity of purposes and processes of school-focused in-service education, i.e. the expert, the resource provider, the promoter (of an idea etc.), the career agent, the link agent (between teachers and schools), the inspector/evaluator, the legitimator, the ideas man, the process helper, the counsellor and the change agent (Eraut, 1977a). The typology, in effect, draws into in-service education many of the intervention roles developed within innovation and intervention theory in an attempt to move towards developing a theory of in-service education.

The models identify disadvantages with intervening prescriptively in the client's life, of taking the 'expert's' role in intervening, and in providing answers to questions. Instead, the interventionist aims to seek questions which are perceived by the client as relevant to his needs, to investigate answers to these questions collaboratively and to place the onus for action on the client himself. The notion here is that where work is related to personal experience and perceived needs and occurs in the context in which experience and needs occur (i.e. the school or department), the client's personal investment in the learning enterprise will be maximized. Indeed, it has been speculated that a significant proportion of the learning associated with change, in practice, takes place in the context of use (Eraut, 1982).

The partnership model (Table 4.1) builds upon both these client-centred models by developing further strategies for challenge and support within the notion of teacher autonomy. It recognizes the need for teachers to retain a high degree of control over the direction of their work and the confidentiality surrounding their contributions, whilst at the same time having access to appropriate critical support.

In this model, since teachers are seen as active causal agents in their own learning, the in-service design cannot be either masterminded or unilaterally controlled by the interventionist consultant/teacher educators. The work must, therefore, be collaborative, with a maximum flow of information between the stakeholders (in the case of this course the participant, school, LEA and University). To achieve this it is necessary to set up channels of communication through in-service courses which enable teachers and consultants to engage in a continuing dialogue about the nature of teaching and learning within agreed contexts. For both perceptual and practical considerations of time and energy the active support of external agents from outside the subject's immediate world is essential. Their presence is necessary:

(a) to establish and sustain a responsive, mutually acceptable dialogue about classroom, staffroom and school events in their context;

(b) to audit the process rather than the product of possibly biased reporting;

(c) to create a situation in which the teacher is obliged to reflect and confront thinking and practice (unlikely to happen in the crowded school day);

(d) to act as a resource which the teacher may use at times appropriate to the needs which he perceives;

Table 4.1 The Management of Professional Learning

Professional learning assumptions	External intervention (challenge and support)
Teachers have the capacity to be self-critical.	They should be offered the means by which they can begin to engage in deliberative inquiry.
Teachers are motivated to learn by the identification of a problem or issue which concerns professional role. (Internal commitment to learning arises out of this.)	They should be offered the means to reflect on their thinking and practice. (The perceived needs of the clients — the teacher and the school — are of paramount importance in beginning this process.)
Effective learning occurs in response to the exploration and confrontation of past and present practice.	Teachers should be offered affective and appropriate moral and critical support in processes of internalization rather than identification or compliance. This support should be provided by peers from their own and other schools and 'critical friends' from other agencies who would work in a partnership with them.
Decisions about change in thinking and practice should arise from reflections on and confrontation of past and present practice.	They should be offered appropriate support in developing strategies for planning; negotiating and implementing work in their own and others' schools.
Transformation in thinking and practice is a necessary part of a teacher's continuing learning process.	Teachers and schools should be supported in the testing or validation of their critical theories through the provision of external consultancy (learning networks, consultants, knowledge brokers).

(e) to support the teacher in planning, implementing and evaluating school based developments.

Where I refer to consulting or consultant, I intend, like Steele (1975), the emphasis to be on a particular process, not on a strict occupational role:

> By the consulting process, I mean any form of providing help on the content, process or structure of a task or series of tasks, where the consultant is not actually responsible for doing the task* itself but is helping those who are. The two critical aspects are that help is being given, and that the helper is not directly responsible within the system (a group, organisation or family) for what is produced. Using this definition, consulting is a function, not an occupational role *per se*. (Steele, 1975).

Within this consulting process, described elsewhere as 'involvement with detachment' (Woods, 1979), the kinds and timings of interventions which are made are critical. The building of trust and credibility, and effective support provided by the consultant are paramount.

---

*Anything a person, group or organisation is trying to do.

Steele (1975) identifies a number of functions of the consultant which are additional to those identified by Eraut (1977b) and which are applicable also to the processes of consultancy which occurred during this in-service course. These functions are discussed below.

Teacher role (Knowledge broker)

'...At times my main function has been simply to teach...I use didactic processes, such as seminars...but...I am defined as the teacher and clients are students...'.

Course as talisman

In my role as talisman it is the fact of my presence that is important. This fact provides a sense of security and legitimacy which allows the client to feel comfortable enough to experiment in areas where he might not act without support. The provision of school-based work as a course requirement, and the peer group support acted as talismen to the participants.

'Shot-in-the-arm' role

It is important that the regular meetings between teachers from different schools should provide a supportive 'nurturing' atmosphere where trust could be engendered. In order to achieve this, the meetings were held outside school for extended periods. Camaraderie and critical friendship were encouraged through cross-school, small group discussion and inviting other sympathetic outsiders associated with the themes of the course to attend, thus providing added legitimization and moral support. This moral support was particularly important as the project developed, when some teachers felt 'negative effects of innovation' (Nisbet, 1974), e.g. an increase in work load/anxiety.

Clock role/collector

There have been projects where my most important role seemed to be that of a timer or clock for the client system to watch. When there was a regular schedule of visits that I would make to a system...My presence (or the thought of it coming soon) served as a spur to clients to be thinking and experimenting so that they would have something to show me for the time in between my visits (Steele, 1975).

It had been negotiated that teachers keep diaries and that the school-based tasks be documented. This proved to be invaluable for all concerned, so that while the clock role described by Steele above might be taken to imply power and control, the consultant in this project was seen more as 'collector' in fulfilment of a properly negotiated initial contract.

Critical friend role

In an enterprise in which a number of people give of their time, energy and expertise for a common purpose it is necessary to establish at the outset what each wishes to gain. For although the purpose should be mutually agreed, what each participant will wish to gain from the process may be different. The question of gain is important and is part of the 'practicality ethic' of teachers identified by Doyle and Ponder (1976). They argue that teachers judge the worth of an innovation or 'change in classroom procedure' (such as in this project) according to its practical use to them.

There is a need for the consultant to establish from the beginning a 'private' relationship with each client as a basis for building confidence and trust, so that, for example the individual client or client group will know that whatever is said and whatever information is collected will be under his/her control. (Will anyone else see the videotapes of classroom teaching or the report of the school? If so, who, and at what stage?) Care must be taken that those who deliberately place themselves in a 'vulnerable' position where their work may be subject to judgment by unknown (or even known) others are reassured of the confidentiality of the material. 'Action research cannot be undertaken properly in the absence of trust established by fidelity to a mutually agreed ethical framework governing the collection, use and release of data' (Elliott, 1978).

Many programmes of professional development are based on what I believe to be a myth — that one can simply sit down with others, work out aims etc. and implement them. They do not take into account such concerns as anxiety, status and identity (Hoyle, 1970). In work which is concerned with a questioning of the teacher's self-image, the affective relationship is of prime importance. The importance of the affective area is rarely made explicit in the documentation of professional development work. Yet, it is clearly crucial for the in-service educator to consider the attitudes of the teacher, not only to the process of innovation, but also to the interventionist role of the consultant which is part of that process. How does the teacher perceive the consultant? Is he an authority or a threat? Is he a process helper or a judge with alien values.

The implication of the discussion so far has been that in-service education represents intervention into teachers' professional learning lives and therefore must take account of both principles of teacher learning and change and consultancy roles. The partnership model and the principles which underpin it may be translated into different kinds of in-service events at different levels, but certain of its features are under threat. The final part of this chapter will focus on the contexts in which the management of professional learning now occurs.

In Support of a Mixed Economy

For some years now there has been a continuing debate concerning the relative effectiveness and efficiency of different forms of professional development opportunities for teachers. This debate has centred implicitly upon notions of purpose, ownership, relevance and utilization. Whilst all would agree that the ultimate purpose of in-service work is to enhance the quality of education for pupils, the means by which this purpose is best achieved most effectively and efficiently are in dispute — hence the variety of activities, courses and conferences. Traditional, off-site professional development in the form of secondments to institutions of higher education has been criticized because these seem to have benefited the individual more than the school — although this must, in no small measure, be associated with a lack of forethought by the school and the seconding LEA. Because these courses have been designed usually by those who are often far removed from school and classroom life they have also been criticized for their lack of relevance. School-based in-service — the other end of the continuum — has itself been criticized because of its parochialism (Henderson and Perry, 1981). The central issues in both kinds of extreme have been need identification, ownership, application, and, implicitly, 'value for money' (interpreted as accountability to employers).

Increasingly, the argument has been made that, with limited financial resources available, professional development opportunities can only be supported centrally where they can be seen to relate directly to the needs identified by national or local government and schools. This apparently minimizes perceived problems of knowledge transfer (from in-service activity to classroom teaching) and, in theory at least, increases the ability of those nearest to the situation of need to control the design and processes of their own professional development. This view has been supported by the introduction of a system of financing in-service work, known first as Grant Related In-Service Training (GRIST) and more recently as Local Education Authority Training Grants Scheme (LEATGS). In this scheme LEAs have been given direct responsibility for managing the in-service work of their schools, and are held accountable for this annually by central government (DES, 1986). 'Categorical funding' of in-service is now a reality. National priority areas are identified annually by central government and resources provided, and the annual submissions required by DES from LEAs are required to be based upon systematic needs identification processes in their own schools. The net effect of this has been that, while the ideal is still to match institutional and individual need, where this is not possible, the former prevails. There has been a growth in school-based work and short courses designed for particular purposes and a decline in full-time students registering for courses in institutions of higher education. Pressures have mounted upon LEA officers and advisory and inspection services to add managing and monitoring the new system to their existing duties, and on higher education to adapt to the new ground rules with modularization of courses, accreditation and validation schemes. As the realities of full cost funding for in-service work are faced in LEAs, and 'managed time' becomes the norm, as 'cost centres' are established in universities, polytechnics and the other institutions of higher education, so the real financial cost of designing, delivery and evaluating in-service is being recognized.

In those areas where there is a tradition of collaboration between higher education, schools and LEAs (which, for example, involves joint planning meetings to design in-service work, 'needs identification' groups consisting of LEA, schools and higher education representatives, visits to schools by higher education colleagues and vice versa) the temptation will be to move towards more resource-led in-service in which work is 'commissioned' by schools and LEAs whose role becomes that of 'purchaser'. Contracts will be put out to tender and 'value for money' in the limited short term economical sense of numbers and costs may become the governing factor. External consultancy, whether it be in the form of advice, research, subject-specific input or evaluation, is now being costed; and this and other types of collaborative work will become more difficult to pursue because of conflicting economic forces. The assumption that the shift from one less than adequate system of programme design (dominated by higher education and LEA) to another (dominated by DES, LEA, and school) will result in more effective in-service work is yet to be tested, for

> the real crunch comes in the relationship between these new programmes or policies and the thousands of subjective realities embedded in people's individual and organizational contexts and their personal histories. How these subjective realities are addressed or ignored is crucial for whether potential change becomes meaningful at the level of individual use and effectiveness (Fullan, 1982).

The course which has been described attempted to address these 'subjective realities', whilst also taking direct account of institutional and LEA need. The expense involved in collaborative planning processes and the related time taken in contracting must be measured against the perceived learning of the course members and their impact upon school. 'Cost effectiveness' is not simply a matter of finance but of effective learning and change.

References

ALUTTO, J. A. and BELASCO, J. A. (1972) 'Patterns of teacher participation in school system decision-making', *Educational Administration Quarterly*, **9**, winter, 27–41.

ARGYRIS, C. and SCHON, D. A. (1976) *Theory in Practice: Increasing Professional Effectiveness*, San Francisco, Jossey-Bass.

BANKS, H. (1988) *Evaluation Report: 10 Day Regional Primary School Curriculum Leaders' Management Course*, School of Education, University of Nottingham.

BRADLEY, H. (1988) 'Partnership in the development of school management'. In: POSTER, C. and DAY, C. (Eds.) *Partnership in Education Management*, London, Routledge.

DAY, C. (1987) 'Professional learning through collaborative in-service activity'. In: SMYTH,

J. (Ed.) (1987) *Educating Teachers. Changing the Nature of Pedagogical Knowledge*, Lewes, The Falmer Press.

DES (1986) Local Authority Education Training Grants Scheme: Financial Year 1987–88, *Circular 6/88*. London, HMSO.

DOYLE, W. and PONDER, G. A. (1978) 'The practicality ethic in decision making,' *Interchange*, **8**, 3, 1–12.

DUKE, D. L., SHOWERS, H. K. and IMBER, M. (1980) 'Teachers and shared decision-making: the costs and benefits of involvement, *Educational Administration Quarterly*, **16**, winter, 93–106.

EBBUTT, D. (1982) 'Educational Action Research: some general concerns and specific quibbles', *Teacher-Pupil Interactions and the Quality of Learning Project, Schools Council Programme*, Cambridge, Cambridge Institute of Education.

EISNER, E. W. (1979) *The Educational Imagination*, London, Collier-Macmillan.

EISNER, E. W. (1984) 'Can education research inform educational practice,' *Phi Delta Kappa*, **65**, 7, 447–52.

ELBAZ, F. (1983) *Teacher Thinking: A Study of Practical Knowledge*, London, Croom Helm.

ELLIOTT, J. (1976) 'Preparing teachers for classroom accountability', *Education for Teaching, Journal of the National Association of Teachers in Further and Higher Education*, No. 100, summer, 49–71.

ELLIOTT, J. (1977) 'Conceptualising relationships between researcher/evaluation procedures and in-service teacher education', *British Journal of In-Service Education*, **4**, Nos. 1. and 2, 102–183.

ELLIOTT, J. (1978) *Who Should Monitor School Performance?* Mimeo, Cambridge Institute of Education.

ELLIOTT, J. (1983) 'Self-evaluation, professional development and accountability'. In: GALTON, M. and MOON, R. (Eds.) *Changing Schools... Changing Curriculum*, London, Harper and Row.

ELLIOTT, J. (1984) 'Improving the quality of teaching through action research', *Forum*, **26**, No. 3, 74–7.

ERAUT, M. (1972) 'In-service education for innovation', *Occasional Paper 4*, NCET.

ERAUT, M. E. (1977a) 'In-service courses: their structure and functions'. In: RICHARDS, C. (Ed.) *New Contexts for Teaching, Learning and Curriculum Studies*, Association for the Study of the Curriculum.

ERAUT, M. (1977b) 'Some perspectives on consultancy in in-service education', *British Journal of In-Service Education*, **4**, pp. 45–99.

ERAUT, M. E. (1982) What is learned in in-service education and how? A knowledge use perspective. *British Journal of In-Service Education*, **9**, 1, 6–13.

FENSTERMACHER, G. (1983) 'How should implications of research on teaching be used?' *The Elementary School Journal*, **83**, No. 4, 496–499.

FULLAN, M. (1982) *The Meaning of Educational Change*, New York, Teachers College Press.

HENDERSON, E. S. and PERRY, G. W. (1981) *Change and Development in Schools*. London, McGraw-Hill Book Company (UK) Ltd.

HOOSE, E. R. (1974) *The Politics of Innovation*. Berkeley, CA., McCutcheon.

HOYLE, E. (1970) 'Planned organisational change in education', *Research in Education*, **3**, May, 1–22.

ILEA Report (1984) *Improving Secondary Schools*. Report of the Committee on the Curriculum and Organisation of Secondary Schools. London, ILEA.

McCormick, R. and James, M. (1983) *Curriculum Evaluation in Schools*, London, Croom Helm.

MacDonald, B. (1973) 'Innovation and incompetence'. In: Hamingson, D. (Ed.), *Towards Judgement: the Publications of the Evaluation Unit of the Humanities Curriculum Project*. 1970–72, Centre for Applied Research in Education, Occasional Paper 1, University of East Anglia.

Morrison, T. R., Osborne, K. W. and McDonald, N. G. (1977) 'Whose Canada? The assumptions of Canadian studies', *Canadian Journal of Education*, 2, 73–82.

Nisbet, J. (1974) 'Innovation-bandwagon or hearse?'. In: Harris, A., Lawn, M. and Prescott, W. (Eds.) *Curriculum Innovation*, London, Croom Helm.

Phillips, D. C. (1980) 'What do the researcher and the practitioner have to offer each other? *Educational Researcher*, 9, 11, 17–20, 24.

Polyani, M. (1967) *The Tacit Dimension*, Garden City, New York, Doubleday.

Reid, W. A. (1978) *Thinking About the Curriculum*, London, Routledge and Kegan Paul.

Schon, D. A. (1983) *The Reflective Practitioner: How Professionals Think in Action*, London, Temple Smith.

Schwab, J. J. (1969) 'The practical: a language for curriculum', *School Review*, 1, 1–24.

Simons, H. (1982) 'Process Evaluation in Schools'. In: McCormick, R. (Ed.) (1982) *Calling Education to Account*, London, Heinemann Educational Books.

Smyth, W. J. (1984) 'Teachers as Collaborative Learners, Clinical Supervision: a state of the art review', *Journal of Education for Teaching*, 10, 24–38.

Steele, F. (1975) *Consulting for Organisational Change*, Massachusetts Press, University of Amherst.

Stenhouse, L. (1975) *An Introduction to Curriculum Research and Development*, London, Heinemann.

Woods, P. (1979) *The Divided School*, London, Routledge and Kegan Paul.

Yinger, R. (1979) Routines in teacher planning, *Theory in Practice*, XVIII, 163–169.

Zaltman, G., Florio, D. and Sikorski, L. (1977) *Dynamic Educational Change*. New York, Macmillan.

5

Process Consultation in School Self-Evaluation: Some Second Thoughts*

David Hopkins

The focus of this chapter is process consultation, the development of skills such as team building and problem solving within a school staff as part of their involvement in a school self-evaluation project. School self-evaluation projects usually occur for specific purposes such as ensuring that the school is operating well (accountability purpose) or as a precursor to changing aspects of the schools organization or curriculum (development purpose). Our concern here is with school self-evaluation as a means of developing a competence within a school staff for problem solving and action planning, the process side of any change or evaluation effort. The chapter falls into two major sections: the first gives a context for process consultation and school self-evaluation, and the second describes experiences with process consultation in a particular school self-evaluation project. In what follows, I first distinguish between the task and process dimensions of school evaluation, then examine the contribution of organization development to school-based review, and third present a conceptual framework and method for doing such evaluations. I then define process consultation as a concept and describe the workshop design used in the process consultation. My hope is that the chapter will illuminate this important aspect of engendering a capacity for change within schools.

School Self-Evaluation and the Task Process Distinction

School self-evaluation has over the past decade become a clearly etched feature on the educational landscape. The reviews conducted by Elliot (1980/82) and James

*A previous version of this paper co-authored with Colin Vickers, was published in the *Cambridge Journal of Education* 16, 1986, with the title 'Process Consultation in School Self Evaluation'. I am grateful to Colin for his collaboration in the process consultation activities described in the paper and for his support and enthusiasm in preparing the original draft. I am also grateful to the *Cambridge Journal of Education* for allowing me to reprint the original material here.

(1982) suggest that the appearance, if not the reality, of school self-evaluation is widely accepted in Local Education Authorities and schools in the United Kingdom. In a more recent international review I found evidence of school self-evaluation activities in 12 'western' OECD countries (Hopkins, 1985a). This range of practice although fairly similar in technique, i.e. schools engaging in a process of reviewing their organization or curriculum (or parts of it), is often different in purpose. The most notable distinction is between accountability and development purpose. So for example the accreditation schemes in the US are a major part of an explicit accountability programme; many of the school self-evaluation schemes in the UK also perform this function. On the other hand, schemes for school-based review (a synonym for school self-evaluation) in many European countries, particularly Belgium, the Netherlands and Denmark, are an esential part of an equally explicit school improvement programme.

But in practice most school self-evaluation projects embody some form of development and accountability function, and can be classified accordingly, as in Figure 5.1. So, for example, School A's evaluation scheme has a major development purpose – it could be a pilot school in the Guidelines for Review and Internal Development in Schools (GRIDS) project – but it is also minimally accountable to itself and its community. School B's evaluation scheme on the other hand is accountability orientated – the LEA requires a regular and validated evaluation – but as a consequence of doing the evaluation a group of staff worked on improving an aspect of the school's curriculum. Although we are primarily concerned in this chapter with evaluation schemes that have a development purpose, the message applies equally to those that do not. But if such schemes adopt the practices outlined below, then it may be that their purpose will also change.

When a school self-evaluation has a deliberate development purpose another distinction needs to be drawn: that between the task and process aspects of school development. For example, a school may choose to undertake a curriculum review in order to improve certain aspects of the presented school curriculum. In this case the review would have as its main purpose a set task, a substantive change in say the fourth or fifth year option pattern. Alternatively, but less frequently, a school may engage in a self-evaluation not with any specific task element in mind but as part of a more generalized attempt to enhance the organizational capacity of the school, to make it more receptive to change and more effective at problem solving. In this case the process of review or evaluation, the ability of a school to problem solve and plan systematically, is the major purpose of the exercise. Put another way the task–process distinction reflects whether the evaluation is part of an innovation strategy (task) or the innovation itself (process).

This distinction apart, the research literature consistently suggests that any intervention such as School-based Review (SBR) needs to include both task and process elements (Fullan, Miles and Taylor, 1980). Elliot (1982) commenting on his large-scale survey of SBR activities in Britain makes a similar point, that teachers are far less resistant to SBR when it is connected with curriculum review.

Of course these two elements coexist: one cannot engage in curriculum review

Figure 5.1   Scheme for classifying the twin purposes of school self-evaluation

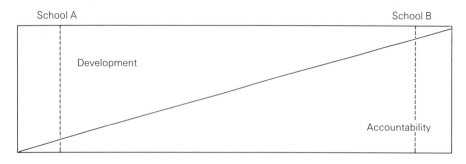

effectively without following some systematic evaluation process; similarly there is no point in transforming a school's capacity for problem-solving if there are no problems to solve. However, our experience suggests that it is the process side of school self-evaluation that has received least attention, particularly in the UK. The purpose of this chapter is to emphasize the process aspects of school self-evaluation and describe one way of developing the expertise of a school staff in this area within the context of a particular school self-evaluation project.

School-Based Review and Organization Development

Over the past twenty years organization development (OD) and allied techniques have provided the main approaches to transforming a school's capacity for problem solving. Although one can trace the development of OD back to the social psychological writings of Kurt Lewin and the establishment of the National Training Laboratory in the immediate post-war period, it was only in 1971 that the first mature expression of OD in education occurred with the publication of *OD in Schools* by Schmuck and Miles (1971). Almost a decade later in a systematic and thorough analysis of OD in schools (in the US and Canada) Fullan, Miles and Taylor (1980) reported that on the basis of their evidence OD in schools had 'diffused to a larger extent than we and others had realised'.

Runkel and Schmuck (1984) describe their approach to educational OD thus:

> In our work, we have usually used the following small steps as the primary ingredients of our OD strategy:
>
> 1 *Clarifying communication*: Clarity of communication is essential to any lasting organisational change. Members of the school must learn to clarify the communication they get from one another. Internal communication networks must operate at high fidelity, and external channels must map the environment accurately.
> 2 *Establishing goals*: Educational goals are usually ambiguous and diffuse. Organisational members can learn to clarify and share their

objectives and to increase their sense of 'owning' the goals and integrating their efforts.

3 *Uncovering conflict and interdependence*: Clarifying communication processes and objectives will lead to increased awareness of conflict and interdependence. Confronting conflicts and exploring interdependence will help to establish norms and roles that will aid the school in accomplishing its educational tasks.

4 *Improving group procedures*: Most organisational activity occurs in meetings of face-to-face groups. Meetings are rarely satisfying or productive for all faculty members; they are often frustrating. New skills for facilitating task productivity and group maintenance can help any meeting to be more satisfactory.

5 *Solving problems*: Adaptability implies active engagement in continuous problem-solving cycles for identifying, analysing, and acting on environmental contingencies. OD can help schools to extract creative solutions that yield a higher rate of success than the solutions that merely extrapolate past practice.

6 *Making decisions*: OD almost always disperses influence much more widely throughout the system than is usual in present day school organisations. Power need not be decreased on one job to be increased in another, although sometimes it is helpful to reduce authority if it is not based on knowledge and competence. Schools must learn alternative styles of making decisions to assure commitment from those who must carry out the decisions.

7 *Assessing change*: Change for its own sake is not necessarily useful. Change should solve, or at least reduce problems. Schools must choose criteria for evaluating progress toward long-range and short-range goals.

One of the most important and effective consultancy strategies is survey feedback (Hopkins, 1982). Survey or data feedback is the systematic collection of information, which is then reported back to appropriate organisational units as a basis for diagnosis, problem-solving and planning. Bowers and Franklin (1972) describe survey feedback thus:

> Change is throughout a rational process that makes use of information, pilot demonstrations, and the persuasive power of evidence and hard fact . . . where the survey feedback is employed with skill and experience, it becomes a sophisticated tool for using the data as a springboard to development.

The correlation between this description of Bowers and the process of school evaluation is striking, and provides a strong argument for those involved in SBR to utilize survey feedback methods in their work (Hopkins, 1985b).

The purpose of this review of OD has been to illustrate that a body of technical knowledge is available for utilization in SBR efforts. The intention has not been to advocate the adoption of OD as a package, but to point to its utility for review in schools. OD has its critics: some say that it cannot work in organizations like schools, and many object to its apparently technocratic ends/means orientation. These criticisms are a valid commentary on the mainstream use of OD as a management tool especially in the United States. This particular view is not being advocated here because (a) the values it espouses are inimicable to education, and (b) schools as organizations are not amenable to such interventions. This discussion has drawn on the work of Matthew Miles, Philip Runkel and Richard Schmuck who have adapted OD techniques and applied them to education. Their concept of OD is as a democratic process designed to humanize schools.

More recently SBR has tended to supplant OD as a more appropriate means for school improvement and internal development. SBR is a school improvement strategy that involves a whole school staff in a systematic review of current practice for the purpose of developing and implementing action plans for improvement. As such SBR places great emphasis on effective staff collaboration which means in most schools that skills in communication, problem-solving and team building have to be consciously developed. In this respect SBR utilizes many of the techniques of OD and process consultation (Schmuck and Runkel, 1985), so much so, that some regard SBR as a type of OD intervention. Both SBR and OD do share the meta-goal of enhancing a school's capacity for problem-solving and the vision of the relatively autonomous school. But in practice SBR is less dependent than OD on technology and external expertise (both of which are very expensive and time consuming) and more concerned with starting at a rather more informal level, and with internal school development and control.

The School-Based Review Process: A Matrix and GRIDS

Figure 5.2 is a conceptual framework within which these issues can be considered. It is a matrix arrangement that identifies the major roles involved in SBR and the main components of the SBR process (for further details see Bollen and Hopkins, 1987). The roles and functions axis, i.e. those involved in the SBR process and performing specific functions, contains an ever increasing list of people. The axis describing the process of SBR is in fact more than that because it constitutes a generic school improvement strategy. When the two are fitted together a myriad of interactions, encapsulated in cells, are produced. These cells represent the totality of SBR experience, but of course not every cell is represented in any one SBR project. It is probable that in analyzing various SBR projects fairly consistent patterns of cells will emerge that characterize different approaches to SBR.

An example of an actual approach to school self-evaluation, rather than a conceptual framework, is provided by the GRIDS project in England and Wales. GRIDS is a pilot project which was funded by the Schools Council to develop and evaluate self-review materials that schools can adopt for SBR purposes. The materials are designed to be free standing and to engage the school in a problem-solving exercise that can be utilized with different problems in the future. The approach taken to institutional review and development in the GRIDS project is an incremental one. It has been conceptualized as a one-year process with five main phases as illustrated in Figure 5.3. The GRIDS materials are contained in two handbooks: one for primary (up to 11 years of age) schools and another for secondary (11–18 years of age) schools (McMahon *et al.*, 1984). The focus is firmly placed on internal school development and there are a number of key principles that underpin the materials and which are central to the GRIDs method. These are that:

1 the aim is to achieve internal school development and not to produce a report for formal accountability purposes;
2 the main purpose is to move beyond the review stage into development for school improvement;
3 the staff of the school should be consulted and involved in the review and development process as much as possible.;
4 decisions about what happens to any information or reports produced should rest with the teachers and others concerned;
5 the head and teachers should decide whether and how to involve the other groups in the school, e.g. pupils, parents, advisers, governors;
6 outsiders (e.g. external consultants) should be invited to provide help and advice when this seems appropriate;
7 the demands made on key resources like time, money and skilled personnel, should be realistic and feasible for schools and LEAs.

The purpose of briefly describing the matrix and GRIDS is to illustrate approaches to SBR that emphasize the process aspects of a develomentally orientated approach to school self-evaluation. Both GRIDS and the matrix underscore the importance of staff development and the acquisition of specific organizational skills. These skills, although most probably new to most staff, are also professionally important and useful in a range of educational situations. The matrix diagram (Figure 5.2) gives an indication of the range of skills that SBR develops in a staff, and the SBR process that has been described is specific about providing training in such skills. Some of the skills that have been identified are negotiation, communication, team building, action planning, decision making, developing and analyzing questionnaires, feeding back information to small groups, designing in-service programmes and evaluation. Although not everyone will develop each of these skills, an awareness of their importance will be generated inside the school and a reservoir of expertise within the staff developed. Also, in many instances the role flexibility inherent in SBR means that an *ad hoc* group of staff (often young and relatively inexperienced) will be responsible for managing the review. This gives these individuals valuable management and organizational experience that will contribute to their future careers.

In the following section task and process consulting at a micro-school level are reviewed. Further, a number of the skills mentioned above are described as well as one method of acquiring them.

Figure 5.2 *Process and roles in School-Based Review: A matrix*

PROCESS	SUBJECT to review	DOING the review	MANAGING the review	SUPPORTING the review	CONTROLLING the review	INFLUENCING the review
Start Conditions — Past Experience, History						
Preparation (Readiness) Phase:						
— Initiation						
— Negotiation over —						
* participation						
* control						
* training						
— Decision to proceed						
Review (Initial) Phase:						
— Planning for Review						
— Decision on Instrumentation						
— Data Gathering & Analysis						
— Reporting of Findings						
— Decision to Proceed						
Review (Specific) Phase:						
— Setting Priorities						
— Planning for Review						
— Mobilisation of Resources/Expertise						
— Training for Review						
— Gathering Information						
— Validating Conclusions						
— Feedback & Evaluation						
— Decision to Proceed						

Development Phase:
- Establishing Policy
- Planning for Implementation
- Training (Inset) for Implementation
- Implementation of Policy with particular reference to:-
  * school organisation
  * materials
  * teaching style
  * knowledge utilisation
  * acceptance of change
- Monitoring and Evaluation

Institutionalisation Phase:
- Monitoring of Action
- Utilisation of SBR Process in other areas of curriculum and school organisation
- Development of problem solving capacity as an organisational norm within the school

Figure 5.3   *GRIDS stages and steps. Optional paths are indicated by broken arrows.*

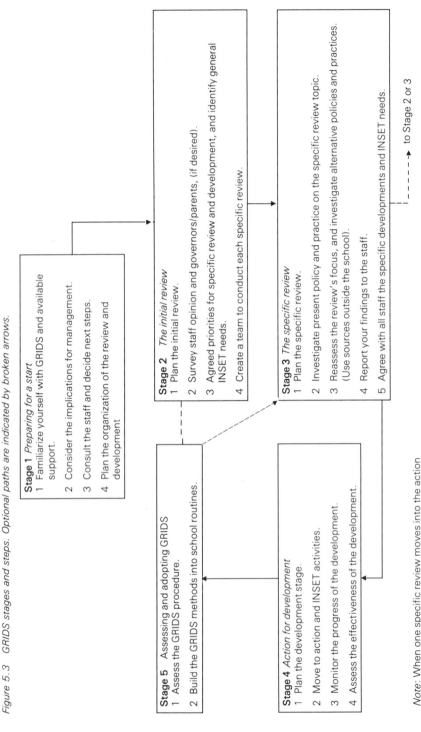

Stage 1 *Preparing for a start*
1 Familiarize yourself with GRIDS and available support.
2 Consider the implications for management.
3 Consult the staff and decide next steps.
4 Plan the organization of the review and development

Stage 2 *The initial review*
1 Plan the initial review.
2 Survey staff opinion and governors/parents, (if desired).
3 Agreed priorities for specific review and development, and identify general INSET needs.
4 Create a team to conduct each specific review.

Stage 3 *The specific review*
1 Plan the specific review.
2 Investigate present policy and practice on the specific review topic.
3 Reassess the review's focus, and investigate alternative policies and practices. (Use sources outside the school).
4 Report your findings to the staff.
5 Agree with all staff the specific developments and INSET needs.

Stage 4 *Action for development*
1 Plan the development stage.
2 Move to action and INSET activities.
3 Monitor the progress of the development.
4 Assess the effectiveness of the development.

Stage 5   Assessing and adopting GRIDS
1 Assess the GRIDS procedure.
2 Build the GRIDS methods into school routines.

- - - - ▶ to Stage 2 or 3

© SCDC Publications 1988

Note: When one specific review moves into the action for development stage another topic can come under specific review. There is no need for one GRIDS cycle to be completed before another begins. Lessons from the first review will improve those which follow.

Process Consulting as a Concept

Within the GRIDS model is the opportunity to review and to improve aspects of the schools's organization and curriculum. This approach focuses on an internal procedure for review, that can lead towards school autonomy. Both product and process elements are evident. Task and process consulting are external resources which can be employed, and are indeed encouraged, in the GRIDS process.

It is task consulting that is best known in schools. Most schools are looking for improvement. Characteristically the staff choose a curriculum focus (e.g. Primary Science) as a result of the 'gap analysis' completed in the GRIDS model. Occasionally cross-curriculum topics like school organization or discipline are chosen. In most cases a degree of expertise exists in the school to assist with the review and the ensuing action. Staff are also accustomed to requesting outside support (e.g. local advisers) to deliver new ideas for curriculum development and implementation. An example would be the county English adviser asked to give new ideas to infant school teachers interested in improving pupils' writing. This could clearly be defined as task consulting, with the adviser attempting to guide the staff towards a product (i.e. writing in this example).

More pertinent to this chapter is the process consultant, the affective partner in the GRIDS process. Process consulting belongs to a new era in school management. Process consulting is part of an ethos which espouses the importance of staff development as a prerequisite to curricular change. Therefore, process consulting and its methodology is not for the 'faint-hearted leader'. Process consulting also provides school staff with the opportunity to develop new skills that relate to the implementation of curriculum change. Among these skills are:

1 recognition and planning for curriculum change;
2 interpersonal skills for school staff;
3 team building;
4 systematic problem-solving.

The process consultant can approach the development of these skills in two ways: either through isolated skill development (e.g. human relation activities), or through skill development based on current curriculum development activities (e.g. GRIDS project focusing on Primary Science).

In the first situation a process consultant attempts to take staff through a number of exercises or workshops which are hypothetical, perhaps impersonal and often low risk. An example of an activity would be a communication exercise designed to improve staff listening skills. The exercise might be followed by a short lecture on listening skills. Staff are encouraged to retain these skills for future use. For the second situation the process consultant 'ups the ante' by attempting a similar array of exercises and activities, but in this instance the focus is no longer hypothetical. Listening exercises exploit a perceived need in the school's communication. Team building activities ask staff to 'risk a little' when they share some of their personal perceptions and beliefs as a prerequisite to better staff relations. Because the second approach involves experiential learning, the exercise increases the personal risks for the staff involved. The headteacher of a secondary school, for example, risks unwanted change when allowing a process consultant the opportunity to show staff more about participative management and consensus decision making.

Process consultants can come from within or outside of the mainstream of the educational field. But, because of the degree of personal risk involved, process consultants need to be well-versed in adult teacher/training techniques, flexible in their approach to satisfy client needs, and particularly aware of group process. Currently the process consulting which has been embarked upon in British schools is a reflection of the very early (i.e. 1970s) activities undertaken as part of OD in US schools. Many of the exercises currently in use in Britain, for example, are part of the elementary and high school curricula in the US (Johnson and Johnson, 1982). These basic, yet useful exercises, are complemented by more intricate models (e.g. Herschey and Blanchard, 1982 and the series *Annual Handbook for Group Facilitators* (Pfeiffer and Jones, 1969 *et seq.*). Process activities have been treated with some scepticism. So perhaps the best way to judge the efficacy of this experiential learning tool for staff development is to describe the design of some of our recent workshops.

Workshop Design

A series of process consultancy workshops was recently conducted in an LEA that was embarking on the GRIDS project. There was a great diversity between the four primary schools we visited. The overall process consulting design, however, remained consistent. This design was as follows:

Step 1 school visit by consultants to learn more about school needs (e.g. school climate, school objectives, staff agenda, headteacher's agenda, GRIDS task focus);

Step 2 consultant meeting to plan workshop design (consideration of new information);

Step 3 specific workshops presented for school staff;

Step 4 optional return to school for further process/development assistance.

The first step is crucial for the ultimate success of the workshop particularly when staff are initially sceptical. Process activities are a novelty for most British educators. The initial visit can often allay fears and help establish a contract between those involved. Even volunteer workshops, like the ones we are describing require the consultants to respond to certain agreed needs. Reciprocally, the school staff agree to initial participation and outline the facilities that can be made available. A few of the questions typically asked by process consultants illuminate the commitments that need to be made:

1 How much time will be available?

2 Will all the staff (including the head) be available?
3 Can we use a larger open space?
4 How far have you proceeded with the GRIDS?
5 Are you having difficulty identifying how to develop and initiate strategies?

One of the 'secrets of success' in process consulting is to know your audience. Is the assumption about the need for some team building confirmed by discussion with the staff? Is the school climate relatively open to participatory learning? Is the organizational climate autocratic or democratic? At what stage is the school with respect to the GRIDS process?

The four schools we worked with presented a range of situational differences. Leadership styles varied with each head. All four heads were relatively new to their schools, and one was a first-time appointee. There was a mix of male and female staff in three of the schools. In one school the entire staff was female including the head. All four schools had a positive school climate from the consultants' view; the staff in particular appeared committed to their schools. In each case the schools had become involved in the local GRIDS project because they had been identified by the local authority as having a potential for 'success'.

Although the staff agenda and the headteacher's agenda for 'process assistance' were similar in each of the four schools, there was some diversity and difference. As in most schools, there was variation between the head's perceptions and those of the staff. This is fertile ground for the process consultant who can use group techniques to both maintain diversity of opinion but consolidate the efforts of the individuals involved. The task focus of each school was fairly traditional, (e.g. primary sciences, language). As part of the GRIDS project in this LEA a task consultant had been found for each of the schools.

The second step in the process is planning by the consultants. The information and the perceptions gained from initial visits were brought together in a preliminary workshop design. Both of the consultants adopted a style whereby each produced a draft of the proposed workshop which was then discussed. Responses to questions asked in earlier visits to the schools were addressed. Modifications with respect to content, order and presentation were made and agreed upon. Although time-consuming, this collaboration had a distinct advantage: the cumulative expertise of the consultants invariably led to a stronger workshop design. Following the planning meeting(s), it was agreed to prepare the pertinent materials for the forthcoming workshops and to keep in touch.

Workshop Activities

The day has arrived. Transportation is arranged. Chart paper has been set aside. Markers are in hand. Sufficient 'handouts' are ready for the workshop. Cue cards are prepared. Material to be displayed has been printed on chart paper with prompts or notes written carefully in pencil under the headings to be used.

The four schools required different approaches. The two-hour workshop design which follows is therefore a composite of features from each of the four workshops. The following is an overview of the workshop design.

    1 Introduction of facilitators (5 minutes)
    2 Statement of purposes (5 minutes)
    3 Get-to-know-you or ice breaker activities (15 minutes)
    4 Communication exercises — broken squares (15 minutes)
    5 Communication lecturette (5 minutes)
    6 Problem-solving questionnaire (5 minutes)
    7 Problem-solving model — lecturette (15 minutes)
    8 Problem-solving sequence:
       (i)   defining problem — resolution activity (15 minutes)
       (ii) forcefield analysis (10 minutes)
       (iii) brainstorming solutions (5 minutes)
       (iv) criteria for selection (5 minutes)
    9 Problem-solving — lecturette (10 minutes)
  10 Evaluation and closure (10 minutes)

Responsibility for each of the stages was undertaken by one of the two facilitators. What follows is a more detailed description of the activities.

    1 *Introduction*: the two facilitators, after informally greeting each of the participants, initiate the workshop by introducing each other. The biography is minimal, stressing only qualifications for leading this type of activity and personal background. It is important to engender credibility and a degree of warmth at this stage.

    2 *Statement of purposes*: In this case there were two:

       (i) developing problem solving skills; and
       (ii) team building.

    The format of the workshop, the time frame and 'ground-rules' are negotiated and the commitment of the staff to this is solicited.

    3 *Get-to-know-you/Ice breaker activities*: An example of a 'get-to-know-you' activity would be 'six squares'. Participants divide a page of paper into six. Then they move about the room 'meeting' six people. Each time they meet a colleague they asked them an interesting question recording a key phrase on their paper with their colleague's name. After six or seven minutes the group is bought back together so that the facilitator can debrief the activity (e.g. what did different people learn about John? Jane? Howell?).

    There are a large number of alternatives for this part of the design. Cooperative games are sometimes used if more vigorous activity is included. This stage of the design is sometimes known as the 'warm-up' phase.

    4 *Communication exercises*: Most problem-solving and group process are

enhanced by improved communication skills. 'Broken squares' is an activity which requires groups of five. Participants are given packages filled with various puzzle parts which can only be pieced together when participants are willing to share puzzle parts. No talking is allowed. Frustration and 'power plays' often take place. Success is achieved when individuals are cooperating.

This activity is debriefed. A sentence starting, for example, 'Right now I feel . . . ' may be used to solicit responses from the group. The consultant may prod a little by focusing on specific points of functional breakdown. If there are extra participants beyond the five per group, then people can be used as observers.

5 *Communication lecturette*: The consultant can utilize the experience of the previous exercise to illustrate a number of points about communication. For example, the need to have a 'two-way communication' among a school staff. Barriers to communication, like poor listening and too much educational jargon when speaking to parents, are also discussed. The focus of this short lecture is to point out the implications of positive communication.

6 *Problem-solving questionnaire*: The participants are presented with a ten-item questionnaire which establishes how the individual behaves in a problem-solving situation. This information is not discussed; rather it is used as baseline for comparison workshop.

7 *Problem-solving model*: A model approach to problem solving is presented. Experience has shown that participants are aware of many of the components of the model yet lack a framework from which to proceed. Participants receive a handout.

8 *Problem-solving sequence*: Elements of the problem-solving model are employed. The entire sequence is explored; due to time constraints, however, there is active participation only in selected steps. For example:

(i) *Defining the problem*: Many problems are not clearly defined. This was a major focus for this series of workshops. A resolution activity was employed. Members of the group would be asked to take three or four minutes to describe three areas for improvement in, for example, their environmental science programme. They would write down the three areas on a page, in point form. After four minutes individuals would be paired up. They would have three or four minutes to agree upon three areas for improvement. After this time two pairs would be brought together. They would have three or four minutes to develop three areas for improvement. Considerable negotiation takes place. In approximately 10–15 minutes the group will have generated a number of resolutions to the problem.

(ii) *Force field analysis*: 'Forces' acting upon certain goals or aspects of the problem are now scrutinized. A force field analysis is undertaken. The facilitator asks for restraining and facilitating forces acting on one aspect of the problem. For example, curricula implementation of environmental science could be restrained by limited resources yet facilitated by the availability of a naturalist in the local community.

(iii) *Brainstorming solutions*: A classic OD technique. The process consultant takes three minutes to solicit all possible ways of overcoming part of a problem. These suggestions are carefully recorded by his partner. All suggestions are recorded. No editing of content is allowed. All members of the group are encouraged to contribute. The facilitator can throw in an idea or draw out the reluctant member if required.

(iv) *Criteria for selection*: With many ideas now available, the brainstorming list is reviewed to determine the possibility, feasibility and desirability of each alternative. Care must be taken not to dismiss what, on first view, may appear to be a frivolous suggestion. The 'crazy' suggestion may prove to be the innovative spark required to solve a difficult situation. The alternatives, once vetted, are available to the decision makers for action.

9 *Problem-solving lecturette*: This aspect of the workshop provides the consultant with an opportunity to fill in gaps with respect to the problem-solving cycle (in this case the selection of alternatives, evaluation, and feedback components). Also the entire workshop can be highlighted. Both facilitators can contribute at this point and questions and comments can be entertained.

10 *Evaluation and closure*: It is important that the workshop ends as it began — positively. Closure activities must be well chosen as the ending should provide the participants with an opportunity to express their feelings and to see their way clear for future action. Sometimes the facilitator might engage the participants in a 'psychological contract' whereby each participant selects a skill or an attitude examined during the workshop and promises to employ this in the future. They recognize the resources and the people that will be needed to make this successful. A simpler evaluation or closure activity would be to have each participant respond to this sentence: 'One thing I have learned today . . . '.

In each of the four schools, we offered to return in order to assist with specific needs. This was an optional feature of the design. In other situations it could be a requirement of the contract. Reasons for a series of consultant visits would be continuation and development of process skills or the need for counselling with respect to specific organizational needs.

Evaluation

In this chapter, I have made a case for, and described, an example of process consultation. Process consultation is a necessary adjunct to many educational innovations, although in this paper we have concerned ourselves with school self-evaluation, in particular GRIDS. In our ideal 'relatively autonomous' or 'problem-solving' school, the staff would by definition be experienced in the skills and training associated with process consultation. This chapter has been prepared in an effort to encourage other schools to move towards or attain this ideal. But we must remember that process consultation is not an end in itself. It is essentially facilitating; it needs to be combined with a task. This task could be an aspect of the school's curriculum, organization or climate, and the role of process consultation is to service this end, but in so doing to make the school more effective at handling change and innovation. Success in this endeavour also rests with careful planning by the process consultant who should be sensitive to the needs of the school. As the name 'process consultation' infers, this type of training is dynamic in nature and it responds to the client. Often the strength for change, the seeds for autonomy, belong to the school staff already. The process consultant can provide the catalyst for growth and development within the school context.

In conclusion, here are some comments made at the end of a workshop by participants when completing the statement 'One thing I have learned about GRIDS after taking this workshop . . .':

> 'I have learned to be aware of research into leadership.'
> 'I am pleased with our own approach.'
> 'I have learned about starting points in problem-solving.'
> 'I enjoyed the practical exercises like "ice breakers".'
> 'I have learned the value and importance of having a problem-solving structure.'
> I have learned to reflect upon the positive growth that has taken place during GRIDS.'
> 'I have learned about the gain in confidence acquired as part of the process.'
> 'I have learned about the advantages of talking.'
> 'I have learned that these activities can be enjoyable.'
> 'I have learned the (self analytical) possibilities for co-operation and sharing among staff members.'
> 'I am more enthusiastic and efficient as part of GRIDS.'
> 'We are better at staff communication.'
> 'We are teaching science. We are doing it.'

Process consultation is not a sequence of skills taught in isolation. It is an essential part of a real-life experience — in this case GRIDS. It offers a school staff an experiential learning activity based on adult learning principles with magnificent opportunities for school improvement.

Some Second Thoughts

In the three years or so since the preparation of the original paper on which this chapter is based much has changed in the field of school evaluation and there is promise of even more fundamental change to come. In revising the paper for publication in this volume I therefore decided not to rewrite, but rather to add this postcript believing that in three years' time the rewrite itself would be outdated and that in any case much of the original material was still relevant to the current situation.

In this section I want first to make some general comments about developments in technique as regards process consultation in school self-evaluation and secondly to make some suggestions as to future developments which may occur as a result of changes in context. The distinction between technique and context is of course arbitrary and too simplistic, but may be useful for expository purposes. In reality technique and context exist within a dialectical relationship, each influencing the other as we learn more about effectiveness in changing political situations. I want to discuss briefly four different developments in technique which have recently assumed greater importance. The first is the increased involvement of consultants, the second is the need to blend task and process skills, the third is the need for training for school self-evaluation and finally some comments on the skills required by change agents.

The last few years have witnessed an increase in the use of consultants generally and in school evaluation in particular. Generally consultancy has become a more acceptable and clearly-defined role within the UK educational system. The TRIST experience, the change in the funding and structure of INSET, the plethora of curriculum and organizational changes and the consequent changing role of the advisory and inspectorial services have all contributed to a situation where consultancy in one form or another is a much more legitimate educational activity. The literature on educational change (Fullan, 1982; Hopkins, 1987) also supports these developments.

In the area of school self-evaluation also, many of the approaches or models explicitly require the use of consultants, as I found out in a recent review and analysis of some dozen approaches to school-based review (Hopkins, 1988). The 'new' GRIDS materials which have resulted from the second stage of the GRIDS project (Abbott and Steadman, 1988) have sections explicitly devoted to the role of outsiders. Another well-known school self-evaluation model, the Norwegian based IMTEC Institutional Development Programme (Dalin and Rust, 1983) which uses the National Foundation for Educational Research (NFER) for its UK dissemination, also emphasizes the consultation role as an integral part of its school development programme. The consultancy role in school-based review therefore seems to me to be increasingly well integrated into school evaluation designs and legitimated as a necessary role within the educational system.

My second point is to emphasize again the need for consultants to possess both task and process expertise. This point was made in the original version of this chapter and still remains a crucial factor in the success of consultancy. All too often consultants lack process skills and this seriously inhibits their effectiveness in assisting with curriculum implementation. Alternatively, I have seen many process consultants in action who ignore the substantive context of the curriculum or innovation they are supposed to be facilitating and then quickly lose credibility with those they are trying to help. The third point is a corollary to the second and is to do with the nature of the process skills required by consultants. Recent studies of educational change agents (Miles *et al.*, 1988) suggest that there is a cluster of skills that characterises effective change agents. These skills are best summarized as trust, confidence building, diagnosis, coordination, working in groups and resource utilization. Trust and confidence building refer to inter-personal skills that relate to the consultant's ability to project a warm, empathic personality that puts people at ease and generates feelings of efficacy. Diagnosis is the ability to look beyond the immediate situation, to identify fundamental issues and to analyze them within a problem solving context. This ability requires formidable analytic, contextual and substantive skills. Coordination, working in groups, and resource utilization refer to a cluster of skills related to 'getting work done'. A predisposition for action, leadership and organization, planning and management are required here. Taken together this list of skills is multi-dimensional and normally requires specific training even in already highly skilled and experienced consultants.

Finally and again related to the previous two points is the need for training in evaluation techniques for teachers involved in school self-evaluation. Our work on SBR for the OECD International School Improvement Project (Clift, 1987) suggests that a major reason for the low level of success enjoyed by school evaluation initiatives in the UK is a lack of skill on the part of the teachers involved. As Clift (1987) comments:

> In no case was training in the skills necessary for school based review offered: indeed there is no realisation on the part of those in authority that such training might be necessary (p. 58).
> This failure to operate in the way intended seems to be due to teachers' lack of experience and expertise in the process of SBR . . . (p. 60).
> SBR requires that teachers be trained for it . . . . A search for objectivity is the keynote (p. 64)

Obviously a major role for the consultant is to provide training for teachers involved in school evaluation. Taken together these more technical issues related to consultation for school evaluation suggest that consultation is becoming increasingly important and needs to include both process and substantive expertise. We are also becoming clearer about the skills required by consultants and the training they need to be providing to those involved at the school level.

The issues related to context are more to do with how the external environment is shaping the nature of school evaluation and, consequently, the role of the consultants involved. In this respect I will again briefly discuss four issues: first, the increasing links between evaluation and school improvement; second, the increasing emphasis on evaluation and monitoring in the UK system; third, the emerging role of school development plans and performance indicators; and finally a comment on accountability. As the research into school improvement continues we are increasingly realizing the importance of embedding strategies for improvement within the rhythm of the school organization. This is certainly the case with SBR. My own work suggests that SBR is much more effective when it is linked to ongoing staff development and to substantive and organizational changes. This embeddedness will become increasingly important as we move towards improvement strategies that directly address the culture of the school organization. For school improvement efforts which ignore these deeper, organizational conditions are doomed to triviality.

These issues that relate to research and the knowledge base are complemented by a policy orientation that increasingly emphasizes evaluation and monitoring. Most of the recent National Curriculum and organization developments include provision for evaluation and monitoring at a variety of levels. I personally believe that current evaluation efforts are under-resourced, technically naive and under-conceptualized. Despite these limitations evaluation is here to stay and new forms of evaluation need to be developed to serve more effectively contemporary demands. I suggest that these new strategies will involve more emphasis on school self-evaluation, increased collaboration between teachers, consultants and inspectors, explicit links with school development activities and relatively simple but systematic evaluation techniques (Hopkins, 1989). This will involve teachers and inspectors in acquiring new skills and consultants will be required to help them to do so.

A major focus for this incipient style of evaluation will probably be school development plans. In their simplest form school development plans are a set of curriculum and organizational targets with implementation plans and time lines set by the school on an annual basis within the context of local and national aims. The plans are usually based on a three-year cycle with details for the first year and contingent aspirations for the subsequent two years. They may or may not include details of specific performance or process indicators, staff development needs and resource (both human and financial) implications. School development plans are a relatively new phenomenon in the UK. The Education Reform Act (1988) and a number of the other recent curriculum and organizational initiatives, however, have required or will require the use of school development plans in one form or another. The LEA Training Grants Scheme, TVEI Extension, the National Curriculum, Teacher Appraisal and Local Management of Schools, are examples of initiatives that require overt planning at the school level. These plans, as well as being a blueprint for implementation, also provide a basis for evaluation and monitoring both in the school and LEA.

There is also a similar emphasis on performance indicators in a number of contemporary national educational initiatives. If these indicators can assume a more qualitative nature, be based on targets identified in school development plans and be subject to ongoing self-evaluation at the school level, monitored by the inspectorate, then we have a means of bringing together a number of previously disparate areas of activity that could have a powerful impact on school development (Hopkins and Leask, 1989). This is because such a focus operates at a number of different organizational cultural and curriculum levels within the school at the same time. The consultant would have a major task in facilitating these complex activities.

Finally a word about accountability. Accountability has assumed a different character since it appeared on the UK scene, in the wake of Callaghan's Ruskin speech, some dozen years ago. In the context of contemporary policy, accountability has a potentially much sharper edge, being linked as it is to funding and specific educational targets. Although I believe that the educational system has been for too long not accountable enough. I also believe that bureaucratic evaluation of the cost–benefit type is potentially disastrous. This is because it distorts not only the teaching–learning process but also the infrastructure required to improve the quality of education at the school and local level. I would want to argue therefore for a form of professional accountability linked to serious and reasonable development plans at the school level within the context of national priorities which are evaluated by teachers and others who have acquired new skills and are professionally empowered as a result of being involved in this process. Clearly consultants have a major part to play in this scenario.

In writing these few paragraphs I have been struck by how much has changed in such a short period of time. I am also struck by how much more change is on its way. Despite increasing centralization, many of these changes, as I hope I have hinted at, can have a powerful and positive impact on school development. Whether this happens or not depends very much on the way consultants facilitate the process of school self-evaluation within our education system.

References

ABBOTT, R. and STEADMAN, S. (1988) *The GRIDS Handbooks* (Primary and Secondary versions) (2nd. edn.) York, Longman, for the SCDC Publications.

BOLLEN, R. and HOPKINS, D. (1987) *School Based Review: Towards a Praxis*, Leuven, Belgium, ACCO.

BOWERS, D. and FRANKLIN, J. (1972) 'Survey guided development: using human resources measurement in organisational change', *Journal of Contemporary Business*, **1**, pp. 43–55.

CLIFT, P. (1987) 'LEA Initiated School-Based Review in England and Wales'. In: Hopkins D. (Ed.) *Improving the Quality of School*, Lewes, The Falmer Press.

DALIN, P. and RUST, V (1983) *Can Schools Learn?* Windsor, NFER Nelson.

ELLIOT, G. (1980/82) *Self Evaluation and the Teacher: an annotated bibliography and report on current practice*, 4 vols., London, Schools Council.

ELLIOT, G. (1982) 'Looking at the field: accountability in professional self development; alternative models for teacher and school evaluation'. *Journal of Evaluation in Education*, **1**, May, pp. 2–5.

FULLAN, M. (1982) *The Meaning of Educational Change*, New York, Teachers' College Press.

FULLAN, M., MILES, M. and TAYLOR, G. (1980) 'Organisation development in schools. The state of the Art', *Review of Educational Research*, **50**, pp. 121–83.

HERSCHEY, P. and BLANCHARD, K. (1982) *Management of Organisational Behaviour*, (4th ed.) Englewood Cliffs, NJ, Prentice Hall.

HOPKINS, D. (1982) 'Survey feedback as an organisation development intervention in educational settings: a review', *Educational Management and Administration*, **10**, pp. 203–16.

HOPKINS, D. (1985a) 'School Based Review: an international survey and analysis', *Compare*, **15**, pp. 79–93.

HOPKINS, D. (1985b) *School Based Review for School Improvement*, Leuven, Belgium, ACCO.

HOPKINS, D. (1987) *Improving the Quality of Schooling*, Lewes, The Falmer Press.

HOPKINS, D. (1988) *Doing School Based Review*, Leuven, Belgium, ACCO.

HOPKINS, D. (1989) *Evaluation for School Development*, Milton Keynes, Open University Press.

HOPKINS, D. and LEASK, M. (1989) 'Performance Indicators and School Development'. *School Organisation*. 9, 1, 3–20.

JAMES, M. (1982) *A first review and register of school and college initiated self-evaluation activities in the United Kingdom*, Milton Keynes, Educational Evaluation and Accountability Research Group, Open University.

JOHNSON, D. and JOHNSON, F. (1982) *Joining Together – Group Theory and Group Skills* (2nd edn.) Englewood Cliffs, NJ, Prentice Hall.

MCMAHON, A., BOLAM, R., ABBOTT, R. and HOLLY, P. (1984) *Guidelines for Review and Internal Development in Schools*, (Primary and Secondary versions), York, Longmans for the Schools Council.

MILES, M., SAXL, E. and LIEBERMAN, A. (1988) 'What Skills do Educational "Change Agents" need? An Empirical View', *Curriculum Inquiry*, **18**, p. 157–93.

PFEIFFER, J. and JONES, J. (1969 *et seq.*) *Annual Handbook for Group Facilitators*, La Jolla, CA, University Associates.

RUNKEL, P. and SCHMUCK, R. (1984) 'The place of organisation development in schools'. In: HOPKINS, D. and WIDEEN, M. (eds.) *Alternative Perspectives on School Improvement*, Lewes, The Falmer Press.

SCHMUCK, R. and MILES, M. (1971) *O.D. in Schools*, La Jolla, CA., University Associates.

SCHMUCK, R. and RUNKEL, P. (1985) *The Handbook of Organisation Development in Schools*, (3rd ed.) Palo Alto, CA., Mayfield.

6
Working with the FE College:
Some Experiences and Reflections

Colin Turner

Introduction

This chapter is based on my experiences of working alone or with other consultants in colleges of further education over the last five years. During that time I have learned my trade. I do not know of any way of learning about consultancy other than by going out and doing it. I believe that most learning comes from getting things wrong, and I certainly stumbled into some pitfalls that lie in the path of all novice consultants. I always ensured that I had a consultant to my own consultancy, though often unofficial and unpaid, and when I was working in partnership we always used each other to help analyze and learn from our own mistakes and confusions. In this chapter I have summarized much of the learning that came from these painful and sometimes comic, but always creative, experiences. I have therefore two strong recommendations for those who wish to become consultants in schools or colleges: firstly, accept that you will only learn by doing it, not by reading books; and secondly, when you are working as a consultant, always have available a skilled person who can facilitate your learning from the process as it occurs.

The Further Education Context

Colleges of further education or technical colleges are not very much like schools. They are considerably larger, much more wide-ranging in their work, more complex in their management and administration. Their client group is more or less universal, from the age of 14 up to among the oldest people in the country. A typical college might have 1,300 full-time and 8,000 part-time students, 200 or more full-time staff and very many part-time staff. Its major sections would most likely include engineering, business studies, catering, hairdressing, art and design, construction, social work and health studies, science and humanities. Students attend the college on many different contracts — as full-time students for periods of up to four years, short training courses of a few days, part-time day and evening students, trainees on various schemes of the Training Agency, sandwich courses combining work experience. The college will use several major national examining bodies offering a bewildering variety of qualifications — the major ones are GCSE and GCE 'A' level, Business and Technician Education Council (BTEC), Royal Society of Arts (RSA), City & Guilds, and Certificate of Qualification in Social Work as well as the Training Agency schemes. Most colleges have several sites, often some miles apart.

These characteristics of further education colleges make for administrative and organizational complexity. Although most colleges operate what is a recognizable hierarchic system of organization through departments or sections and with three or four management levels, they are best described as loosely coupled bodies. Departments have considerable autonomy and there are small units or annexes which may be almost totally detached from the system. The staff do not consist, as in a school, of a homogeneous group of trained teachers with various academic specialisms, but largely of people trained in other skills and professions who happen to have decided to teach. The staff-room will typically contain, for example, accountants, lawyers, engineers, nurses, social workers, graphic designers and beauty therapists. There are very powerful occupational sub-cultures in the college, and a staff member's loyalty and affiliation is as likely to be to his or her department as to the college. Indeed it may well be that only to the senior management is there any sense of a total college.

So for the consultant, working in schools and working in colleges are two very different experiences, although, of course, the principles of good consultancy do not change whatever the environment. In my experience there were two significant factors to come to terms with in colleges. Firstly, simply to understand the complexities of the workings of the college was in itself a major task. Secondly, as a consequence of the great variety of activity and organizational arrangements, the range of possible problems faced by senior and middle managers was very wide. I am not suggesting that consultancy is more difficult in colleges than in schools, but it does operate in a more confusing environment.

Consultancy in Colleges

Why do we think that consultants might be useful in our colleges? What are they supposed to do? How are they trying to benefit the college? What kind of behaviour is particular to the consultant? In setting out to answer these questions in the following pages, we might start by reminding ourselves that other people besides consultants visit colleges. Inspectors visit to inspect, researchers to research facts, technical experts to solve technical problems. Frequently the use of the word 'consultant' is extended to cover almost everyone who visits the college for any purpose. One principal claimed he was a consultant because he consulted his staff before taking decisions. So to avoid confusion we will define a consultant narrowly and suggest that the narrower the definition the closer we get to the real value of the consultant in college. Our experience is that consultancy only has any useful effect when the issues that are being addressed and the solutions that are being suggested are primarily coming from the client (i.e. the college staff) and not the consultant. To believe that the consultant has some special skill or insight which enables him or her to tell the college what its problems are and then work out the solution is to misunderstand the nature of the consultancy process. The college may be very impressed with the insight and wisdom of the consultant, but in our experience it will have minimal effect on the college. Unless the consultancy deals with the issues that are the concern of the college managers and results in solutions that are theirs and really owned by them, then almost certainly nothing will change. So we can consider a spectrum of consultancy types from client-based at one end to consultant-based at the other, similar to the non-directive to directive continuum of Kubr (1983) (Figure 6.1).

The most effective consultancy in colleges has in our experience been at the process consultancy point. That is not to say that we refused to give relevant facts or identify some useful resources, if in the process of the consultancy that became relevant. Our prime method of working, however, has been to help college managers work on the issues that they saw as central to the development of their colleges. We would help them clarify their thoughts, intervene to confront them with processes they wished to ignore, work on their relationships with other key workers — in fact generally to help them refine their understanding of the issues and to remove the blockages which were in the way of their successful progress. Then we helped them come to their own solution of what needed to be done. This may sound very supportive but it is often an uncomfortable and stormy process. For example, in one college the situation that was getting in the way of the managers sorting out their problems was the bad relationship between the principal and vice-principal and until we helped them face that, little progress could be made.

Our definition of consultancy, therefore, is that it is a contract to help clients within their organizational roles to reflect on, own and resolve their problems. It is important to emphasize the key words in this sentence. It is a *contract*. It is clear who the *client* is. The consultancy concerns the person's *organizational role*, his work functioning, and not him as a private person. The problems are *their's*, i.e. the clients, not those defined by the consultant, the consultant *helps* the client think about and resolve the problems but doesn't do it for the client, and the purpose of a consultancy is *resolution* of problems. Table 6.1 helps to make this point. Of the possible types of consultancy it is only that labelled 'process' which results in real learning for the client.

The Consultancy Model

There are a number of models that are useful in thinking about the stages of consultancy. The one I found most suitable for work with colleges which is adapted from the work of Schein (1969) is shown in Figure 6.2.

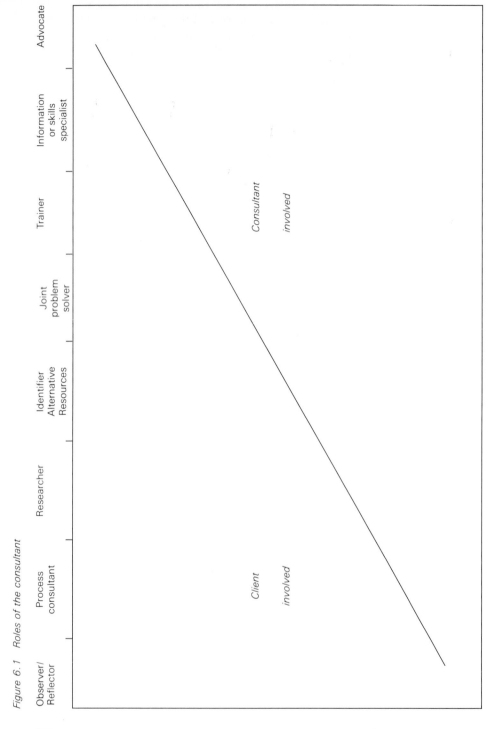

Figure 6.1 Roles of the consultant

Table 6.1 Consultancy — a sketch map

	Executive	Specialist	Advisory	Process
Consultant's role	Analysis, diagnosis, deciding solution, implementing action	Fact finding, analysis, diagnosis, presentation of package solution	Fact finding from client, proposing solution based on persuasion to accept advice	Exploration, reflection, assisting client to generate options
Client's role	Passive	Presentation of own identification of problem, acceptance or rejection of solution	Supply information accept/reject/modify solution	Examining, extending insight, perceiving solution, implementation
Problem ownership	Handed over to/taken by consultant	Temporarily handed over to consultant	Shared	High responsibility for client to retain
Client's commitment to action	Unquestioning acceptance	Often limited	Takes on trust consultant's previous experience	High — own solution fitting own perception of situation
Learning	Little. Mostly related to deciding whether or not to encourage/discourage consultants to change style in future	Deciding if consultant is any good	How to handle same situation again	Transferable to other situations

Figure 6.2   *The stages of consultancy* (adapted from Schein, 1962)

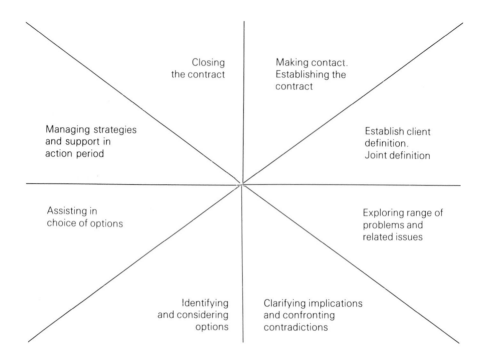

Stage 1: Making contact. Establishing the contract

It goes without saying that the initial meeting of prospective consultant and client is very important. Both sides have to be comfortable with each other. If the client does not really like or trust the consultant there is no point in going on any further. Similarly if the consultant does not feel the client is someone he or she can work with, then this is the point to terminate the relationship. If the initial contact is successful then the two can work on the contract. Some of this can be in written form, some by working things out in discussion but the key things that have to be clearly established are:

Who is the client?

In one consultancy all our initial discussions were with the Vice-Principal, and yet our invitation was from the Principal. We needed to clear that up. In the event it transpired that the Principal was not really aware of the implications of a consultancy, particularly as it affected his own position, and we were in danger of colluding with a political strategy of the Vice-Principal to win a power struggle. In another case, we discovered the Principal had only met us because the LEA had instructed him. Was he or was the LEA our client?

What is the consultant coming in to do?

It needs to be clearly established what the consultant is there for. General phrases like 'help' and advise' will not do. If the Principal wants to work on the problems he and other senior managers have in running the college, that is one kind of consultancy activity. If the Principal wants someone to talk to the staff and find out why they are discontented, this is another activity altogether. This is the point at which to establish whether the consultant is required as a catalyst to the senior managers, a researcher, or in some other role. On one consultancy where this was not made explicit enough, it was clear after a time that the Principal wanted us as a communication channel to his staff because the communication system was so poor. We were not prepared to find out and pass backwards and forwards what people were thinking and wished to have said, though we were prepared to work with the managers as they set out to improve their communications system. However, in this case the Principal could not come to terms with the fact of his poor communications with his staff and so the consultancy was aborted at that stage. The golden rule is to get it clear at this stage.

What is the responsibility of the consultant?

This is the point to establish what the consultant is offering, when and how often he will work in the college. If the consultant is using the model of process counsellor and is therefore not taking responsibility for offering diagnosis and solutions, then this needs to be stated at this point. Otherwise the Principal might assume he has brought in a paid expert who will sort out his difficulties for him. Likewise the two sides must establish clearly how often the consultant will be in the college, how long the consultancy will last, and what the consultant will provide in the way of reports.

What resources will be made available?

Normally the most important need for the consultant is access to people, both individually and in meetings, and this has to be negotiated and agreed at this point. In one consultancy, we were unable to get access to a committee where the major work was taking place on the issue we were supposedly consultant to. When we pointed this out, attempts were made to divert us to all sorts of other activity, and it became clear that for reasons we never did fully comprehend, the Principal was determined not to let us work with that committee. When this remained the case even after we had confronted him with the situation, we had no choice but to withdraw, though he was willing to find us plenty of other tasks to keep us occupied in the college.

Is the client college ready for the consultancy?

Just as a person will look at new cars well before he or she actually intends to buy one, so colleges invite a consultant in well before the staff are ready for working on the task involved. Our own experience is that lack of security and trust among staff have been the most common cause of non-readiness. If a college is going through a bad period when staff feel uncertain about their future and unsure whether they can trust the management to look after their interests, then they are not likely to welcome a consultant. In that situation all the consultant can do is to negotiate a contract which is about the lack of trust and security, and openly work on that.

How is the consultancy going to be introduced?

The consultant needs to work out with the client how the consultancy is going to be communicated to the staff, and to whom. Also how is the consultant to be introduced into the college? In one college I was insistent that I met the senior teachers and they agreed to the consultancy before I went ahead, but in another when I failed to handle this matter properly, I found myself interviewing key people who not only did not know who I was or what I was doing there, but even that there was a consultancy set up at all. I learnt not to take at face value, statements from Principals about what they had told other staff about the consultancy.

It is very common to short-circuit the process of establishing a contract. It is not something that can be rushed, and it may take several visits. The consultant must deal with the client's (and sometimes his own) impatience in wanting to get on with things. Our experience is that more consultancies go wrong because of failures at this stage than at all the other stages put together.

Stage 2: Establishing the definition of the problem

The client will propose his or her definition of the issues that the consultancy will address. The consultant's job in this stage is to test out that definition until both are agreed that they have isolated the real issue. This is not to say the issue will not be redefined in the course of the consultancy but at this stage this is the best definition they can mutually achieve. Problems we experienced at this stage were.

The reluctance of the Principal to define accurately what he was concerned about

For example, I was presented with the problem that, although the college was fortunate in having very hard-working and successful heads of departments, some new integrated courses required some better mechanisms for making decisions about the curriculum. There was a failure in coordinating courses that requried staff from more than one department. In fact the Principal was worried by a long-standing problem that the heads of department were so competitive they could never work together. Once that issue had emerged and been established as the real, if unspoken, problem, then we could get on with the consultancy.

Unawareness of the real problem under the presented problem

In the above instance, the Principal knew but was reluctant to state the problem that worried him. However, the real problem can be suppressed out of awareness. In one college the apparent problem was that a particular level of staff were overloaded with work and were complaining, so that the Principal wanted help in redesigning their job description and role. The real problem was that they felt under-appreciated for the work they did. The college had no effective way of making these staff feel valued and important.

Unwillingness of the client to see himself as part of the problem

Principals may well identify problems in their college but cannot see that they are the main cause of them. For example, in one college, there was a series of symptoms of trouble — for instance, low morale, poor performance — which the Principal defined as the problem. In fact the real problem was partly in the Principal's management style, and as a result of that, partly in his very bad relationships with his two deputy Principals.

Unwillingness of the client to define the problem specifically

It is not uncommon for the client to ask for generalized help. 'Things don't seem quite right'; 'We need to check out the whole organization'; 'I want to generally improve things'. The skill of the consultant is in getting an agreed specific problem as the issue to work on. In one college, I spent several sessions trying to pin down the Principal on the specific concern he had. His requests were for 'a bird's eye view of the place', 'a disinterested observer's comment on the organisation', 'a snapshot picture' and such unhelpful briefs. In my inexperience, I forced the issue too strongly, and was to my initial delight given a specific problem to work on. It was several weeks before I realized the problem was irrelevant to the central concern of the college which was about managerial decision-making. I missed all the clues that with more experience I would now pick up and play back.

Putting the onus of problem identification on the consultant

Often as a result of the point made immediately above, the consultant is invited to give his or her opinion of what the problem is. Some Principals will see that as the consultant's job. Regrettably some consultants will be only too eager to define what the problem is. Note that I am not saying the consultant should never make suggestions for the client to consider, but the primary process should be for the client to work at and then own the issue that is the real concern, and the consultant should check this by questions, analysis, asking for evidence, noting symptoms, until both are happy that they are ready to go forward on that definition.

The first two stages form the *Identification* section of the consultancy cycle, and when completed the consultant can move into the next section of *Examination*.

Stage 3: Exploring the range of problems and related issues

The work of this stage is to extend from the definition of the issue to all the relevant factors that are involved. This will involve the collection of all associated data, both objective and subjective. This does not have to be the sole responsibility of the consultant, but he or she must ensure that the work is tackled. The consultant's key role may be to suggest the variety of methods that can be used in data gathering — for example diagnostic instruments, brainstorming, time diaries, as well as the ubiquitous questionnaire and interview. There will be a premium on the skills of active listening and careful observation to elicit all the data, and the consultant's job is to manage that process. The Principal or other staff may well be uncertain or unwilling to probe into some areas, and may well prefer to follow up very factual data rather than feelings, impressions and emotions. However, these latter are no less, and may be more, important. The stage of collecting data moves into the next stage without a tidy division. It generally works out that while data is still being collected, its evaluation starts taking place, and this generates the need for new data.

Stage 4: Clarifying implications and confronting incongruities

This stage is about evaluating the data, exploring and clarifying its implications for the central issue, giving feedback where it is needed to facilitate progress on the central issue. Most issues are embedded into a network of systemic relationships, and attending to one issue will generally have consequences on other parts of college operations that may not be obvious at first sight. We found that our commonest activities at this stage were bringing out into the open, contradictions or incongruities which were so taken for granted that they were not noticed. For example, in one large college we were working on the central issue of staff morale and commitment, but although management had been very worried about this for some time, they had no coherent personnel policy or any single manager responsible for personnel. A simple test is to ask what resources have been or are being committed to working at the problem in terms of time, energy, finance and expertise. If there is very little evidence of this, one is entitled to ask whether the management really see it as a critical problem. If they do, being confronted with the contradiction of defining it as important but making no resources available to help solve it, will open a new opportunity for moving forward.

The problems we encountered in these two stages of *Examination* were not dissimilar to those of the next two, which we can label *Development*. Therefore, we will consider them all at the end of the sixth stage.

Stage 5: Identifying and considering options

At this stage the issues have been defined, they have been set in a context of related issues, and their implications have been considered. The next task is to identify the available options. The function of the consultant is to help the clients develop as wide a range of options as possible. For this purpose he or she can bring into the process some technical skills in option development such as brainstorming and creative thinking techniques. Problems the consultant may have to tackle at this stage are as follows:

1 *Narrow focus on possible options.* There may be some impatience with developing a number of options. The feeling may be that the fewer there are to consider, the more manageable and comfortable is the process.
2 *Evaluation of options before the full range is identified.* The consultant may have to work hard to prevent the client assessing and either rejecting or accepting suggestions as they come up. There may be a tendency to go for the first apparent solution that is suggested and stop the search at that point.
3 *Predilection for or pre-decision on the way forward.* Very often managers carry around prototype decisions in their heads, and may well have more or less made up their mind during the previous stages of the consultancy. For example, in one college we were considering the job dissatisfaction of the staff in a particular role. We had brought to the surface a lot of the problems they saw, but in trying to generate options it was clear that the Principal had already developed a plan which assumed that changes in organizational structure were the way forward. It was very difficult to get

her to hear and note some of the other options which were being suggested, such as changes in their communication pattern.

4 *Resistance to training for option development*. Developing lists of options is dependent on using appropriate techniques, and the consultant can change role to give short training sessions on how to use brainstorming, how to develop lateral or creative thinking, but there is sometimes resistance by managers to take this time out and move into a learner role.

Stage 6: Assisting in the choice of options

There is a danger that the two stages are not clearly separated, and that choice is being discussed while the search for options is still taking place. The consultant can greatly assist his or her clients by working to prevent premature consideration of choices. Our experience is that most Principals want to get to a solution as soon as possible. Perhaps they have a role image of the Principal as a decisive decision-maker, and this encourages them to cut through the search for options so as to 'get on with the job'. Evaluation of options is fraught enough without confusing it with the search for options.

In choosing the best options, clients may need help in evaluation techniques. There are many described in the literature on management, all of which in one way or another work systematically and logically through the nature of the problem, the costs, benefits and contingent implications. The difficulty for consultants is that they know that the field research suggests that most management decisions are not made like that, but by a quick, gut feeling of the manager, which is based on a mixture of intuition, previous experience, favoured management style, and personal predilection. A consultancy may be one of the few occasions when a more considered process can be encouraged. Given the amount of work that has already taken place, it seems wildly inappropriate to make snap decisions, and the use of, for example, force-field analysis would extend the depth of decision-making and probably the quality of the decisions taken. We often found it useful at this stage to take the client through the processes we had gone through so far.

1 Review of problems and means of tackling it agreed in contract.
2 Clearer perception by consultants of problems after data collection.
3 Analysis of key elements of problem supported by evidence.
4 Joint establishment of possible causes and consequences.
5 Decision by client on course of action.

The last point is very important. The consultant may be under strong pressure to recommend or even make the decision on a course of action. To do so would negate the whole process up to that point. The ownership of the solution is critical to everything that follows. If the Principal feels he or she has made the choice, then there will be a personal commitment to its implementation and success. If, however, the choice is seen as that of the consultant, even if the Principal has taken part in the analysis and has agreed the action, then there is likely to be less commitment and someone else to blame if the action starts to run into difficulties.

Difficulties and pitfalls

During the stages of *Examination* and *Development*, we have experieienced many difficulties and pitfalls for the consultant. One set we can describe as being trapped or blocked. This takes several forms:

(a) *The de-powered client*. One experience was to discover that the client, although apparently having the appropriate power for his or her status, in fact had very little power or influence, and we were really working with the wrong person.

(b) *Being set-up*. Another experience was to learn, rather painfully, that we were part of a hidden set-up. We were being manipulated in an organizational power game. For example, I was invited into a consultancy, which it soon appeared was to distract the attention of some of the staff while other internal changes were being made.

(c) *Being kept in the dark*. Without such conscious manipulation, it is also possible that the consultant is kept in the dark about key facts. For example, in one college I was working with the senior management team without knowing that the Principal was expecting to leave for another post any month. I would have worked quite differently if I had been given that information.

(d) *Being given too much information*. In most colleges, I was the recipient of masses of written information and suggestions that I ought to speak to almost everyone. I found it hard to explain that I did not need it, that I was not a new member of staff, and that the kind of information I needed was qualitatively different from that of a researcher into the organization. I suspect that sometimes I was given a mass of reports and other information to keep me quiet, so that I would not be disturbing people by tackling the real issues that were around.

(e) *Plastic rapport*. I have experienced situations where I have been treated in a very welcoming and friendly way, but it is only skin deep. By preserving the appearance of affability, the members of the college aimed to divert me from doing any real work with them. I had to learn not to collude with this seduction.

(f) *Encountering defensive positions*. I experienced very strong defensive positions in some colleges, not from the managers who had worked through the contract with me, but from others in the organization. Sometimes this simply reflected their own sense of insecurity, but often it was as a result of past experiences of outsiders (not necessarily consultants) whose unskilful activities had made staff very suspicious of anyone who might come in and change things.

(g) *Treated as a dustbin.* I was occasionally blocked by being treated as a kind of dustbin for all the internal conflicts of the college, often concerned with personal fights or disappointments. I had to learn not to accept the role of medicine-man for the college, but to limit myself to the contract and the agreed issues.

External events sometimes took the interest of the Principal out of the consultancy. However important it may look in January, key events in June may suddenly cause attention of the staff to be switched to a new challenge. For example, in the middle of one extended consultancy, the college Principal became involved in some planning for merging with another smaller college, and I found it difficult in keeping interest going in the consultancy issues, even though they were of a very important nature.

Most consultancies depend on the enthusiasm of one or two key people in a college. If one of them leaves midway through the process, the consultancy can be left floundering. The movement of key management staff in colleges is frequently underestimated. In a number of the colleges with which we were involved, the Principal or Vice-Principal moved to another post during the period of the consultancy, and in most cases this effectively brought the consultancy to a stop. In other cases the Principal was away from college for an extended period due to serious illness. It is a reasonable estimate that there is at least a fifty per cent chance that a key manager will leave during an extended consultancy of eighteen months to two years.

Keeping objectivity is always difficult. The consultant has to walk a tightrope since establishing good relations and trust with the Principal is a great help to the consultancy process, but if this develops into friendship, then this can begin to cloud common sense. This is particularly likely to happen if, as in one college where I worked, the Principal was new and the staff were fairly hostile to her and suspicious of her reforming intentions. Necessarily I had to work very closely with her and was in danger of becoming a support for her rather than a consultant. Likewise the consultant will see this among staff, where loyalty can get in the way of objectivity.

It is during the stages of *Examination* and *Development* that the consultant may need to confront the client or clients with aspects of their behaviour. It requires skill in feedback techniques, and it is tempting for the consultant to ignore or avoid such issues by dismissing them as not critical or important.

There is a danger in being a compulsive consultant, needing to be very active and mistaking mere activity for real work. Clients are also likely to be trying to convince the consultant they are serious about doing something by indulging in lots of activity, which actually is not taking the process forward at all. Getting more information is one of the compulsive activities to give the appearance of work while actually avoiding the issues. In one college we had great difficulty in avoiding this. Although we got initial agreement on the nature of the issue to be addressed by the consultancy, the senior managers were very reluctant in practice to work on it. Their avoidance strategy was to instigate numerous surveys, devise and send out questionnaires, set up wide-ranging but unfocused interviews. There was plenty of activity, all to no purpose but allowing the staff of the college to delude themselves that something was happening. In the event, as we could not move the managers from their belief that they were doing something about the problem nor get them to focus on the real issue, we had to admit defeat and retire.

In the four stages we are considering, the particular skills of the consultant that are likely to be in demand are those of listening, eliciting information (of feelings as well as facts), of recognizing and removing blockages, confronting, holding onto objectivity, and offering specific problem-solving techniques.

Stage 7: Managing strategies and support in the action period

The last two stages can be described as the *Implementation* phase. This is the time for action, firstly in planning it, and in the final stage, taking it. The consultant may bring the contract to a close at this stage of planning action, if that is what the contract stated, but more often that will not be until the final stage.

The consultant is supporting and facilitating the Principal in planning the actions that are to be taken. The great temptation is for the consultant to want to insert ideas of how he or she would do it. Even more so than the evaluation and choice of options, the consultant must leave this to those who have to direct and manage the action, and who are accountable for its consequences. The consultant helps the Principal in thinking through the strategies of implementation, estimating the response of various sections of the work-force, making resources available, and setting actions in a time-scale.

Stage 8: Drawing the contract to a close

As the plan of action is put into operation, the cycle is completed and the consultant needs to draw the contract to a close in a clear and satisfactory manner. The two key parts of this are:

1 The consultant should instigate a review of the consultancy process with the client, checking out how the whole process has gone, the difficulties, the successes, the lessons both sides can learn. This will enable both sides to feel that the process has been properly completed.
2 The consultant should then leave. There is a great temptation to hang around, to check how various things are working out, to continue relationships that have been formed. The consultant must be disciplined enough to avoid this, and cut the connections. If there is more work to do, then a new contract can be formed; if the consultant visits the organization as part of his or her job, then it must be in that role and not as consultant.

Summary

This is only one model of the consultancy process. There are others. However, they will all, in one way or another, pay attention to the initial contract, the definition and exploration of the problem, the generation of options, and the planning and implementation of action. The points I have tried most strongly to emphasize are: getting clear the role of the consultant as distinct from the technical expert, the counsellor, the adviser, and the researcher; giving responsibility for the decisions at all stages to the client organization, so that it has ownership of the solution; and the traps that lie in wait for the unwary consultant. In any particular circumstances, the process of the model may need to be modified for pragmatic reasons, but we believe that the above statements should always be attended to, and the skilled consultant is one who can ensure that this is so.

References

KUBR, M. (Ed.) (1983) *Management Consulting: A Guide to the Profession*, Geneva, Internal Labour Office.

SCHEIN, E.H. (1969) *Process Consultation: Its Role in Organisation Development*, Reading, Mass., Addison-Wesley.

7
Some Aspects of the Tutor's Role in Initial and In-service Education

Howard Lewis

The purpose of this chapter is to review some recent thinking about and developments in the role of the higher education tutor both in the area of initial teacher education and in in-service work. Since the tutor is an external agent to schools yet offers advice to students and teachers about how to work within schools, he or she qualifies as a consultant. It is not possible to explore the full range of work of a tutor since this is extremely variable. The chapter will therefore examine two major areas of a tutor's role, both school-based: that of supervisor to students in initial training, and that of team member working with students, teachers and pupils.

Initial Education: Criticisms of the Tutor's Role

That aspect of a higher education tutor's role which consists of paying occasional visits to students in initial training working in school has been subjected to some criticism in recent years, often based upon research findings. Zimpher *et al.* (1980) state bluntly in an ethnographic study that during an eleven-week practice in school: '... student teachers weren't understanding the criticisms of the supervisor and weren't able to make any changes in their teaching styles and weren't willing to do anything but satisfy the cooperating teacher'.

Support for such findings also comes from statistical studies. For example, Morris (1974) sought to discover the importance of the university supervisor to the student working in school. Morris was especially interested in the extent to which the supervisor affected the student's ability to adapt himself or herself to different situations. Two null hypotheses were stated:

1 There is no significant difference between the classroom performance of student teachers who receive supervision from the university supervisor and the performance of those who do not.
2 There is no significant difference between the adjustment of student

teachers who receive supervision from the university supervisor and the adjustment of those who do not.

Two groups of about fifty students each were used, assigned randomly. The first group received the usual support from university-based tutors, and the second received support exclusively from the cooperating schools. Neither null hypothesis could be rejected by Morris's results.

Work has also been carried out by Hoste (1982) who mounted a research project as part of a larger project on curriculum evaluation in teacher training. Again one of the major aims was to examine the effect on students of college courses and of supervisors. Although he was originally concerned only with the influence of an environmental course upon students, a main thrust was to use students' self-reported sources of ideas for their teaching practice. Supervisors did not feature strongly in their contribution towards the students' preparation for school practice or towards the students' actual teaching.

A much larger study was carried out by Yates (1982) which looked at all teacher training institutions offering the Bachelor of Education degree or the Certificate in Education. He focused on teaching practice, its organization and also on how students were supervised. Though all institutions were originally invited to participate, the research was finally based upon a random sample of 100 teachers and the same number of university and college supervisors plus 500 students. The findings included the student opinion (held by 72 per cent of them) that the teacher to whom he or she was attached was of more help than the supervisor. In addition the students generally thought that the cooperating teacher was better placed to spend time observing them when they had charge of a class and also to discuss such lessons with them than the supervisor. Just over 70 per cent of the students claimed that: 'the amount of time their cooperating teacher spent in observing them was sufficient for judging their work'. However, only just over 30 per cent of the student teachers thought that this was so with their college or university supervisor. Just over half (53 per cent) of the students said that teachers spent enough time discussing their teaching with them as against 24 per cent who thought this of their supervisor. Other percentages also favoured the teacher at the expense of the supervisor. For instance, 78 per cent of the student opined that the evaluation of their work by the teachers was valid, whereas only 47 per cent viewed the college supervisor's evaluation as being more valid.

Findings which seem to point to the function of the college- or university-based tutor acting as a supervisor to pre-service students as being rather ineffective have encouraged some writers to call for the role of the teacher to be increased (often at the expense of the supervisor). Student opinion reigns supreme. If he or she is more often in the company of the teachers and also values the teacher's opinion more, surely students would value such a development. 'Considerable gains,' according to Partington (1982), 'can be achieved for the student in school-based rather than university-based teaching practice supervision'. He conducted an experiment heavily reliant upon statistical analysis in which he handed over one-quarter of one year's post-graduate certificate students exclusively to teacher-tutors. The benefits he claims for the teacher-tutored group were that there was a reduction in the students' concern about assessment and that this group contained more students who felt happier about their first year in teaching. He added that for the cooperating teachers there were advantages for their own professional development.

Such findings as these have often led their authors and others (Bowman, 1979; Patty, 1973) to draw the conclusion that supervisors are redundant and that teachers alone should be invested with the responsibility of overseeing students in school. In addition Bowman has pointed out the negative side of supervision for the college or university tutor. In reality, he asserts, such a function harms a tutor's career. Supervision of students in school is never recognized by a college or university hierarchy as an activity worthy of credit in the promotion stakes. It ranks in importance even below good teaching by tutors. Moreover supervision appears as a non-activity by those outside the education service. It rarely achieves any prominence, so ignorance of it remains profound. Bowman also makes the point that any supervisor would in any case be hard put to it to carry out his or her job effectively. The amount of time put aside for supervision of students is eaten into by travelling from one school to another. His rough calculation makes interesting reading:

> Assume that the supervisor makes four additional visits and spends an average of ninety minutes per visit at the school — probably a generous estimate. But assuming this, the supervisor has spent six hours in the supervisory process. Not really. Included in the visit must be time for the amenities of greeting and exchanging pleasantries with the building principal, sitting through recess periods and restroom breaks, a needful conference with the student teacher, another with the cooperating teacher, and perhaps a third with both of them. After all this is deducted, there is probably left over for the four visits a grand total of 100 minutes. Even during this period an observation of a typical classroom performance may not have occurred. But this is the system.

Finally he makes a point of increasing relevance to institutions of higher education in the present political and economic climate: 'the supervision of student teachers by university personnel represents a needless drain upon dwindling resources'.

In short, critics of what remains the standard method of looking after students on school practice ask the disturbing question: is the supervisor necessary?

The Other Side of the Coin

My major purpose in this section is to suggest reasons why the system is as it is and to suggest also that it is built on foundations too often ignored. In order to redress the balance to some extent — though only in passing — it had better be said that the research evidence does not all point in one direction. Teachers have not always been found to be more influential than supervisors (Boschee *et al.*, 1978; Nelson and Ahmed, 1972).

Perhaps one of the greatest dangers of excluding the tutor from the supervision process is the divorce of the learning within the institution of higher education from that taking place in school. In fact of course this learning should form two mutually sustaining parts of a whole experience and the tutor is the best placed to ensure that this marriage is effected. Giving the teacher exclusive responsibility can easily lead to the situation that obtained before the creation of institutions devoted to the preparation of teachers. Students come to see their situation solely as that of apprentice teacher (attached to a master craftsman) who has to be inducted into the teaching ritual. I shall return to this point later. For the moment I wish to explore the idea of master teacher. The main difficulty with such a concept is that, unlike other crafts with their long-defined skills, no one is yet able to translate vague positive qualities of so-called good teaching into an easily-defined and concrete set of skills for master teaching. Any teaching apprentice therefore may try modelling himself or herself inappropriately. The other result is that no one teacher is likely to possess all the necessary skills to a level of excellence.

It might be possible to lessen the worst effects of apprenticeship. For example teachers could be helped to understand what went on in the institution. Nevertheless organizational difficulties would remain great and in effect what would be happening would be a significant change in workload from tutors to teachers. In fact teachers would have to modify considerably what they saw as their job since they would be taking on the education of students in training in addition to the education of their pupils.

A further argument in support of the separation of functions rather than their being merged in one person is that some of the functions that enhance the education of a student in training can only properly be performed by someone external to the school. This consultant role is analyzed by Zimpher *et al.* (1980). They first link it to the work carried out in the institution of higher education by saying that the supervisor defines and communicates to both the teacher and student their respective roles. Without such guidance, of course, both would be left in a kind of limbo operating as best they could. Presumably the result of allowing both teacher and student to define their own roles would be that considerable variation in practice would arise. The supervisor function therefore ensures uniformity and it follows from this that a certain standard is set. A second function unique to the supervisor was that of phasing the student into the teaching. Both teacher and student were found to be anxious for the latter to be involved as soon as possible in full-time teaching. The supervisor alone had the responsibility of ensuring that such involvement came at an appropriate time.

The most obvious function associated with the supervisor, and which was third on the authors' list, was that of evaluating the student's performance. Teachers can perform an invaluable service for students; there is no doubt about that. However, the strength of their position — intimate and frequent involvement in the work of the class and the student — can also make it more difficult to stand back from the particular classroom situation, whereas the outsider status of the tutor occasionally enables a fresh perspective. The authors found, for example, that teachers tended to avoid negative criticisms of students, presumably because by dint of working closely with the students, they had come to some extent to regard them as colleagues and therefore found it less easy to point out faults. Nevertheless the teacher–student relationship rarely reaches real intimacy since Zimpher *et al.* found that the final function unique to the supervisor was that of confidante to both parties and this enabled better communication between the two.

Some writers have sought to enhance the role of the tutor as consultant by concentrating upon the liaison of what are often the two major aspects of the higher education tutor: pre-service and in-service work. In some unique writing on the matter Stones (1984) effects the bridge by claiming that all teaching is based upon certain underlying principles which should be studied in order for improvement to be forthcoming:

> I view pedagogical skills as the *deep structures* of teaching ability...They constitute the underlying grasp of principles by teachers, and their practical application lies in helping pupils to learn by teachers' deployment of a variety of *surface* activities i.e. teaching methods. Thus teachers with an understanding of these deep structures would manifest them in the way most appropriate to a specific teaching situation. Since every lesson must of necessity be unique, given the complexity of abstractions inherent in these interactions, every approach to teaching must of necessity also be unique. Thus equipping a student teacher with highly specific 'tips' might work in some conditions but could be disastrous in others. The implementation of a teaching plan, and its consequent interactions based on a grasp of a body of general principles, will equip students to take into account the nature of the uniqueness of the specific situation and provide guidance about the necessary appropriate action.

Certainly Stones seems to put his finger upon a weakness endemic in the system of the supervision of students and in courses that aim to improve the skills of practising teachers. There is often a desire to maintain good personal relationships above all else especially in the case of supervisors (Terrell *et al.*, 1985). Stones (1979) has elsewhere explored the area of pedagogy and produced checklists of skills against which classroom performances may be measured. He has also produced (Stones, 1984) checklists for supervisors to look at their own performance. However, the sub-title of his book on supervision is 'a *counselling* and pedagogical approach' (my emphasis), indicating that he also considers that the interpersonal relationship role of supervision is important. Blumberg (1976) too has concentrated upon this latter aspect of a supervisor's work in pre-service and in-service.

Some authors (for example, Emans, 1983) claim that (even without following

Stones' ideas on deep structure) there is no obvious difference between pre-service and in-service education and Emans goes further to advocate a less passive role for the tutor-consultant. He maintains that the tutor should become nothing less than 'the major change agent for schools and for teacher education'. However, to enhance the supervisor's role he suggests extensive alterations:

1 The functions of college supervisors be changed so that they would have less direct responsibility for the immediate and direct supervision of student teachers than they presently have.
2 College supervisors serve in an in-service mode by working with school personnel on curriculum development and the improvement of teaching.
3 College supervisors focus attention on the interpretation of the theory and research that comprise the knowledge base for education.

Clearly Emans suggests a shift in balance from the pre-service part of a supervisor's work to the in-service part. A supervisor should be familiar with research findings — something a teacher cannot be expected to be — and so should be able to interpret such findings and bring them to practitioners at the chalkface. The tutor is therefore that part of the system which links the higher education sector to the primary or secondary sectors. Obviously by concentrating only on the pre-service element of his or her job, the tutor can only fulfil partially the potential of the role. In order to bring about change in the system the tutor needs to have access to practice in schools and more particularly to serving teachers. Emans chooses to compare the tutor in his or her new fully fledged role with the agricultural agent who often works out of agricultural colleges. They possess an expertise valued by farmers. Thus tutors could become even more valued by teachers if in turn their expertise is drawn upon.

In-service Education: One Example

In fact there already exists a movement within the British educational context which places particular emphasis upon the dual role of tutors. This is IT-INSET (Initial training — Inservice education and training), an approach propounded by Ashton *et al.* (1983). These authors claim to have identified several recent trends in the British education service which have come to a head in IT-INSET. Certainly the movement was strong enough to receive funding from the Department of Education and Science for nine years (1978–87). About twenty institutions training teachers in Britain claim to have adopted the approach. It undoubtedly was boosted by the government's dark threat to close courses if their tutors did not possess recent and relevant experience of the classroom since IT-INSET allowed tutors to work in schools. It has therefore become firmly established with its philosophy influencing recently validated degree courses and with the development of regional organization after the period of direct DES funding ceased. It is worthwhile, therefore, spending a little time in examining this latest attempt to bring together pre-service and in-service work.

Work in schools becomes central to this approach which, claim Ashton *et al.*, offers a 'more professional focus' for the education of teachers. They reject the more traditional belief that schools are sources to illustrate theory — usually derived from great educational thinkers. Instead it is the schools themselves which generate the theory which is derived from practical situations. For obvious reasons therefore the importance of periods spent in school is increased.

The authors discern a parallel development in in-service education as this too has become ever more interested in what actually goes on in the classroom. The principal concern for teachers is solving problems generated by pupils at work in the school. In consequence there has been a movement away from the type of in-service course which takes a teacher to listen or work alongside a group of other teachers away from the pupils.

Thus the authors echo Emans in so far as they see a greater bonding of pre-service and in-service as a healthy development. At first sight, however, there appears little novel here since tutors have always worked in both areas. Perhaps the most important departure resides in the fact that the tutor should be doing both aspects of his or her work at the same time. IT-INSET is based upon a concept of teamwork which has teacher, student and tutor working together in the classroom. The teacher's task is critical — in theory at least — at the outset since it is the teacher who is supposed to identify the area for the team to work on. The teacher after all knows that classroom well and is most immediately concerned by it. Thereafter, however, the roles of the three participants are less traditionally defined; one might well take over, albeit briefly, the function of another in an effort to solve practical classroom problems. Thus a teacher could become the student or the student the teacher. So too, a tutor can adopt either role. The three thus become a team of (approximate) equals as each works with the others.

Nevertheless such a method of working does not in itself mark off the organization of IT-INSET from similar forms much favoured in the past. It is a long established tradition for tutors to work alongside students, and indeed teachers, in the classroom. What do distinguish the latest forms from previous similar forms of classroom-based organization are, firstly, the systematic review of what goes on in the classroom and, secondly, the desire to alter the consultative role of the tutor; neither change is effected easily as we shall see later. Both aspects nevertheless modify the tutor's role.

By systematic review is meant the deliberate effort by team participants to collect data about what is happening in the classroom and thus to move away from the more usual impressionistic accounts that pass for valid observations of classroom activity. We have here a strong parallel with Stenhouse (1975) and his well-known call for the creation of the teacher as researcher. He suggested such data gathering methods as video and audio recordings as well as perceptions from pupils in an effort to get the teacher to investigate the reality rather than myth of school life. He recognized that the target of teacher-researcher is as yet unattainable but proposed that teachers rely upon researchers in the interim in order to gain the necessary skills. Laudable as Stenhouse's ambitions are, they appear excessively optimistic. The day when a majority of teachers regard their classrooms as fertile breeding grounds for validly verifiable hypotheses does not appear to be about to dawn. The IT-INSET form of organization does, however, provide an example of the sort of Stenhousian interim (which in fact seems more likely to be the ultimate stage of development) in that the tutor–teacher–student team should be research orientated. Within such a team the most likely member with research knowledge and/or experience is the tutor and it is he or she, therefore, whose consultant role is reinforced.

Paradoxically this might provide a source of tension within the team if the pure model of IT-INSET is to flourish and this leads us into the second aspect mentioned above of the IT-INSET tutor role. In contrast to many earlier versions of tutors and students working (sometimes) with teachers in school when the tutor's expertise — normally in an area of the curriculum — was recognized and exploited, IT-INSET urges tutors to become one of the team rather than the leader of it:

> If the team is to function effectively, it must be run on democratic lines, and this will not guarantee the tutor the 'chair' at team discussions let alone the last word on everything discussed . . . the leadership role will circulate, in action and in discussion. (Poulton, n.d. p. 14).

The fear that the tutor might take a dominant role is based principally upon the contention that by following an expert 'it might be of greater long-term value for the teachers to learn of the students' problems in tackling the issues than to receive any pseudo-definitive solutions'. (Ashton *et al.*, 1983, p. 3)

A brief case study might help to highlight the above points and illustrate the general method of working. This is offered not by any means as an example of first-class IT-INSET in action but simply as an actual piece of teamwork which also contains elements which could have been better done.

A case study

The work hereafter briefly outlined took place in a suburban primary school in the Midlands. The team consisted of two primary postgraduate certificate students, a teacher and the author as the tutor. We worked for ten weeks in a spring term with eight-year-olds on a science topic, air, chosen by the teacher. LEA support was forthcoming in that supply cover released the class teacher for an extra session per week so that the team could meet to review progress and plan ahead.

Having been given the topic, the team decided to begin the process by selecting experiments and demonstrating them to groups of pupils. The areas to be covered were: (1) burning oxygen, (2) 'pouring' air (underwater), (3) air in gaps, and (4) the effects of moving air. The first three were done in the classroom whereas the fourth was done outside — fortunately it proved to be a windy day. The pupils rotated between the experiments throughout the morning. In the subsequent meeting of the team, it was felt that although the pupils had been keenly interested in each experiment, the pupils themselves should be more actively involved. We also wanted, however, to continue with centring the lesson around practical sessions. In fact the school possessed sets of science workcards one set of which dealt with air so we decided to use these after choosing the most promising ones. In the event seven experiments were prepared by the team setting up the equipment and the children following the cards — a competent reader in each group ensured that the rest followed. The role of the team was to help out if necessary, though in fact our main task was that of checking on progress by posing the occasional question to members of the pupil groups.

The next step for the pupils would be to look more deeply into one particular aspect of the topic, and so it was thought useful if each team member could spend a whole session leading some work of a practical nature which nevertheless could be carried out by the children. This would lead to four weeks' activities since each team member would take one quarter of the class each week so that the whole class would have experienced the complete set of activities. The four areas under investigation were: (1) falling objects, (2) paper plane construction, (3) moving air and its propulsive qualities, and (4) boomerang construction. Since the author was involved in the last named, it is this which will be outlined. At first pupils were invited to design and fly their own but though designs were sometimes imaginative, none passed the flying test and thus a design for a four-bladed boomerang was presented to the group who dicussed it and then set about constructing it and thereafter flying it. In fact just like their earlier design it was a small boomerang made out of cardboard so it was possible to try it out in the school hall.

Unfortunately by allowing the pupils *carte blanche* to experiment initially, the time for reflection and final discussion was drastically reduced and so it was decided to omit this first part in future sessions so that pupils had a better opportunity to reflect upon their work. In fact greater emphasis was put on the simple mathematics of the construction since there was plenty of uncertainty about this aspect; that is, the difference between centimetres and millimetres, the properties of a square and rectangle, how to find the centre of a square, marking and cutting along straight lines. There was also a greater emphasis upon discussion within the new group so it could be checked whether pupils understood the major processes. The term's work ended with a presentation by the class of the various experiments and the progress that had been made.

Although each team member emerged from the term's sessions feeling that both they and the pupils had benefited, we did not always agree on the best method of procedure. For example, I was keen to check upon progress, and thus introduced into the team discussions the scientific processes outlined in *Science in Primary Schools* (DES, 1983) and later in the term a checklist based upon Harlen (1977), *Raising Questions*. In fact team members were not enthusiastic to do anything formal to judge pupils' progress, relying principally upon personal impressions and written accounts by the pupils of their work (though the latter were in fact produced for the class teacher on another occasion in the week). Further, an attempt in the latter part of the term to get a team member to act as a non-participant observer in order to report on the teaching and learning was not eagerly adopted. This was partly because the organization of the classroom activities had become locked into the four team members heading a group and so extracting someone to observe would mean that not all the class would experience all the activities. However, this was not the only reason. After the cycle was completed, it was again suggested that the detached observer be used and the team now agreed. However, this particular session was due to be seen by some visitors, and the Head, acting through the class teacher, let it be known that she was anxious to have all team members participating in the actual teaching. This was an interesting development since it raises several issues not least the effect of outsiders on a school. This is a case, of course, of image management. Nevertheless it also brings to the fore the *expectations* of all participants in such a team venture, particularly when linked to consultants or outsiders — a point I shall return to shortly.

Conclusions

I have tried examining two major aspects of the higher education tutor's role and used school-based work as the focus and unifying factor between these two aspects. It is interesting to note in passing, and before returning to look again at some points raised earlier, that the tutor can well spend a major part of his or her work outside the home institution. Yet it is still sometimes thought by teachers that tutors are somehow cut off from the realities of the chalkface. No doubt the argument would be that part-time working in classrooms is not the same as full-time working. But the query in reply to that might be (and I shall pursue this no further) that this is so, but does one need to be working full-time in the classroom to know reality (and where does this leave other members of the teaching profession, for example headteachers)?

Although I do not wish to maintain that the tutor's role is immutable, I do believe that it is stronger philosophically than is often admitted. Hence suggestions for reformulation of the tutor's role are rife — including the exclusion of the tutor from pre-service work. Basically the difficulty with excluding the tutor as supervisor from the school-based work of the student on a pre-service course is that the student should be being educated and not just trained. The school-based experience, essential though it is, is not the whole story. By this I do not mean *only* that there is a theoretical input which is also essential but *also* that school-based experience can only offer a partial view of the whole. Nevertheless it is not rare for a student to consider himself or herself as an apprentice who must rapidly learn the techniques demonstrated by the cooperating teacher. The wider question of change for the good enters here and leads to the question whether an apprenticeship system would be more or less likely to encourage change and improvement within the education system. Surely the outsider's view is essential here. It is more important for a student to question present practice than to imitate it.

As stated earlier, the trouble with the position adopted by those that advocate an exclusive hegemony for practising teachers (Partington, 1982; Jeffcoates, 1988) is that it tends towards exclusivity and divorce (of one element of the educative process from another). Certainly institutions involved in the pre-service education of students (and then not all of them) have only in recent years come to appreciate that school-based work by students is not just an appendage but an integral part of the overall course, and thus such work often feeds work done in the training institution. Part of this recognition comes in the way tutors increasingly work in schools, and this brings me to the second aspect of the tutor's role.

At the end of the case study I said that the expectations of all participants in such work had to be aligned. To promote such an alignment there is a case here for a contract clearly stating the obligations of each party (essentially the outsider(s) and the receiving institution). This links furthermore with the mixed reception accorded to the idea of monitoring progress, happily experimented with by some, ignored by others. Despite having spent time on accustoming the school to the principles of the IT-INSET teamwork, systematic inquiry into the methods adopted and progress of pupils remained only partially explored. The over-riding consideration was the actual teaching, ensuring that pupils were occupied: both perfectly legitimate concerns particularly for the class teacher and, as I have already said, for students in training. Systematic investigation of the processes within the classroom was therefore of secondary importance to them and the emphasis upon this aspect of the work came rather late in the day. The idea therefore of a written contract might well have the merit of literally putting in black and white the expectations of each party. Naturally it would have to be a negotiated document, not one imposed from outside, but it would need to be established from the outset. It is worth noting here that the idea for such a contract would be expected by all parties to emanate from the training institution and tutor, not elsewhere.

Another point that should be made in regard to the IT-INSET way of working is that the focus of the enquiry is supposed to be chosen by the teacher. During my particular involvement in the case study this posed no problems but in reality I consider it to be too restrictive. The idea behind it is of course a laudable one, namely to ensure that the work undertaken would be relevant to the teacher rather than being imposed from outside and, by allowing the teacher the choice, he or she would feel part of the enterprise from the beginning. Nevertheless since IT-INSET places the emphasis upon teamwork, I do not see why one member of the team should have on every occasion the exclusive right to choose the subject-matter. Kelly (1985), who in fact is talking about action research, puts her (and, as it happens, my) point of view forcibly: 'Nor does action research take as axiomatic that teachers should generate their own research problems, or that the research should be approached from the practitioner's point of view'.

In fact it is clear from present practice that it is not rare for those institutions working in the IT-INSET mode to adopt such a position in reality. The entry of action research at this point is a useful reminder that school-based teamwork is often preoccupied (and the case study gave an instance of this) with action to the detriment of research. It is here again that the training institutions and tutors have a particular responsibility. The argument for analytic reflection as a part of teaching is surely won but it is the tutor-as-consultant who should be taking the lead here and setting up a framework for this to happen. Such procedures have probably emanated from action research more publicly than from IT-INSET (Elliott, 1981). It is interesting to compare what I believe to have been the frequent (though not exclusive) case in IT-INSET with the classification of action research offered by Ebbutt (1985). He insists that to qualify an activity as research, teachers must write a report of the activities and that such reports should be open to public scrutiny. I do not wish to pursue here whether all work conducted by teams in schools should aspire to be research (though I confess I find such a notion attractive), but I do wish to make the point that it would be a pity if such school-based work did not add to the *general* store of knowledge about classroom processes. The implication is that such work should be rigorous and public (i.e. written). As it has often been done in the past, school-based teamwork involving outsiders would not fit any of the categories suggested by Ebbutt.

Finally, the higher education tutor can derive little of his or her authority from a position of status within an educational hierarchy. The position is, therefore, essentially that of negotiator when related to school-based work either in pre-service or in-service work. The tutor remains a true consultant.

References

ASHTON, P. M. E., HENDERSON, E. S., MERRITT, J. E. and MORTIMER, D. J. (1983) *Teacher Education in the Classroom: Initial and In-Service*, London, Croom Helm.

BLUMBERG, A. (1976) 'Supervision as interpersonal intervention'. Abstract presented to the Convention of the American Educational Research Association, San Francisco, California.

BOSCHEE, F., PRESCOTT, D. R. and HEIN, D. D. (1978) 'Do cooperating teachers influence the educational philosophy of student teachers?', *Journal of Teacher Education*, **29**, pp. 57–61.

BOWMAN, N. (1979) 'College supervision of student teaching: a time to reconsider', *Journal of Teacher Education*, **30**, pp. 29–30.

DES (1983) *Science in Primary Schools: a discussion paper* HMI Science Committee, London, HMSO.

EBBUTT, D. (1985) 'Educational Action Research: some general concerns and specific quibbles'. In: BURGESS, R. G. (Ed.) *Issues in Educational Research: Qualitative Methods*, Lewes, The Falmer Press.

ELLIOTT, J. (1981) *Action-Research: a framework for self-evaluation in schools*, TIQL Working Paper No. 1, Cambridge, Cambridge Institute of Education.

EMANS, R. (1983) 'Implementing the knowledge base: redesigning the function of cooperating teachers and college supervisors'. *Journal of Teacher Education*, **34**, pp. 14–18.

HARLEN, W. (1977) *Raising Questions*, London, Oliver and Boyd.

HOSTE, R. (1982) 'Sources of influence on teaching practice in the evaluation of courses in teacher education', *Journal of Education for Teaching*, **8**, pp. 252–61.

JEFFCOATES, R. (1988) 'Surplus to requirements', *Times Educational Supplement*, 24 June 1988.

KELLY, A. (1985) 'Action Resarch: what is it and what can it do?'. In: BURGESS, R. G. (Ed.) *Issues in Educational Research: Qualitative Methods*, Lewes, The Falmer Press.

MORRIS, J. R. (1974) 'The effects of the university supervisor on the performance and adjustment of student teachers', *Journal of Educational Research*, **67**, pp. 358–62.

NELSON, N. J. and AHMED, A. (1972) 'Educational values of student teachers before and after student teaching', *College Student Journal*, **6**, pp. 72–7.

PARTINGTON, J. (1982) 'Teachers in school as teaching practice supervisors', *Journal of Education for Teaching*, **8**, pp. 262–74.

PATTY, A. H. (1973) 'Classroom teachers will replace college supervisors', *Contemporary Education*, **44**, 179–83.

POULTON, A. (n.d.) *Doing IT-INSET: No. 2, Tutoring*, CEDTE, School of Education, University of Leicester.

STENHOUSE, L. (1975) *An Introduction to Curriculum Research and Development*, London, Heinemann.

STONES, E. (1979) *Psychology of Education: a counselling and pedagogical approach*, London, Methuen.

STONES, E. (1984) *Supervision in Teacher Education*, Windsor, NFER-Nelson.

TERRELL, C., TREGASKIS, D. and BOYDELL, D. (1985) 'Teaching practice supervisors in primary schools: an ethnomethodological perspective', *Research Report*, College of St. Paul and St. Mary, Cheltenham.

YATES, J. W. (1982) 'Student teaching: results of a recent survey', *Educational Research*, **24**, 212–15.

ZIMPHER, N. L., DEVOSS, G. C. and NOTT, D. L. (1980) 'A closer look at university student teacher supervision', *Journal of Teacher Education*, **31** (4), pp. 11–15.

8
Mental Health Consultation in Education: Theory and Practice

Joan Figg and Rob Stoker

Introduction

A Definition of Mental Health Consultation

Consultation takes many forms as will be apparent from the first chapters within this book. The focus of this chapter is on one particular type of consultation referred to as mental health consultation. Caplan (1970) describes this form of consultation as:

> A process of interaction between two professional persons — the consultant, who is a specialist, and the consultee, who evokes the consultant's help in regard to a current work problem with which s/he is having some difficulty and which s/he has decided is within the other's area of specialised competence. The work problem involves the management or treatment of one or more clients of the consultee, or the planning or implementation of a programme to cater to such clients.

Caplan goes on to describe the interaction as being one in which the consultant takes no direct responsibility for implementing the remedial action for the client and also makes the point that the consultee retains full professional responsibility for the client. The focus of the work within mental health consultation is to help the consultee with the current work problem but above and beyond that to engage in an educative process which will add to the consultee's knowledge and allow him or her on future occasions to be able to deal better on his or her own with the particular category of problem. Central to the philosophy of this form of consultation, then, is the fact that it is a community method which is pro-active in nature and has as its goal the spreading of the application of the specialist's knowledge through to those who consult with him or her.

The background to the model developed by Caplan and his colleagues was initially the post-war years in Israel. There he was involved in a child guidance centre where one of his duties was to include the supervision of the mental health of approximately 16,000 new immigrant children in the Youth Aliyah organization. The combination of the sheer number of potential clients, combined with transportation difficulties in Israel, meant that the small team of psychologists spent their time most effectively talking with the adults responsible for the management of the children rather than taking direct referrals on the children themselves. From these activities emerged a picture in which it was recognized that the dynamic responses of the adults played a crucial part in the successful management (or otherwise) of the children in their care. Thus by the psychologists helping the adults to look at their own dynamic responses to their care situations, it was possible to help them in their management not only of certain identified individual children but with much larger numbers of children as well.

Caplan draws up a model of consultation where four types of consultation are likely to occur. He points out, though, that this is a purified model and that in practice consultation sessions will not fall neatly into one clear category. The categories are:

1 *Client-centred case consultation*. This is the traditional type of specialist consultation in medical practice, in which the consultee asks the consultant for his or her expert opinion and this is then provided. It may be through this form of consultation that the consultee increases his or her experience with this case and can then apply that experience to future situations.

2 *Consultee-centred case consultation*. In this process the problem being presented by the consultee has to do with a particular case, but the focus of the consultation is on trying to understand the consultee's difficulty with the case and in trying to help him or her remedy this. Caplan identifies four main areas of difficulty and these are: (a) lack of knowledge about the type of problem being presented by the client; (b) lack of skill in making use of such knowledge; (c) lack of self confidence; and (d) lack of professional objectivity due to the interference of subjective emotional complications.

3 *Programme-centred administrative consultation*. In this form of consultation the consultant helps the consultee with a work problem in the area of planning and programme administration. The consultant helps by using his or her expert knowledge of administration and social systems, as well as that of mental health theory and practice. The work of the consultant allows the consultee to manage the implementation of the particular programme in question and this may also prove useful in his/her implementation of other programmes in the future.

4 *Consultee-centred administrative consultation*. In this form of consultation the focus is on helping the consultee to gain better understanding of the difficulties and shortcomings that interfere with his or her grappling with the tasks of programme development in organizations. Caplan points out that as well as lack of knowledge, skills,

self confidence and objectivity in individuals, other issues can arise which may be more linked to group activities (e.g. poor leadership, authority problems, lack of role complementarity, etc.)

The work of Caplan was further developed within the context of the US educational system by Meyers *et al.* (1979) and Meyers (1981). Meyers *et al.* proposed a model with four levels of service which increased in the amount of indirect service provided. The levels were defined as:

Level 1 — Direct service to the child. This includes traditional psychodiagnostic techniques.

Level 2 — Indirect service to the child. This involves somebody other than the consultant, usually the teacher, gathering the data and running an intervention programme.

Level 3 — Direct service to the teacher. This is analogous to Caplan's consultee-centred case consultation.

Level 4 — Direct service to the organization. The primary goal is to influence the organizational climate as a whole.

Both Meyers and Caplan attach considerable importance to the psychodynamic processes that occur between consultees and members of their client group. The focus of consultation sessions is often likely to be in the realms of the feelings generated within teachers, and as such is perhaps a more unusual approach than many and one that may be seen as threatening to some of those staff who work within educational settings. This will be due in part to the simple fact that it is not at all common for teaching staff to spend very much time looking at areas such as their own feelings.

Traditional educational psychology practice

Educational psychologist engage in a wide range of activities in the course of their work. Professional journals provide exciting examples of new developments in professional practice, including the moving away from the assessment of individual children into the assessment of schools as complex organizations and the production of strategies to help those organizations manage the task more effectively.

Despite this the substantial majority of educational psychologists engage in traditional individual assessment work that follows a referral to the psychological service as a support agency. Typically the educational psychologist will be in contact with the school and will agree to a referral to his service as a result of hearing details about a case, or may simply receive a referral through the post system direct from the school without a great deal of discussion beforehand. It can be argued that traditional referral procedures of this kind work well both for the school system and for psychological services. The schools, having become concerned about an individual child, can almost literally 'post' their concerns to somebody else in a support agency and in the posting feel themselves relieved of some of the burden of concern and responsibility. They are now able to refer to somebody else as being responsible for the next stage of action. Psychological services may look upon the arrival of referrals as a critical component of their *raison d'être*. Referrals represent a quantifiable unit of demand which emphasize the fact that educational psychologists are desperately needed because of their particular area of expertise.

Typically, though, demand outstrips supply and this can lead to frustration on the part of schools as clients who are wanting more of a service than they can actually obtain. The process that often unfolds is that the school makes a referral to the educational psychologist and waits a while before an appointment is arranged to see the identified client (in a school situation this being always a child). What then usually occurs is that the educational psychologist arranges to see the child and carry out a detailed assessment (either with the child as an individual, or within the context of the school setting, or more often combining both) and will provide feedback and a report to the school. Consequences after that will depend on the circumstances of the particular case. Naturally, the more successful the educational psychologist has been the more his or her services are required and so the more demands there are put upon him or her. This can in turn generate further frustrations on the part of the schools and it can be seen as a parallel to the position that Caplan was in in Israel in the late 1940s.

The adoption of mental health consultation within the practice of a team of educational psychologists

As has already just been mentioned there are similarities between the dilemma faced by successful traditional referral work within educational psychology and the dilemma faced by Caplan in Israel. In both situations experts in the area of mental health and psychological processes are responsible for very large client groups within the population. The adults responsible for the client groups are asking for a considerable amount of help to the point where the level of demand is much greater than the mental health experts can manage to meet. The two authors of this chapter have both gained experience in application of mental health consultation and were excited by its potential application within educational psychology. The appeal of the model was that it comes with a clear framework and attempts to disseminate problem-solving skills within the community rather than retaining them within a field of 'specialized experts'. It was apparent that whilst some problems being presented to educational psychologists did indeed require quite specialized forms of intervention and help, a very large number of problems took forms that could be used as learning situations for the teaching staff to be able to manage their jobs better, thereby gaining greater satisfaction and also higher levels of skills.

It was felt by the authors that one of the possible mistakes of the practice of educational psychology in the past was to make those who referred to the service increasingly dependent on it by passing the work issue to somebody else to solve. It was therefore felt that within the school setting mental health consultation would provide the opportunity for educational psychologists and teachers to work jointly at disseminating higher levels of skills back into the teaching force. With a client population of approximately 15,000 school-aged children and the staff of thirty-one primary schools, six secondary schools, a further education college and numerous special schools and units, it was felt that the impact of successfully applying mental health consultation could be enormous.

It was from this background that the authors implemented the model of mental health consultation at a primary school level and a secondary school level.

Primary School Consultation Service

The consultation service has been established with the specific aim of applying the concepts of mental health consultation. The town concerned is in an area of high unemployment (at present running at approximately 20 per cent) and represents the area covered by the psychologists who work as part of a team offering a service to the community.

There were two stages to the implementation of the consultation service, the first being a developmental phase where an initial service was offered to five of the total of thirty-one primary schools, and then a second phase where the service was made available to all thirty-one primary schools. Service delivery to secondary schools is pursued along different lines and will not be discussed here. In the initial phase the headteacher of each of the five schools was consulted about the new service before its start date and the educational psychologists met with each whole staff group for discussions about how the service would operate in detail.

The service itself is essentially very straightforward to describe. Each week the educational psychologists from the team make themselves available at the local teachers centre and any member of staff from within the primary schools is welcome to come and join them. There are three sessions in the course of the week, each lasting two hours and thus totalling six hours of meeting time available each week. Whilst any member of staff can arrange to come along at short notice (as close as fifteen minutes away from the start of one of the sessions) an appointment diary is operated to ensure that nobody is left waiting unnecessarily. In practice this means that teaching staff typically telephone several days prior to a consultation session and book one of four possible thirty-minute slots.

The core activity of the consultation service is a period of time when the educational psychologist and a member of staff from the primary school meet to look at a problem that is being defined by the member of staff. Typically the session will involve a teacher (and sometimes headteacher) defining an area of concern and the psychologist will be listening as well as asking for elaboration on certain points. There will then usually be a stage when the psychologist reflects back to the member of staff the psychologist's understanding of the area of concern and his or her observations of some of the processes that appear to be significant and which may help to gain insight around the problem. The third and final phase of the session will usually involve the teacher looking at the range of options open to him or her, although there will be no pressure for any decision to be taken during the meeting session. The psychologist will take brief notes concerning the session on the standard consultation service form and will send a copy of this summary to the teacher. The fact that both consultant and consultee have a copy of the summary is useful in that it provides both with a record of the issues which arose and any decisions on action that were taken towards the end of the session. It is also a useful point of reference with regard to evaluation of the service.

It will be useful now to relate the practice of the consultation service to the preceding section looking at mental health consultation and traditional educational psychology practice. The objective in deciding to run the consultation service was to apply the concepts of mental health consultation to the direct support work to schools and their management of the work tasks. The critical part of the consultation service is the session in which the educational psychologist and teacher discuss a problem that is being presented by that member of staff. In the context of Caplan's model, the main activity of this session is consultee-centred case consultation. On occasions consultee-centred administrative consultation also takes place. The activities can also be described within the framework used by Meyers *et al.* (1979) where the main activity is at level three (direct service to the teacher) but where there may also be some involvement at level two (indirect service to the child).

One of the more exciting aspects of the setting up and running of the consultation service is that it has involved organizational issues which impinge upon the activities above and beyond the level of individual schools and can be understood in terms of Meyers *et al.*'s level four activity (service to the organization).

At this point some examples of the ways in which consultation sessions unfold will be useful. On one occasion the deputy headteacher (also the teacher in charge of special needs within school) of a large primary school came to the consultation service and spent approximately fifteen minutes discussing a young girl aged six years. The content of the presentation had to do with the fact that the young girl was using no language whatsoever in school, although it was reported that she did use language at home. Within the consultation the clear signs of frustration on the part of the deputy headteacher were commented on and this in turn led to an acknowledgement of the fact that the young child's refusal to use language had developed into a power battle between the deputy headteacher (who was also the classteacher) and the girl. The member of staff felt that this was an issue, and also that the power battle extended to the work of the speech therapist, who appeared to be engaged in a struggle to extract language from the girl who apparently 'had' it whenever she chose to use it.

Within the very brief duration of the consultation session the deputy headteacher developed a series of strategies that would reduce the conflict between the young girl and the adults around her and further provide a likely environment for speech to occur. Shortly afterwards a phone message came through to the educational psychologist informing him that the child had suddenly started to produce normal language within the classroom. Of particular significance here is the fact that the consultation sessions lasted a mere fifteen minutes, and seemed to lead to the required change in approaching problem. If the consultation service had not been running, it may well be that the case would have been referred through the traditional procedures and led to much more lengthy involvement, with an assessment and a spotlight being focused on the child. This in turn might have exacerbated the problem. Obviously it is to be hoped that the deputy headteacher gained from the experience not only in terms of helping this particular child but also of understanding one of the processes that may lead to problems occurring within a primary school. This may then enable her to tackle better a range of problems in the future.

The headteacher of a Roman Catholic primary school came to the consultation service and presented a very different problem and this in turn led to a different outcome. This time the consultation session lasted thirty-five minutes and involved a description of a boy aged ten who engaged in a range of sexually explicit behaviour around the playground and classroom of the school. In the discussion that followed the consultee explained that this had created some very strong reactions on the parts of some of the staff at the school and the headteacher was unsure of the best way of dealing with the very agitated situation. The consultant reflected back to the headteacher the concerns that were generated in the adults around the child (and certainly wondered whether the description involved some projection of the headteacher's own anxieties) and they went on to discuss more details of the very difficult home background concerning the boy. As well as the anxiety related to the sexualized behaviours, it emerged that there was a lot of pressure being put upon the staff of the school to provide an unusual amount of supportive help for this boy because of his home situation.

Towards the end of the consultation session the headteacher made a direct request for the psychological service to come and join with herself and the staff group at a meeting being run as part of their in-service training programme. It was agreed that the meeting would focus directly on the issue of teachers' own feelings and responses that followed on as a result of the behaviour of the children in their charge. The staff meeting took place some weeks later and was led by the educational psychologist (with the support of a colleague as a group process consultant).

A further case example involved a class teacher who attended the consultation service for thirty minutes. There were two concerns expressed about a ten-year old child, the first of which was parental anxiety about the rate of learning development, which the teacher did not share. The second concern had to do with the boy's social and emotional adjustment and in particular his isolation from male peers. During the discussion that followed the teacher went on to describe a range of actions that she had already undertaken to try and tackle the problems. One of the more significant interventions by the teacher was the setting up of group exercises which focused on topics such as friendship. During the consultation it became apparent that the teacher was already engaged in some very successful strategies for tackling the problem that she was describing. Indeed the issue for the consultant was initially to wonder why the consultee had brought the case along for discussion. It emerged that the main need for the consultee was to seek reassurance that the strategies already employed were correct, so that she could return to those strategies with reinforced confidence. Within the consultation session the issue of the importance of professional confidence was discussed and acknowledgment given that the present strategies appeared to be working well. Towards the end of the session the classteacher decided not only to continue the existing strategies but to employ new ones to involve the mother and step-father and help boost the boy's own sense of security.

Consultation sessions not only focus on feelings but also they will often tackle cognitive and learning development. In one case, the teacher in charge of special needs in a large primary school came to discuss the severe under-achievement (and combined low attendance) of a child aged eight years. The session lasted quite a while because from the presentation it appeared that the main requirement was for the development of the necessary knowledge and skills to run a curriculum-based assessment. Thus within the session the educational psychologist explained how the school could identify reliable performance levels in curricular areas of literacy and numeracy and how they might set about establishing objectives that could be pursued over a six-week interval. Built into this was a monitoring system that would allow the school to compare performance prior to the running of the educational programme with performance upon completion of the educational programme. The consultee's request, supported by the consultant, was to run the programme for the duration and then return to the consultation service for a discussion of the rate of development.

Comments on consultant/consultee processes

It is well worth commenting upon the experiences of the consultant working within the framework of the consultation service. Several points emerge as a result of that experience.

Moving into a new role

The relationship between the consultant and the consultee takes a very different form during the consultation session. Where traditionally a member of staff within a school would look towards the educational psychologist as somebody to provide expert advice and opinion, suddenly this is no longer the case. Instead the reflective technique, combined with the consultant commenting on process issues, puts very different demands on both consultant and consultee. It moves away from the tempting clarity of assessment details in a report form through to the complex issues of personal dynamics influencing a work situation. Whilst the mental health consultation model offers an enormous amount of gain to schools and educational psychologists in their combined areas of work, it is certainly also very demanding and exhausting. Some of the exhaustion on the part of the consultant is inevitably due to the work of resisting the temptation to provide expert 'advice' on those occasions where it would threaten to undermine the professional work of the member of school staff. Some of the exhaustion on the part of the consultee, on the other hand, is likely to arise from the desire for the consultant to take over and own the problem, only to discover that he or she is not willing to do so.

Contrast between model and working practice

Experience of working as a consultant highlights the fact that any model is a purified form of what actually occurs in reality. That is to say whilst there are phases during the consultation session work that are clearly, for example, consultee-centred case consultation, this often moves across a blurred boundary into programme-centred administrative consultation or consultee-centred administrative consultation. At other moments, it can be difficult to escape the fact that the process occurring within the session is actually moving away from consultation into other activities such as socializing or advice giving.

Conflict of role within consultation sessions versus outside consultation sessions

Whilst there can be role conflict within the consultation session, it is also quite clear that role conflict occurs between meetings with school staff at the consultation service and meetings with them elsewhere. Equally, it is not always possible to maintain a clear consultancy role within one area and move completely out of that in other areas of one's work. This is difficult for the educational psychologist, but also for the members of staff who use the range of services available. Thus they may see the educational psychologist as mental health consultant in one context, and if following on from this there is a need for direct educational psychology assessment of a child, then the teacher may see the psychologist in this very different 'expert' role and be left wondering whether this is the same or a different person in front of them! One possible way of helping with this conflict is to ensure that whoever acts in a consultancy capacity with a group of schools and their staff, does not at the same time operate as the educational psychologist involved in school assessments. However, levels of staffing and a variety of other constraints may make it difficult for a psychological service always to keep these roles apart.

As we mentioned earlier the consultation service was initially set up with a small group of schools and then expanded to cover all primary schools within the team's area. A critical change occurred at the time of the extension of the service to the complete group of schools. Specifically, the decision was taken to make the consultation service the main, and indeed only, form of initial discussion between schools and the psychological service concerning work issues. As such, from the day it started, the existing referral form used by schools was formally discontinued. In its place there was offered a much more readily available form of contact with the psychological service. Paradoxically the main form of contact had been through the sending of referral forms to the service and waiting for a response. Now, suddenly, the opportunity to send a problem through the post to a different agency had gone and in its place there existed a forum for joint work on problem-solving. Paradoxically the whole move towards much more rapid access to the psychological service occurred at a time when staff shortages had led to a rapid decline in the service to 60 per cent of its normal capacity. At this level an organisational change occurred affecting the full range of interaction between all of the primary schools and the psychological service. The change has been radical both at a superficial level (the complete disappearance of referral forms) and at a more profound level (the whole process of interaction over problem-solving between primary school staff and members of the county psychological service).

Application of Mental Health Consultation to Secondary School Adolescent Disruptive Behaviour

The school support team consists of a group of teachers, educational psychologists and social workers who have been using the concept of consultation to look at the problem of adolescent disruptive behaviour. The organization and design of the team took into consideration the main elements of the consultation process, the specific contribution of Caplan (1970) and mental health consultation, it's modification by Meyers *et al.* (1979) for schools, as well as aspects of organizational development and elements of the change process itself. As the work of the school support team developed we used seven stages that the consultation process might go through in order to conceptualize our work. These were:

1 entry into the system;
2 orientation to consultation;
3 problem identification;
4 problem definition;
5 developing an intervention plan;
6 assessing the impact of consultation;
7 concluding the relationship.

For the school support team it was at Stage 3 that the critical link between Caplan's four categories of consultation and Meyers *et al.*'s level of service delivery was used.

The school support team is a team of teachers drawn from five of the six comprehensive schools in the town and its sole aim is to reduce disruptive behaviour in those five schools. It has been operational since September 1985, planning began in September 1983, and the description that follows covers the period up to March 1988. Teaching staff have changed each September since 1985, and this is an established pattern which will continue. Except for the full-time post appointed by the education authority, the staffing concerned is all part-time and the time given varies from one session, or half a day per week, to three sessions, or one-and-a-half days per week. It is proposed that approximately one-quarter of the teaching staff will be new at the beginning of each academic year. These teaching staff members are all volunteers and this is an important element which will continue.

Since September 1986, there has been the appointment of a full-time teacher to the project who is a permanent staff member. In addition there has been input from a social worker from the county psychological service and a half-time educational psychologist who has been the project leader. For the first eighteen months of the project the resources mentioned above, i.e. teaching time, were the only resources we had to draw on. We had no buildings, capitation, books, secretarial support, etc. We were not acknowledged as part of the county's provision for disruptive children and therefore had no entry point to the local education system. We were solely being supported at a locally-agreed level between the five headteachers and the senior educational psychologist.

When we started, this project had virtually no resources except the support team teachers themselves. Therefore there was a necessity that the direction of work focused quite clearly at Level 3, i.e. we explored in great depth the area of consultee-centred case consultation with these teachers. As we have mentioned earlier Caplan described four basic reasons why people might seek consultee-centred case consultation. They were (a) lack of knowledge/understanding, (b) lack of skill, (c) lack of confidence, and (d) lack of objectivity. We intend to take Level Three out of order and describe it first as it was so important for us.

Level 3 — Direct service delivery to teachers as it applied to the school support team

Lack of knowledge/understanding

In stark contrast to the access normally available for teachers working with difficult youngsters in secondary schools to psychological services (we include contracted time here), the arrangement of staffing described above allowed there to be a free interchange over individual cases. Not only did the timetabling allow the consultee to be free during normal school hours but the psychologist was also timetabled to be available for consultation during the school day. This eliminated the problems such as rushed breaks, no place to meet, and no commitment to the consultation. The psychologist was able to share psychological information, interpret disruptive behaviour, give information about adolescent development in a relaxed way, being confident that the outcome would not be another referral to the psychological service and an increase in the psychologist's own stress over workload. In addition the team met weekly where an acknowledged part of the session was to allow for case discussions over particular difficulties. Here again there was an arena to influence the acquisition of knowledge of the consultees in a consultative manner.

Lack of skill

This was a very important area of development, and we certainly underestimated the amount of work that was needed in this area for the support team teachers, but we also underestimated their willingness and amazing motivation to work. The main areas which have been covered, have been initiated from case-based discussions, and needs mentioned by the school support teachers for additional skills in order to change the behaviour in their clients. The list of areas initiated in this way and covered over the years, have included basic theory underlining behaviour modification programmes, observations and analysis of behaviour, analysis of classroom interactive behaviour, experimental awareness training and an examination of the implications of social skills for support teachers themselves and their clients, counselling techniques with clients, relating at a meaningful level to parents, teaching the importance of effective lesson organization, of appropriate non-verbal behaviour and of management techniques in the classroom. The peer-professional, collaborative nature of the consultant–client relationship certainly 'freed' and allowed the professional teachers to increase their skills base. It also allowed the educational psychologist in an easy and non-threatening way into an area of sharing knowledge.

The allocation of the school support team is so arranged that the school-based team teacher-volunteers always work in at least one other comprehensive school than their own, and never in their own on individual referrals except with at least one other colleague. This arrangement allows for a sharing of ideas across institutions which has also helped with increasing teachers' skill base.

Lack of confidence

Much of what was described above applies in this section as well. Increased accessibility and availability allow the consultee to relate to the consultant at an individual level. The consultant previously had seldom been able to establish this relationship working other models of service delivery with secondary schools. It allows time for the consultant to listen and encourage the consultee. The weekly group meetings also allow the group to help each other in sharing and developing confidences.

Lack of objectivity

This is an important area where we do feel that this integrated model of shared responsibility for disruptive youngsters has proved very useful. It allows the consultee the fundamental opportunity of relinquishing many of the allegiancies and alliances which often inhibit him or her in dealing with children in the classroom. The consultee can establish a 'proper' professional identity and distance, and work in another school on a disruptive problem, freed of many subconscious difficulties they would have if working on exactly the same problem in their own schools. Increased objectivity and confidence in the situation is then transferrable back to their own school, and role conflict in the area of authority is reduced. What has been found is that support team teachers not valued for their own levels of professional management of children in their own schools have been highly valued and have worked very well in other schools, this also has increased personal confidence. Dependency is not a problem since the model of referral is absolutely clear and the case responsibility is always with the consultee. Anger and hostility again seem to be reduced by the shared support and professional distance which the model allows.

Having taken Level 3 out of sequence we now want to return to Level 1, 2, and 4.

Level 1 — A direct service to the child — Application in the school support team

Depending on the nature of the problem some of the work in schools has been at Level 1. At this level the consultant (support team worker) works in school collecting first-hand data about a child and his or her problem, and from this first-hand data works directly at changing agreed behaviours. One example would be an observer working inside a classroom recording behavioural events and then working with the child to modify these behaviours. Others would include direct intervention with the child, offering counselling support, remedial programmes, direct social skills training, and group work sessions. All of these activities are at Level 1 and are activities that support team members have directly involved themselves with.

Level 2 — Indirect service to the child

When providing an indirect service a consultant uses somebody else to gather data from the child in order to define the problem precisely (via observation by teachers, other students or the children themselves) and uses a caretaker (a teacher, for example, in our case) to carry out the derived intervention plan. An indirect service is often an economical, efficient way of using the consultant's time, the primary goal is to change the child's observable behaviour in the classroom. Consultation based on indirect services to the child like this, often emphasizes extra personal factors in a child's environment, and might lead to questioning for instance, the curricular content or teaching techniques at the child's school. As far as the school support team is concerned we would say that together with Level 3, which is a direct service to teachers, Level 2 in fact, is a main part of the work which has been carried out. Into this area fall other behaviour modification programmes initiated where the contact has been between school teachers and child. It would, therefore, also include remedial programmes carried out by school teachers, and additionally a range of other activities, for example, counselling, and social skills training where the class teacher has been willing and has the skills to work directly with the child. The role of the school support team member has not only been as consultant in these cases but sometimes as the invaluable supply teacher who covers and allows direct intervention by the class teacher.

Level 4 — Service to the organization

This represents the most indirect form of service to the child, the primary goal is to influence the organizational climate as a whole. It is in this area that the theory and implication of organizational development, which was mentioned earlier, comes to the fore. There are three main factors which should be covered before any proposed administrative consultation is embarked upon. These are determining:

1 whether you have the sufficient systems knowledge to be able to analyze and assess the system;
2 whether you (the consultant) have enough commitment and interest because this type of consultation can be very demanding;
3 whether you have enough time and flexibility, because time estimates of administrative consultation always prove to be underestimates.

The goal of this kind of intervention is to improve the organization's problem-solving skills through a better understanding of organizational processes. In this way the ability to repeatedly solve new problem situations is enhanced. Few educational psychologists are experts in school administration and they should be hesitant about direct advice to administrators. What the psychologist as consultant brings to the consultation is not expert knowledge of administration but resources for the process of problem-solving, thus the consultee-centred approach is process not content-oriented. Although some organizational interventions may be initiated by mental health professionals, a more desirable situation occurs when the organization itself recognizes the existence of some problem and seeks a psychologist to help them. As far as the school support team is concerned we have had one enquiry from one of the schools to look at their expressed needs for enhancement of skills in identifying and acknowledging disruptive behaviour. They quite clearly were wanting to work within their own system. The other area where we have been asked actively to look at an administrative level of intervention was one school which has asked us whether we would be able to compile curriculum material based on the work we do ourselves with children, to use in a modular approach in their own school.

The last area of consultee-centred administrative consultation that we want to describe is that carried out between the project leader/psychologist and the five headteachers of the contributing comprehensive schools. It has been a long intensive consultative process but always with the aim of affecting teachers' and children's behaviour at an organizational level. The beginnings of organizational change are now being seen, which include:

(a) regular meetings with the five headteachers to look at the provision and needs of disruptive pupils in the town;

(b) capitation arrangements and financial commitment to support the needs of these youngsters;

(c) timetabling changes to allow support team members time to work in the unit;

(d) the headteacher's group having presented an agreed request to the LEA for time from the county's peripatetic behaviour support team, and all the headteachers agreeing that a full responsibility for allocation of this time is given to the school support team;

(e) our negotiating with the LEA to establish a full-time post to the project;

(f) our negotiating with the LEA to provide central off-site accommodation for the school support team;

(g) a sharing of resources: most, or more needy schools have benefited.

Because of the increased demand and allowances being made by the LEA (behavioural support team teachers, and the full-time post), there has been an administrative change in the headteacher's commitment to the project. They have now established a management group which consists of a representative headteacher, the project leader and an administrator. This has also led to other areas of organizational influence and possible levels for change:

(a) influence on the LEA to see this model as an organizational innovation which could be used to influence children in other parts of the county;

(b) acknowledgment of the involvement of support team teachers in the project as an agreed, county in-service training programme for teachers;

(c) review by the authority of existing provision county-wide for disruptive pupils.

Briefly in summary, then, we have tried to introduce people to the concept of mental health consultation and our application of these in educational practice.

References

CAPLAN, G. (1970) *The Theory and Practice of Mental Health Consultation*, New York, Basic Books.

MEYERS, J. (1981) 'Mental health consultation'. In: J.C. Conoley (Ed.) *Consultation in Schools: Theory, Research, Procedures*, New York, Academic Press.

MEYERS, J., PARSONS, R.D. and MARTIN, R. (1979) *Mental Health Consultation in the Schools*, San Francisco, Jossey-Bass.

Part 3
Training and Development

9
Training Internal Consultants in Schools

Harry Gray

Provenance

There is no tradition of training consultants to work within the educational system in the United Kingdom. Of course, even in industry little that is really systematic goes on, either, although some large companies have made a serious attempt, for example ICI trained their own internal consultants in connection with the radical change in the 1970s and continue with some in-service training as a matter of course (Sworder, 1988). Firms of professional consultants train their professionals in consultancy skills in accordance with the consultancy approach of the company, and naturally, training consultancies train their professionals in the company mode. But the idea of training consultants in education or for work with educational institutions is a comparatively new one. In the past it has just been assumed that one professional educator, such as an adviser, would be able to communicate effectively with another.

To help the clarification of the subject of this chapter I want to base my comments on management consultancy which is the area of which I have most experience, although I believe the principles and processes to be the same for other forms of consultancy. Consultancy in education is so novel a concept* that its various forms are by no means generally clear. When I edited a book on management consultancy in schools recently it became clear that my focus on management was only one of a number of possible forms. The publication of this current volume, also on consultancy in education, reinforces the view that there are several forms of consultancy in education. However, because consultancy of any kind requires special skills it should be possible to devise training programmes of a generic character and in this chapter I try to detail both what training is required for and how it may take place.

---

*Canadian and US colleagues would claim that consultancy in education in North America is well established but I am not certain that the theory is too well developed there.

Internal and External Similarities

This chapter is entitled training internal consultants but the considerations for training both internal and external consultants are the same. For one thing, it is difficult to distinguish who is internal and who external though a good rule of thumb is that an external consultant comes from outside the consulted system and is paid a fee for his services. In education, consultants may be advisers, advisory teachers, teachers expert in a specialized branch of the curriculum (e.g. TVEI), teachers or headteachers experienced in some special management area (e.g. appraisal), as well as outsiders, such as university and college lecturers and professional industrial consultants. Such internal consultants may not be full-time but their involvement with a single school may last several months or even years. When an internal consultant comes from another school, he comes on the same terms as a professional consultant from an outside firm; indeed not to acknowledge such separateness will lead to an impairment of his effectiveness as a consultant. For this reason, the training needs of consultants both internal and external may be treated as the same. Even when a teacher works with colleagues or in his own school he will be best advised to observe the protocols of external consultants if he is to be effective with his colleagues.

Consultants will normally engage in one or both of two functions. They will help the members of the client organization to solve mutually-identified and agreed problems and they will help in training of clients for various management or organizational functions. Such training may be in such matters as curriculum development, appraisal skills, counselling skills, financial management techniques. Occasionally consultants may be employed as researchers on behalf of the school but this will generally be part of a broader consultancy contract. Research alone does not fall into the category of consultancy discussed here, though the interaction between reseachers and clients may. Action Research which is a joint venture between researcher and colleagues is, however, a respectable form of consultancy, though the researcher and client need to share the same value system as well as purposes — which in other forms of consultancy does not need to be the case.

Definitions

Consultancy is essentially a helping relationship where the help is offered by a · professional to another person who may or may not be also a professional within an organizational context. The important elements are that both parties (individuals or groups) are experienced (expert, that is) in their own roles and that they are dealing with organizational issues. A helping relationship that concerns personal issues outside the context of an organization would be counselling. Counselling may be used within a consultancy relationship — indeed it often is — but it occurs because personal issues have arisen in the organizational context. Consultancy does not involve extra-organizational concerns of individuals although it may lead to referral (e.g. when an individual has personal problems such as alcoholism or drug addiction). Consultancy itself will vary from the providing of expert technical advice to personal interaction with a client on problem-solving. However, it is seldom possible to maintain a relationship at only one end of this continuum, even the technical one, hence the importance of generic training for consultants.

A consultant is someone who engages in a professional helping relationship. By professional I mean both that a specific contract to help has been agreed either verbally or in writing for a certain purpose and that the helper has skills as a helper. Consultation cannot occur unless there is a psychological contract even if occasionally this is unstated. Another way of expressing this is to say that a consultant should not work with someone who has not agreed to be consulted. As I have already said, it is customary to identify two provenances for consultants — internal and external. Internal consultants come from within the organization while external consultants come from outside the organization. Any individual can function as a consultant but the problems are different according to the relationship with the organization. Local LEA advisers will sometimes be perceived as within the organization and at other times as outside it; likewise with headteachers who are invited to act as consultants to other headteachers. By and large internal consultants have greater problems of acceptability and credibility than external consultants even when they may be more skilled and expert.

Functions and Purposes

The functions of a consultant are to help a client to solve problems within his organization. This is done by helping the client to understand the problem more clearly and precisely so that the members of the organization itself can come up with a solution or identify a technical solution. The consultant works for the benefit of the client and ideally has no interest in the particular nature of the outcome. Where a consultant already has a preferred solution then he is a reformer — and it may be perfectly correct and proper for him to be so but he is not thereby a consultant in the sense employed in this chapter. (However, in reality, there is something of a reformer in all of us and we cannot avoid having personally preferred solutions to some problems.) In order to help a client to solve a problem, a consultant may have to engage in some research but this will be because he is the best person to do this in the client's best interest. A researcher *per se* is not a consultant though some researchers seem to think they have a right to act as consultants after they have done some research on an organization. Having done research on a topic does not bestow the right to act as a consultant. The results of a consultant's research belong to the client though whatever is generalizable may fall into the public domain.

Problems of Dependency

Primarily the role of the consultant is to help the client by increasing and improving the quality of control the client has over his own organization and over himself in his organization. A danger is that consultants may simply increase dependency or even themselves become just another employee. The consultant relationship should increase the autonomy of both the client and consultant and not lead to greater interdependence. For this reason, part of consultant training is to help consultants to maintain psychological distance, however enticing the client relationship may be. All consultants are naturally drawn to some clients more than others but too close an identification is likely to cloud the consultant's perception. A consultant needs to see and understand but not become functionally involved. When a consultant is perceived as successful, it is tempting to try to renew a contract but this may be quite inappropriate and be an impediment to a client's continued independence. Sometimes, however, a contract should be extended because new work has developed. Training and experience help with such decisions.

Nature of Problems

Consultants do not themselves solve the problems of their client's organizations; they help the members of the organization to do their own problem-solving. But consultants do not necessarily accept the problems of the organization as presented; more often than not a client organization will change its view of the 'real' problem as members work with the consultants. Learning how to evaluate and diagnose the presenting problem is a critical part of the consultant's training. With technical issues, the consultant's skills of diagnosis arise from his technical qualifications but with non-technical problems (e.g. social, interpersonal, psychological) the situation is different. Most problems arise and are presented in a confused or complex form and all problems have personal and interpersonal elements. Few problems are exclusively technical but are enmeshed in organizational dynamics. For this reason it would seem that training in group dynamics (which subsumes organizational and interpersonal dynamics) is a basic qualification for consultants. A knowledge of organization and group dynamics enables the consultant to see behind the information he is presented with and translate it, through his own organization modelling, into the deeper reality of the members of the organization.

The same issues applies to understanding individual clients, especially bosses (which includes headteachers). Knowledge and experience of personal psychology is helpful in identifying what sort of a person the consultant is dealing with and it enables him to have insight into how each person creates his own world — and hence his own world of problems. One of the best ways of learning about how people create their own personal and organizational worlds is through Encounter Groups that concentrate on personal insights. To be able to understand the person who is presenting the problem or issue it is necessary to be able to understand how an individual thinks — about himself and about his world. But it is also necessary for the consultant to have insight into his own personality because he, too, will tend to see people in certain ways and identify problems as of a certain kind. By understanding himself better, the consultant can hold his own interpretation on one side and listen to what the client is telling him, so gaining an insight into the other person's world.

Consultancy and Counselling

Basically, the aforementioned learning processes seem to be the same as those used in counselling training programmes. Indeed they are, but much more limited because the consultant is not a psychotherapist. On the whole, consultants are interested in working with people in organizations rather than with people on their own, so their interest in personal psychology and therapies is more limited. Learning about how organizations work is thus marginally more important than learning how people work. The interest is on underlying processes not surface processes hence the need to understand the psychodynamics of processes, not the descriptive and idealized forms of them that policy and administration studies are often composed of. Consultants are concerned with understanding the various elements of behaviour that go to make up organizational problems. They are not interested in producing glossy, whitewashed solutions. The integrative processes belong to clients, the analytical processes to consultants. That is, the clients identify the nature of their problem and find their own solution; the consultant simply helps in the process of identification.

Key Skills

The key skills of the consultant are listening, reflecting, questioning and confronting. This may or may not require empathy or sympathy but the consultant has to show himself generally supportive, accepting and understanding of his client. A consultant cannot work successfully with a client for whom he does not have respect or regard. Although there will be organizational change as a consequence of a consultant's work, a consultant is not a change agent. A change agent is usually someone who joins an organization in order to bring about certain desired changes but the consultant does not have a previously determined view of what should happen. It can, of course, be argued that the better kinds of change come about as a consequence of consultancy but a consultant is not put into an organization with a power base to bring about change in others. It is precisely because the consultant has no organizational power base — and this applies as much to internal as external consultants — that his or her work is effective in the ways it is. So skills of influencing, persuading, directing, and controlling are not required for consultant training, although an understanding of power, politics and conflict in organizations is.

The important skills are those of communicating with people. A consultant has often to enable clients to confront issues they are unwilling to consider and may have to confront them with the failure to confront! Assertiveness is necessary in that clients will often try to slip away from critical issues and must be firmly encouraged to face up to them. Consultants may also find themselves blamed for failures of understanding that really are at the core of the client's problem. A consultant cannot expect clients to face difficult organizational issues without some resistance so a consultant must be able to stand up against criticism which is destructive and intensive. Clients may project their own guilt, anxiety or sense of blame onto the consultant — and of course the reverse may happen! Outsiders are often able to recognize deep-seated organizational problems, but being able to deal with insiders is a different matter. Consultancy is more than both guess work and accurate diagnosis; it involves working with the client on diagnosing so that the client gains ownership of the problem and a vested interest in a solution. Just telling someone what their problems are doesn't help very much.

When there are human problems to be dealt with in an organization (and few problems are without their human side) a consultant may need to employ straightforward counselling skills (Reddy, 1987). Counselling serves the purpose of helping an individual client, or a group of clients, to think through their problems and come up with solutions. Basically these skills will probably be Rogerian (Reddy, 1987; Gray, 1976) for the simple reason that this approach to counselling is the least threatening and the original contract with the consultant most probably did not include an agreement for clients to receive counselling. The need for counselling arises out of an acceptance of organizational problems and the recognition that there are personal aspects. In my view, a trained consultant will also be an experienced counsellor (though not necessarily a psychotherapist). A trained consultant may or may not be a psychologist; being a psychologist and being a counsellor are not, of course, synonymous. Counselling insights often arise from psychology, and studies of leadership, motivation, personality and often individuals and organizations show a 'dark side' that can best be explained through psychological insights. However, the limits to counselling interventions are drawn organizationally not from the full dimensions of human personality.

Managing the Consultancy

There are certain managerial roles that consultants must observe during the course of the consultancy, beginning with the contracting phase, passing through the phases of consultation and into the termination and withdrawal. The consultant can be expected to have considerable experience of the consultancy relationship but for the client organization this may be the first involvement with the consultant. There are no easy rules for managing this relationship except that it is the consultant's responsibility rather than the client's, even though the client is paying the money.

The contracting phase involves the establishing of a working relationship and building a rapport on which the consultancy can develop. It involves building trust and confidence in the consultant and acceptance on the part of the client organization. The consultant is in a position to state how the negotiation will proceed, who he will meet, how the meetings are conducted and who comes to them. Occasionally (but seldom in education!) the client will have experience of the contracting situation and will steer it appropriately, but usually the level of sophistication is too low for the client to be very useful. Anyway, the consultant must show at this early stage that he is in charge, that he knows what he is doing, not just to build confidence but because once the contract is agreed the consultant will want to let the situation roll and will prefer the client to be — or feel himself to be — in control. This is not manipulation but a recognition that unless the client accepts full responsibility for the running of the consulting process no progress can be made. Gradually during this initial phase the consultant allows himself to be drawn into the culture of the organization so that he can become a dynamic, truly reflective part. The best way of learning how to handle this phase is by working with an experienced consultant and through practical experience.

The consultancy phase is the one for which the bulk of training is required as discussed broadly in this chapter. The final phase requires skills, some of which have already been mentioned, akin to those in the contracting phase. The important quality is for the consultant to maintain his integrity on withdrawal, leaving the client with a sense of independence. Where a report or account has been written this is strictly the property of the client and the consultant should not consider it to be his or to do as he likes with, such as publish in any identifiable way. Some academic researchers who gain entry to organizations through consultancy of one form or another are tempted to consider their consultancy to have the same status as research but this is not so. Leaving behind a good opinion of oneself is an important aspect of consultancy and the skills can only be learned in the field, hence the importance of field work in the training process.

Handling Expertise

Among the problems arising for internal consultants is the difficulty in being recognized not so much as expert but as consultant. The pressures on a colleague are initially quite strong to give quick and accurate information, to answer in a simple way 'straightforward' questions. It is always a temptation to give answers but a consultant wants his client to define and understand the problem for himself so that he can make good sense of answers and solutions offered. When working with colleagues one has to drop into a different way of working, adopt another mode, another register. Of course, there is nothing wrong in giving direct answers so long as they are appropriate, but consultants learn to sense out problems behind the words, to listen to what is not being said. Often simple and obvious requests for information mask deep and complex problems, particularly when they are about how to deal with people. Internal consultants may well be much more useful than external consultants in dealing with intractable and long drawn out problems because initial problems of credibility have been solved. No colleague asks another colleague for help if he hasn't already gone a long way towards trusting him. In many schools the known existence of one or two (senior) staff with consulting experience will provide a ready source of help with organizational problems that would otherwise be neglected.

Reality and Optimism

Consultants have to take a realistic view of what can be done. Heads of organizations often expect too much and are optimistic about what can be done. Training and experience provide the consultant with a realistic sense of evaluation with regard to expectations. Often the consultant is asked at the beginning what he or she thinks can be achieved and more often than not the answer will be that very little is expected. That is partly because asking the question suggests that responsibility is being laid on the consultant and the clients feel themselves almost passive. Training helps to provide a good sense of the slowness of personal change, its great complexity and the fluidity of its consolidation. An experienced consultant will not look for great signs of change but rather for small indications of basic changes in attitude. The expectation that consultancy leads to highly visible immediate change in behaviour is probably false in almost all situations. But the institutional pressure on internal consultants to demonstrate that something positive has resulted from their efforts may be considerable.

Basis of Training

Training involves two levels; the level of basic theory — organization theory, personality theory — and the level of actual behaviour, experiencing the kinds of specific problems that surface. Training enables the consultant to identify surface problems and question their cause according to theoretical modelling. A common example is motivation. For example, a headteacher claims that his staff are alienated and unmotivated in spite of there being no discipline problems among the students. The consultant will want to know if this view is generally shared, who shares it and why; he or she will want to talk to many people to see if the view is corroborated and find out reasons offered. Or he or she may 'play a hunch' that the head has not examined his own relationships with staff and the real problem is one of interpersonal relationships. But alternatively he or she may have discerned that a problem is the nature of the local authority system, that this is an area of selective schools and that this one recruits the least academic pupils. Or he may consider both these possible causes and try to understand their relationship. In any case, though he will use his experience and his understanding of theory to help him understand, he will work with clients on the problems they perceive and the reasons they give. In the end he will work very much with his 'intuition' ('informed experience') and not be at all anxious to come up with neatly packaged solutions. Indeed, most problems unpeel like an onion: there is always another layer.

Internal consultants may work with external consultants and this may be part of (in some cases, all of) their training. The process here is to work with the internal consultant as the key link with the organization, an exemplar of what might be done and achieved. An internal consultant will be able to work as a peer with colleagues but because he is particularly sensitive to the consultant will be more responsive in the consultancy process. When the external consultant has left, the internal may take over with development and training. This has been done in schools where the internal consultant is a trained counsellor who can then use his skills in a more broadly legitimated way.

Ethics

Certain ethical issues arise in consultancy that are particularly important in the consultant–client relationship. Confidentiality is the main issue. Consultants need to observe the strictest confidentiality between themselves and each client. A consultant is not there to spy or to report on individuals; he is not a trouble-shooter who has a master to obey. The strictest impartiality and neutrality must be maintained because no one has any way of predetermining responsibility among organizational members. Those cases where the consultant is in fact a detective or policeman fall under a different form of contract from organizational process consultancy and would not normally involve internal consultants. A second ethical issue is around the integrity of the consultant and the separateness of his own personal values from those of the people in the organization. A consultant is unlikely to act as consultant to an organization whose values he disapproves of but he may work with one when he is not wholly personally in accord with the organization's values but nevertheless admits them as legitimate. One of the values of consultants themselves must be the legitimacy of alternatives and the more experienced consultants will have knowledge of a greater variety of practice than novices. Hopefully experience leads to tolerance and understanding.

On the other hand, a consultant would be asking for trouble if he were to take on a job when he did not feel some degree of sympathy with his clients. Firstly, consultants cannot change basic value systems though they may release basic values that have been subverted. Secondly, values and individuals are seldom separated — it is individuals who express values, not organizations, and one cannot detach oneself from an individual who is uncongenial to oneself. A consultant may also feel physically uncomfortable in a situation and there is no reason why he or she should work in unacceptable conditions just because a client wishes it. A consultant can expect consideration of his/her physical and material needs even if he or she is prepared to forego psychological support. Waiting around in a draughty room until clients show up does little for a good temper nor does the use of a bare room with constant interruptions help with group work among clients. A consultant needs to ensure that he is not subjected to dysfunctional physical irritants. Training should help in the assertiveness necessary to ensure negotiation of appropriate comfort for himself and his clients.

Supervision

In counselling, supervision is generally considered to be essential to maintaining sound counselling practice. A supervisor is someone who helps the counsellor reflect on his own practice with some regularity and frequency and to increase his understanding of how he conducts his counselling sessions. There are various forms of supervision but it is generally agreed that counsellors need the support of an emotionally-detached colleague in coping not only with the process they use but the emotional reactions they experience during counselling. Supervision employed in consultancy would serve much the same purpose, as well as being an extension of training. Supervisors would have to be experienced counsellors as well as consultants because many issues that arise in reflection are personal to the consultant. Because many consultancy issues also have a strong theoretical importance (i.e. there are important aspects of organization and other theory at issue) supervisors need a significant academic background and experience. Supervision is not a way of just checking on a consultant but a means of supporting him. Supervision is not widely practised in consultancy, except perhaps in large consultancy firms as a way of monitoring activity, but once consultancy becomes extensively used in education it would be necessary to ensure that consultants, who now work in professional isolation, receive the help and support they need. Since consultancy is an uncoordinated activity, there being no professional body of educational consultants (although other consultants have their professional associations), supervisors will have to be chosen on an *ad hoc* basis by consultants themselves.

The term often used to describe the approach to consultancy described here is 'process' consultancy (Schein, 1988). In fact, most consultancy is of this kind though there are other forms that consist of giving advice after some time spent on 'objective' analysis. Process consultancy means helping members of the organization to work through their own organizational processes (climate, culture, procedures) to bring about desired change and improvement. So far as schools are concerned, it is unlikely that they will need advice alone, so the main need will be for process consultancy. For example, when locally funded management is introduced (or LMS — the Local Management of Schools in the Cooper and Lybrand phrase) the problems of schools will be process problems — how to implement the procedure or approach in such a way that it will suit the individual school. The consultant will help the school's senior management to work out a process of adaptation and implementation in a collaborative way. Hence the terminology of 'process consultant'.

The Facilitation of Learning

As already stated, basically the skills of the consultant are facilitation skills, facilitation being the appropriate way of helping people in organizations. In fact, the consultant facilitates learning on the part of members. Consultancy theory assumes that people in organizations have the capacity to learn and hence change. In common parlance, it is said the 'organization learns' but as organizations only consist of people, it is the people who learn. Consultants tend to use the same learning model as trainers in management development (Boot and Reynolds, 1983) and in developmental learning or experiential learning (Kolb, 1976). This theory of adult learning assumes a simple learning cycle in which experience is the starting point followed by reflection and theory building (Figure 9.1). What the consultant tries to do is to help his client individually or in small groups to identify their organizational experiences, to reflect on them, to understand them and design strategies for improving future experiences. In this cycle the onus for learning is with the client, the consultant's responsibility is to help the client to learn and he or she does this by directing the reflective process so that the client is forced to deal with the major issues and is deterred from going off at a tangent. The consultant is concerned to help clients explore their own words and language even when they want to avoid doing so. The objective is to help clients to clarify their thought processes so that thinking becomes less sloppy and more precise. In this way the linguistic ambiguities which bedevil organizational thinking are reduced and the collective clarity of purpose ensues. From time to time the consultant will explain ideas by the use of models or concepts to increase understanding and provide a base for action but concepts will arise from cases and examples, not predetermine them. There is a tough intellectual process involved here — a form of applied philosophical analysis — and this is at the core of consultant training.

Figure 9.1   The learning cycle in adult experiential learning (Kolb, 1976)

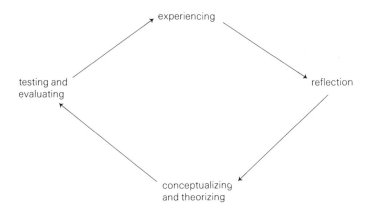

<table>
<tr><td></td><td>experiencing</td><td></td></tr>
<tr><td>testing and
evaluating</td><td></td><td>reflection</td></tr>
<tr><td></td><td>conceptualizing
and theorizing</td><td></td></tr>
</table>

Subjective Theory

Process consultancy tends to be based on a subjective theory of organizations (sometimes referred to as phenomenological theory (Bush, 1986)). This theory says that organizations are subjective experiences, that they exist less (or not at all) in their own right than as in the experiences of their members. And each member has a unique and personal experience of the organization which is partly — and often largely — determined by the kind of person he is. Organizations are thus personally constructed of what we make them. According to this theory, headteachers who see themselves as authoritarian will behave as such; headteachers who believe in collaboration and equity will behave as such. Teachers who believe headteachers ought to be authoritarian will be put out by a head who is collaborative and call him weak and ineffective. And so on. In organizations the members accommodate to their different perspectives sometimes satisfactorily, often unsatisfactorily. Not all differences can be accommodated and conflict ensues either repressed or overt. Consultants try to find out and understand the 'meaning' the organization has for each member and help them to share the meanings. Too often members assume that their meaning is shared when it patently is not. Process consultancy based on this subjective model works with individuals in order to improve the quality of accommodation and cooperation but not necessarily with the intention of changing people from being their essential (and contradictory) selves.

Training Programmes

It is difficult to define the full nature of a training programme for consultants because there are always two elements: professional knowledge and skills, and consultancy knowledge and skills. If we follow the model of school counsellor training as established in the United Kingdom in the late 1960s then we would be talking of a one-year full-time course at postgraduate level. This is possibly too expensive a programme in the present climate although it may well be that consultant skills could be seen as leading to a great deal of cost-effectiveness. But the time required for a training programme is a function of its content and so almost infinitely expandable. In 1987, Lancashire LEA introduced a course in consultancy skills for teachers which consisted of ten weekly sessions of three hours each. The content was entirely process-based and consisted of learning the skills of listening to others and helping them to reflect on their problems or issues. Such a programme would generally be considered too brief for the acquiring of such interpersonal skills. Follow-up research on the course members confirmed that a longer time was needed for individuals to feel confident in their roles as internal consultants or even external ones.

As a consequence of the Lancashire experience the Department of Educational Research at the University of Lancaster has proposed a somewhat longer programme of a part-time Professional Diploma in Consultancy (scheduled for commencement in Autumn 1989). This is based upon some existing courses at Masters Degree level and consists of four units each of thirty hours duration in Organization Theory, Leadership Theory, Consultancy Theory and Practice, and one unit in an aspect of school organization (e.g. Special, Needs) and management (e.g. Policy Making). There is also a practicum leading to the writing of a consultant's report which may be taken in any organization where internal consultant supervision is available. At this stage the contents of such a programme must be open to a great deal of discussion; other kinds of content will be preferred in some instances. But the essential characteristic of the programme is that it is process based (as most counselling training programmes) and students learn through their own experience rather than by being fed information and theory. I have explained this process as it relates to learning about organizations in a paper written some years ago (Gray, 1976) and its relevance to learning consultancy skills seems even greater now.

Selection

It would be foolish to propose a single form of training for consultants. But the current situation is that no specific training exists anywhere in the United Kingdom, and probably not even in North America where new developments usually start off. However, it is clear that there is a demand for process consultancy training particularly in education. Consultancy is the easing mechanism to the implementation of change and when it takes place according to the modes described in this chapter it is likely to be much more successful than the RD&D (Research, Development and Diffusion) model of innovation. The beauty of consultancy is that it always starts where the client is, accepting and recognizing the validity of the client's own view of the situation. Thereafter it stays with the client in a continuing process of client ownership. Probably the personal, qualities that consultants bring to their role are of fundamental importance. Consultants are the sort of people who are content to see themselves as a catalyst; they are not reformers or change agents even though they will have strong and clear organizational and personal values of their own. As with many professional skills areas, maybe selection is more important than training in any case training without careful selection will not be much use. Qualitative and process training is the hardest of all and there is comparatively little instructional (information giving) training in consultant training.

Selection is likely to be on the basis of personal interest. There is little glamour to consultancy in education at the present time and most teachers desiring training in consultancy have either already been involved in some advisory capacity or are senior staff looking for ways of improving the general climate/atmosphere of the school. Most of them will already be people-orientated and a good number will have worked in pastoral aspects of school organizations. Such people are likely to be willing, if diffident, learners with an appropriate disposition to being helped themselves through a learning process. The main problem will be a general reluctance to go back and practise in the school. Over the years, my experience of training teachers in OD (Organization Development) skills in short courses has been that, however much learning an individual may engage in for himself, there is a reluctance to go and practise the skills with colleagues. The situation may be improving now that there is such turmoil in school organizations but it would seem reasonable to suppose that unless there are substantial programmes in training for consultants the idea that consultants, both internal and external, are exceedingly useful in school will not achieve much currency and salience. There is no doubt the interest and talent exists in schools, it is only to be hoped that sufficiently substantial training becomes available to tap this much-needed resource.

Acknowledgments

Many thanks are due to Donald Musella and John Davis of the Ontario Institute for Studies in Education, Toronto for comments on an early draft of this chapter. The final version, however, reflects my opinions and not necessarily theirs.

References

BOOT, R. and REYNOLDS, M. (1983) *Learning and experience in Formal Education*, Manchester, Manchester Monographs.

BUSH, T. (1986) *Theories of Organisations*, London, Harper & Row.

GRAY, H. (1976) 'Training people to understand organisations', *British Journal of In-Service Education*, **3**, 1, 66–71.

GRAY, H. (Ed.) (1986) *Management Consultancy in Schools*, London, Cassell.

KOLB, D. A. (1973) 'On Management and the learning process', *M.I.T. Sloan School Working Paper*, No. 652–73

REDDY, M. (1987) *The Manager's Guide to Counselling at Work*, British Psychological Society, London, Methuen.

SCHEIN, E. (1988) *Process Consultation*. (Vols. I and II). Don Mills, Ontario, Addison-Wesley.

SWORDER, G. (1988) 'Developing consultants in industry'. In GRAY, H. (Ed.) *Management Consultancy in Schools*, London, Cassell.

10
Issues of Effectiveness and Evaluation

Carol Aubrey

Introduction to Effective Evaluation

The final stage of consultation is termination. This usually takes place when the assignment has been completed, when it has been mutually agreed that no further assistance in the implementation of the innovation is required, or when it has been agreed that the consultation process shall be discontinued. The most important part of the termination phase is evaluation. Without it there would be no means of judging the effectiveness of the change process or the justification for the use of resources allocated. The change must be seen as worthwhile and the benefits must constitute a significant improvement to the existing situation.

Evaluation, like the whole consulting process, will be a joint enterprise between the client and consultant. However, in addition to judging the benefits of the assignment, the client will be judging the consultant and his or her performance. The evaluation will consider the accuracy of the original needs assessment, the appropriateness of the assessment of alternative solutions presented in the proposals and the aptness of the intervention chosen, but also it will involve the quality of consultant inputs and the consultant style of work, reflected in the quality of the consultant–client relationship.

Staff Participation

As it is likely that resources for evaluation will be limited it may be essential that the consultant involves personnel throughout the system in the planning and execution of the evaluation. In making a decision regarding the involvement of staff in organizational evaluation, Maher (1982) has suggested a framework, entitled A-VICTORY for assessing organizational readiness for evaluation. This is an acronym for eight factors which seem influential in facilitating evaluation. These are:

Ability	— the availability of staff, method, materials and resources to support evaluation;
Values	— the compatibility of the evaluation with the school's prevailing norms and philosophy;
Idea	— staff perceptions of the credibility of the evaluation for contributing to the ultimate development and improvement of the organization;
Circumstances	— the stability of the school environment for influencing a willingness to engage in evaluation;
Timing	— dynamic, external factors which influence organizational changes, such as changes in legislation;
Obligation	— felt need of staff to evaluate;
Resistance	— degree of opposition among staff to engage in evaluation;
Yield	— perceived benefits or losses to staff engaging in evaluation, such as increased paperwork or external observation of their activities.

The A-VICTORY framework offers a basis to assess organizational readiness, and may help to determine the design of the evaluation.

Evaluation is more likely to be meaningful to those in the organization if responsibility for carrying it out is shared, and means are found for incorporating it into the activities of the school system. It would involve individuals, existing groups or newly-created groups who agree to take on a specific function. Since the operation of a school system is being evaluated, it is appropriate that those affected by it should participate in the evaluation process. Broadly speaking, the focus of evaluation can be a general needs assessment, involving goals for the whole school system, or an individual needs assessment, which focuses on the needs of individual learners, or resource allocation, processes for providing an appropriate service to learners, such as decision-making and administrative procedures, materials of instruciton, teacher effectiveness or pupil progress.

Models of Evaluation

As can be seen, goals tend to be broad and outcomes complex. On the one hand, descriptions of goals, settings, personnel, methods and content may be undertaken, on the other hand recorded personal judgments on the quality or appropriateness of goals, inputs or outputs may be made. The evaluation may be 'formative' if it takes place during the implementation phase with a view to setting up the iterative process of a tryout–evaluation–redesign cycle, or 'summative' if the evaluation is terminal, and focuses on the successful completion of the assignment. Stufflebeam *et al.* (1971) suggested a model known as CIPP: Context — analyzing goals or needs assessment; Input — determining the appropriate design for the chosen goals; Processes — for monitoring the implementation; and Product — for judging the assignment effects.

Models provided tend to be ideal types and do not necessarily allow for the complexity of the educational process. Stake (1972) proposed 'responsive' evaluation, which instead of emphasizing pre-specified intentions and established criteria, relies on observational data and descriptions of activities and Scriven (1973) wrote of 'goal free' evaluation which allows for side effects as well as intended goals. Parlett and Hamilton's (1972/6) 'illumination model' was a response to a dissatisfaction with traditional models and sought to describe the operation of an innovation on the context, organization and practices, problems encountered and solutions obtained from various points of view, as well as outcomes. Methodology was borrowed from social anthropology and the techniques favoured participant observation. In terms of realization, this broad strategy would lead to a combination of techniques being used, serving different functions at different times. It would entail a long, open-ended exploration of different information and activities from a range of personnel involved in order to generate a focused enquiry from general themes which emerged, issues from observations made and problems encountered. From this, the study would generate direct, relevant and systematic data collection and lead to a report responsive to the personnel involved. The amount of time involved would curtail seriously the use made of this model in consultation evaluation.

Probably the most suitable model for consultation evaluation is that of action research, since its focus is on a particular problem in a particular setting and its goal is to provide specific information for remedying it in a particular situation. It is generally collaborative and participative. Information is collected, recorded, evaluated with necessary adjustment which forms the basis of the review of progress. Again, its problem-solving sequence follows closely the five-stage consultation process advocated in Chapter 1.

However, limited time and funds and the particular role designated to the evaluation for the specific consultation will all influence decisions made. Three decisions have to be made by the consultant: the scale and scope of data collected must be determined (a lot of data may be collected from a small sample or an amount of data from a range of sources); the selection of appropriate goals for the evaluation must be made; and the decision taken to place relative emphasis on process or product. Considerable skill will be required to decide which techniques are appropriate, and evaluation strategies to be chosen will be determined to some extent by the knowledge and expertise of the individual consultant.

Relating Stages of the Consultation to the Evaluation

As noted in the case of action research, evaluation which is most suitable to the problem-solving model will follow broadly the sequence of the consultation process. Meyers *et al.* (1979) suggested a seven-stage model which is similar to the one proposed for this book (Table 10.1). Mason *et al.* (1984) have designed a sequence of evaluation activities to correspond to the seven-stage model and which is similar to the model proposed by Stufflebeam *et al.* (1971). In the first three stages the collection of needs assessment data will occur, in a collaborative enterprise between the consultant and client. Objectives to be chosen, the assignment design and the services and training (fourth and fifth stages) to be offered, can be based on the data obtained in the needs assessment. The consultant will confer with the client and staff on the implications of the needs assessment data and alternatives available but the responsibility for choosing between options will remain with the client.

Table 10.1   The consultation process — two models compared

This volume Chapter 1	Meyers et al. *(1979)*
Entry	Entry into the system
	Orientation to the process of consultation
Diagnosis	Problem identification
Action planning	Problem definition
Implementation	Consultation intervention
Termination	Assessing impact
	Concluding consultation

Most of the formative evaluation data will be generated in the fifth and sixth stages and as in previous stages this will take place in an atmosphere of exchange between consultant and client with staff. In the seventh stage consultation with the client and staff will lead to decisions on conducting the summative evaluation of the assignment. The consultant will seek to remain objective and provide advice on what and how the outcome should be judged. In the final stage, the summative evaluation results are interpreted and a final report prepared. The report should offer a written statement of the aims and processes of the evaluation and a summary of the outcomes for the client organization.

Designing Internally-Based Evaluations

Matuszek (1978) has argued that the worth of evaluation activities depends heavily on the use made of evaluation results, and outlines some of the difficulties in designing an evaluation procedure that provides suitable information for decision-making. As the field of evaluation has developed, the utility of some conventional, research design models has been increasingly questioned. Usually consultants and school staff are addressing specific concerns of specific organizations. School administrators themselves, who may not have a strong background and knowledge of evaluation, may be less interested in evaluation of assignments, as a basis for decion-making. Decisions may be made unexpectedly at meetings; if the consultant is there then his or her information is considered, if not, it isn't. Many decisions are made well before the setting in which they are formalized, in casual and unpredictable ways. Again, if information can be supplied in these contexts, it will be considered, if it is presented only at formal meetings, it may be too late. Matuszek described the difficulties of providing information for decision-making. While utilizing Stufflebeam *et al.*'s (1971) CIPP model, she found objectives-based evaluation an unhelpful approach to evaluation planning. Whilst still maintaining the use of the concepts of context, input, process and product data, the evaluation goals were based by her on a number of decisions likely to be addressed by administrators during the school year. These were called 'decision questions' and acted as a reminder to evaluators that the basic purpose of evaluation was to provide information for decision-making. Questions represented actual decisions to be made and could be used as a basis for collecting and reporting data. A tentative list of questions was created from a number of sources, including staff management. One problem with the approach was that it generated questions for which no ready use of the information could be found, or *a priori* questions which might generate an exploration of data for an administrator who had already decided to make the decision. In this case it is unlikely that information will be used which is not in accord with the decision already reached, and information supporting the view point will be used to influence colleagues to share the same perspective!

Once the decision questions are gathered, it is important to determine what evaluation information might be relevant, in relation both to the importance of the decision and importance or relevance of the information the evaluator can provide in making the decision. Prioritizing both decisions and information is important. The evaluator's judgment of the likelihood of the information being used, if provided, is available. Equally it is important to stick to a few big decision questions which can be addressed by the resources available, and for which the desired information can be gathered, analyzed and reported before the decision is made.

When the decision questions have been selected an initial design will be drafted, with specific evaluation information specified for each decision question, with an allocation of resources included and data agreed for completion. It was found easier by Matuszek to structure day-to-day activities in terms of data to be gathered and analyses to be performed, than in terms of reports to be made. At this point the design is reviewed with the client to clarify expectations on the nature of the evaluation and the need for provision of relevant information in time to be useful.

Conclusions

At the level of meta-evaluation, Sanders (1978) cited four categories of standards for judging evaluation efforts:

1. *accuracy standards*, which determine whether the study has produced technically sound information;
2. *utility standards*, which ensure the evaluation is informative, timely and serves the needs of the audience for whom it was intended;
3. *propriety standards*, to protect the rights of persons affected by the evaluation;
4. *feasibility standards*, to determine whether the time and, resources used in the evaluation are relevant and realistic.

Given our existing knowledge of consultation in education it is important to conclude by considering consultation evaluation within the broader context of the implementation of change in education. The state-of-the-art of evaluation is by no means complete and the execution of design and implementation is not likely to be flawless. The knowledge, too, and competence of the particular consultant as well as the amount and quality of knowledge about the organization made available to him or her, will all affect the outcome of evaluation. In fact, human factors surround the evaluation. Evaluation has human designers, human objects of the evaluation and human receivers of the assignment information. In each of these roles, reactions to and attitudes towards the execution of the evaluation are likely to influence results obtained. Since evaluation takes place within an organizational context with its own vested interests and purposes, it too must be similarly structured to take account of existing structural levels and procedures and relate them back to the organizational whole. The structure of the organization is a framework of power relationships and evaluation information represents power. Those with power will seek to obtain control of evaluation information, which may be used in a variety of ways for a variety of purposes, stated and unstated.

Finally, evaluation will be constrained by ethical issues and guards must be taken to avoid invasions of privacy or release of sensitive information. Above all, the effects of experimentation must not interfere with the broad goals of the school to provide for the best educational achievements of all its pupils. That said, it is a professional responsibility of the consultant that the goals of the assignment have been effectively met and the outlay of resources justified. Many consultant assignments remain evaluation. Whilst the role of evaluation may vary from assignment to assignment, arguably it is equally part of the consultant's professional responsibility to take part in evaluation in order to assess its value and judge its worth.

References

MAHER, C. A. (1982) 'Utilization of program evaluation information in public schools. Perspectives and guidelines', *Journal of School Psychology*, **20**, pp. 113–21.
MASON, E. J., DeMERS, S. T. and MIDDLETON, E. J. (1984) 'Integrating consultation and program evaluation in school psychology', *Journal of School Psychology*, **22**, pp. 273–83.

MATUSZEK, P. (1978) 'Designing internally-based program evaluations in school settings', *Journal of School Psychology*, 16, pp. 346–55.

MEYERS, J., PARSONS, R. and MARTIN, R. (1979) *Mental Health Consultation in the Schools*, San Francisco, Jossey-Bass.

PARLETT, M. and HAMILTON, D. (1976) 'Evaluation as illumination'. In: Tawney, D. (Ed.) *Curriculum Evaluation Today*, London, Macmillan.

SANDERS, J. R. (1978) 'School professionals and the evaluation function', *Journal of School Psychology*, 16, pp. 301–11.

SCRIVEN, M. (1973) 'Goal-free evaluation'. In: House, E. R. (Ed.) *School Evaluation: The Politics and Process*, Berkeley, CA, McCutchan.

STAKE, R. E. (1972) *Responsive Evaluation*. Mimeo. Urbana-Champaign: Centre for Industrial Research and Curriculum Evaluation, University of Illinois.

STUFFLEBEAM, D. L., FOLEY, W. J., GEPHART, W. J., GUBA, E. G., HAMMOND, R. L., MERRIMAN, H. O. and PROVUS, M. M. (1971) *Educational Evaluation and Decision-making*, Itasca, IL, F. E. Peacock.

11
Collaborative Consultancy Through Action Inquiry

Gordon H. Bell

What can't be known isn't. (Schopenhauer)

Concerns have been voiced for many years about weak links in our educational system. Gaps between theory and practice, research and its application, policy makers and practitioners, and between training institutions and professionals have long been regarded as deficiencies for which various remedies have been tried. Two recent developments have transformed attempts to bridge these gaps: Grant Related In-Service Training and the Education Reform Act. Both require collaboration (if not co-operation) between central and local agencies and both require detailed consultation between partners in the provision of a service.

Previously, the educational situation of teachers, trainers, pupils and parents depended upon a mixture of voluntary and statutory association. Now the process of schooling is determined contractually against defined criteria of performance. Under such circumstances, organizations have a choice between following rules or determining rules. In the former, tendencies to regimentation predominate in an effort to standardize judgments. In the latter, promoting agreements in judgments is the main intention with a view to discriminating regulation. The attitude proper to the one, i.e. to a civil servant, is in potential conflict with beliefs appropriate to the other, i.e. to a professional. Putting this another way, schools can proceed in the current context as organizations of consent or as assenting bureaucracies. This challenge need not necessarily be viewed as an either/or situation. The alternative form of 'both/and' thinking may not only convert problems into opportunities, it can also eliminate the very gaps that have been commented upon. In short, the prevailing climate within which the question of collaboration and consultancy may be understood comprises both logical and psychological contracts in a re-defined partnership with the State. The task of this chapter is to explore some conditions for unifying these elements. The main aim is to describe a process that has the potential for both training and education, co-operation and collaboration.

What is called Collaborative Consultancy?

I take the purpose of collaboration to be the strengthening of links between partners in the enterprise of teaching. This effort is justified in terms of the transfer of skills, improvements in the texture of professional communication, and the benefits of jointly agreeing principles and procedures. Such benefits whilst being logically connected with the concept of a democracy are psychologically related to conditions for professional effectiveness. For without systematic attempts to collaborate, certain risk factors may readily be identified of which innovation without change, paper tigers, re-inventing the wheel, high impact and low take up, and leadership without ownership are but a few (Bell, 1987a). Collaboration will therefore mean identifying opportunities for co-operation, clarifying roles and tasks, planning action in relation to combined resources, and working out the details of a joint review procedure. These processes are summarised in Figure 11.1.

Figure 11.1   Model of a process for professional collaboration

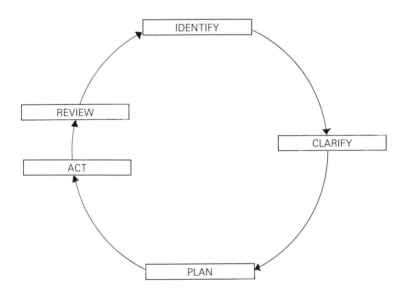

Under present circumstances, I take the central purpose of consultancy to be participation in the management of change with a view to improvement. The consultant, whether insider or outsider, can help bring about those skills essential to worthwhile innovation, e.g.:

— pursuing structural rather than marginal change;
— encouraging resource use to sustain both immediate and self-maintained growth;
— using what is known to inform decision-making;
— ensuring communication amongst partners;
— maximizing opportunities for the transfer of professional knowledge and experience;
— making ethical and staff development issues explicit;
— promoting objectivity through procedures for evaluating and validating outcomes;
— seeking multiplier effects;
— clarifying role relations to minimize conflict.

Occupying such a position within a school is greatly facilitated in the case of the 'outsider' consultant for it offers an enhanced opportunity for realizing two main requirements of effective change: pressure and support (Fullan, 1986). But whatever the location, the consultant has responsibility for facilitating collaboration and cooperation through recognizing and to some extent manipulating the preconditions of successful change.

This will involve judgments on the following selected criteria: that change with a view to improvement is desired, that a critical level of dissatisfaction with the status quo has been reached, that efforts will or have been made to ensure quality and clarity of vision about an ideal future state, that the feasibility of proposed changes has been calculated, and that the costs both material and psychological are less than the benefits (Bell and Pennington, 1988a). Consultancy to meet these criteria will require joint critique of school and professional development, involving the processes of reviewing the situation, challenging assumptions, supporting change, and reviewing afresh (see Figure 11.2).

A strategy which seeks to combine collaboration with consultancy and meet the twin aims of strengthening links and supporting the management of change I have termed 'action inquiry' (Bell, 1985a). The role of consultants on this account, whether they be teachers, advisers, trainers, or other agencies involves facilitating a specific process designed to safeguard quality in the delivery of a service. Whilst there are several versions of this type of 'process consultancy' (Schein, 1969), the consultant adopting such a role essentially prioritizes certain beliefs and values.

The process of action inquiry is basically a belief in the worthwhileness of jointly planning and evaluating change with a view to making professional knowledge and experience accessible. Its underlying values and its implications for partners in the enterprise of teaching go somewhat deeper.

Figure 11.2   Model of a process for school consultancy

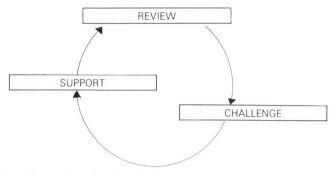

The Values of Action Inquiry

A central problem in the management of educational change is how teachers can gain controlled access to each other's knowledge and experience. This precondition of effective collaboration requires the consultant to create a framework in which a school can develop knowledge of its own practice. I mean here developing practical professional knowledge not simply making assertions, expressing matters of opinion, or depending on statements which rely for their authority on occupying a particular position in a hierarchy. The central feature of this kind of knowledge is that it arises from evidence grounded in the study of a practice. Its main characteristics are derived from investigating problems and issues experienced by practitioners, developing diagnoses of practitioners concerns, and adopting a framework of enquiry which governs the collection, use and release of data (Elliott, 1978).

'Action Research' is the term which has come to be used to describe such a process of research-based teaching and training. The procedure is based on a cycle of fact finding, action planning, implementing action steps, monitoring change, interpreting data, and evaluating outcomes and has become widespread both as a means of improving practice and bringing about collaboration between possibly reluctant partners (Letiche, 1986).

But it is not the only means of developing practical professional knowledge, and it has certain weaknesses. Firstly, it imposes a restricted definition of the purposes of collaboration and requires a certain schedule of activities that must be carried out in a set order. Partners may or may not be ready to take on the extra demands this requires. Secondly, there are many problems of interest to practitioners that are not accessible through the techniques of action research, especially policy issues in circumstances where the collaborating partners do not sufficiently 'own' the practice under investigation. Thirdly, the benefits of becoming a reflective practitioner (Schon, 1983) on which the core values of research-based teaching depend are unlikely to reach maturity by limiting practical thinking solely to the business of testing one's own theories in action.

However, without both intervention and reflection, planned change is not logically possible and without procedures to make accessible to critique the data of

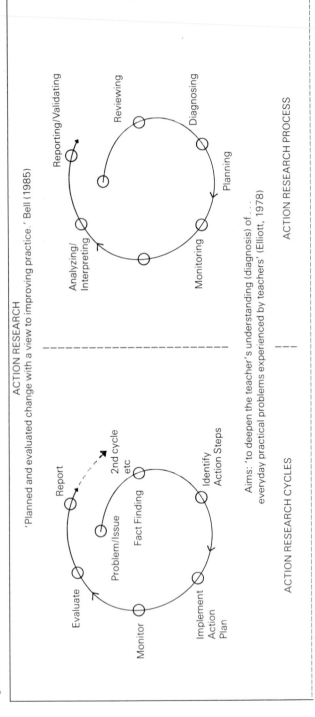

Figure 11.3   Structure and processes of action inquiry

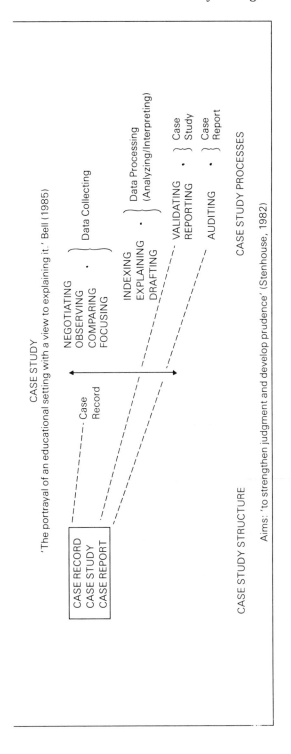

one's practice, professional autism results. What cannot be known through independent scrutiny of the evidence — whether philosophical by reference to reasons, or empirical by reference to the data of observations — does not exist as an improvement except the claim itself. The virtues of having a consultant installing principles and procedures against this not uncommon form of professional terrorism are justification enough.

The further question as to which principles will overcome the weaknesses of action research whilst preserving the benefits may be found in procedures for case studies. Whilst several different forms are advocated (Kenny and Groteleuschen, 1984; Simons, 1980; Stenhouse, 1978; Walker, 1974), there is a conception of 'practitioner case study' where the chief aim is to construct a critical portrayal of an educational situation as a necessary preliminary to effective action. Unlike action research which requires intervention in order to test whether change is an improvement, case study methods use unobtrusive measures in order to appraise what might need to be done. Their usefulness lies not only in improving judgment about priorities for action but also in transferring that experience to others evaluating like situations.

Not infrequently, educationists claim that their circumstances are unique. In one sense this is true and case study provides the means of explaining that uniqueness. But if such a quality were the only attribute of educational situations, there could be no common language developing between partners because the possibility of agreements in judgments has been denied. And this is precisely what we find: jargon — because collaboration in reporting and justifying teaching decisions has not been thought relevant: authoritarianism — because collaborative study of evidence is not thought appropriate — isolationism — because access to critical dialogue about standards is restricted.

If what it is to be a professional is to be able to control and contribute to the knowledge base of one's chosen practice, then the development of a tradition of practitioner research is an indispensable requirement. In present circumstances, Stenhouse's (1975) account of the teacher's role in curriculum research and development in studying the work of other teachers and testing ideas for school improvement through classroom research procedures, has never been more crucial to raising standards. The role of the action inquiry consultant is therefore to enable the necessary collaboration to take place. It will mean seeking to establish the conditions whereby partners in schooling, e.g. advisers, inspectors, professional researchers and trainers can contribute to a systematic study of their own effectiveness (Hampton, 1988). This will, I suggest, be accomplished by enabling participants to gain access to knowledge of their own practice through a planned relation of action research and case study techniques. Such a process of collaborative consultancy through action inquiry is represented in Figure 11.3.

There is some evidence to indicate that whole school improvement can arise through adopting such processes (Bell, 1988). This is, however, a situation that is unlikely to be immediately achieved for reasons explored above. Action Inquiry will have to be built progressively. The evaluated experience of strategies which have been tried out in a variety of settings towards this end are now described.

Approaches to Action Inquiry

The opportunities for collaborative consultancy where the key concern is the management of change with a view to improvement can, I suggest, be classified into five main types:

1 collaborative curriculum development involving inter-professional or inter-institutional cooperation;
2 collaborative evaluation in which the outside consultant supports the evaluation as distinct from research activities of colleagues;
3 collaborative practitioner research in which consultants teachers and other partners including parents might participate;
4 collaborative research development and dissemination where an external agency (e.g. LEA, higher education institution, funding agency) commissions demonstration studies in a framework of responsive sponsorship;
5 collaborative professional study within the framework of an award-winning course. (Bell, 1985b).

To some extent these types of consultancy overlap, but the point of overlap is crucial to an understanding of how action inquiry can be developed progressively. Whilst each one offers a distinctive vehicle whereby schools can develop knowledge of their practice they all involve participants in action learning. The key entry point for the consultant therefore is paying particular attention to ways in which this form of professional development can be facilitated.

Action learning makes explicit to collaborating partners the deceptively simple idea that change means adults learning (Fullan, 1986). Whilst there are several variants (Revans, 1982; Wallace *et al.*, 1988), it provides a technique whereby a group of professionals can help each other to resolve practical problems by pooling knowledge and experience. The action inquiry consultant's aim is to encourage the development of small-scale data collection as the focal point for collaborative analysis and interpretation. In this way, personality issues are controlled, task orientation is increased and an embryonic knowledge base is established.

Action learning is therefore central to collaborative change. On account of this it helps overcome the problems of getting started, gaining access, and building trust. In these respects it meets the requirements of progressively moving towards action inquiry by adopting the characteristics of a 'thinking school' (ACSET, 1984) or 'problem-solving' (McLaughlin, 1976) or 'developing school' (Holly, 1986) in which a gradualist approach to change takes place and where staff are finally willing to explore value differences with a view to agreeing an action plan. The action inquiry consultant is effective to the extent that he or she strengthens the underlying conditions for this type of collegial democracy.

A closer understanding of these conditions may be gained by considering in turn some main methods or organizing action inquiry namely, interactive research and development, site study, school-based projects, networking, and award-bearing courses.

Interactive Research and Development

Within this category a variety of roles is available to the consultant on a continuum which includes being a researcher, support teacher, or curriculum developer. The poles can be represented as two modes: A and B.

Mode A

Where the consultant is cast more in the role of professional researcher, the research activities are mainly seen as the responsibility of the outsider. But typically, the school-based team is designed to be broadly representative and its members are charged with the task of taking joint decisions about research questions, data collection, and development issues. As Lieberman (1986) points out, the benefits of this form of collaborative investigation are that it creates a structure for teachers that facilitates reflection and action on live issues, the team unites staff and encourages professional communication, what is known from research about the situations identified as problematic is applied, and it provides possibilities for participants whether teachers or consultants to assume new roles and exhibit leadership.

But there are costs, the chief ones being the potential for role conflict between researchers and practitioners, and the tensions arising between research and development. Much will depend upon the quality of team functioning. However, even when this is assured differences of perception can arise about the direction of effort especially where a variety of sponsors are involved, e.g. the school, the LEA, the polytechnic or the university. Slippage can develop between the actions of the team and assumptions about the interests of partners. This issue and the related one of whether more centrally-directed inputs should be provided, emerged in a study carried out to test the feasibility of this type of collaboration (Bell, 1982, 1983). As was said at the time: 'Action research can disappear into the sand. Centrally-directed research can disappear into the clouds'.

A balance needed to be struck, and a key factor was seen to be adequate time for negotiating role and task definitions. The weaknesses evident were that teachers' aims were assumed to be positively geared toward achieving defined goals whereas the process consultants were perceived to have adopted a neutral attitude. Central direction was seen to be the answer to motivate, encourage, point in the 'right' direction, sort out mismatches of expertise and provide more specific resourcing. In particular, there was a perceived need for help in establishing a wider forum for debate than the team — a concern that was later to be taken up in terms of the concept of 'networking'.

Such tensions serve to illustrate some of the potential sources of subversion in collaborative consultancy. The quest for quality in the functioning of action inquiry teams will it seems be one of perpetual conflict between the demands to pursue truth built into the concept of research and the requirement to form a consensus built into the commitment to action. Improving information flow by adopting a school-based project approach, where the broader framework enables teams to find more flexible ways of working, is one response I shall later examine in greater detail.

Mode B

In circumstances where the emphasis for the consultant is more towards a support teacher/developer role, collaborative teaching and evaluation is implied. This approach can be particularly useful for bridging certain kinds of gap particularly between advisory teachers, teacher trainers and schools. In current circumstances where it is a statutory condition for the approval of teacher training courses that tutors engage in periodic renewal of teaching experience, collaborative teaching and evaluation offers one model of cooperation.

The role of support teacher as consultant to a process of collaborative teaching and evaluation is essentially one which involves active participation in the management of change. A joint diagnosis of a situation is called for with a view to sharing the task of implementing alternative strategies. The division of effort involves the common distribution of both research and teaching tasks. This role can be clearly distinguished from others by considering the matrix in Figure 11.4.

The demands of collaborative teaching and evaluation can however be considerable. In the study referred to below (Bell, 1987b) a group evaluation of the strengths and weaknesses of this role was carried out amongst an experienced team of consultant/support teachers who had operated in four comprehensive schools for two years. Evaluating the positive aspects of this role yielded thirty-five items with the group voting in rank order: having access to an overview; bridging theory and practice; personal and professional development for self and others; freedom and flexibility to plan and reflect; and having a wide range of involvement in the process of innovation. The negative aspects identified eight key concerns: being placed in situations where the process of collaboration did not spring directly from the participants themselves; having insufficient feedback from and in relation to policy/decision makers; having unclear lines of accountability; constraints arising from existing school structures; no personal support or appraisal procedure; lack of role definition; insufficient status; and the tensions arising between keeping neutral and 'going native'.

Reflecting on the characteristics of a successful support teacher produced seven items ranked in order of importance: being good at public/personnel relations; having detachment; being open to learning; being a good time manager; having empathy; having abilities as problem manager; and being ready to 'muck in'. This evidence can be cross-checked against the views of another group of support teachers who adopted a collaborative teaching and evaluation definition of their role (McKenna, 1988). Their experience can be summarized as the 'four D's' (joint school and consultant): diagnosis; data collection; dialogue; decision making.

Figure 11.4 Role possibilities in collaborative consultancy

FOCUS OF CONSULTANCY

CONSULTANT ROLE	Pupil performance	Teaching style	Curriculum	Whole-school	Policy review
Co-teacher					
Process supporter					
Content adviser					
Staff developer					
Evaluator					
Researcher					

The overall judgment was that the process of 'watching each other' acts as a powerful means of assisting change. The data from observations provided compelling evidence for decision-making and identified a range of choices about what to change. The gains in credibility were considerable both for teachers in securing the grounds of a case for change, and for external supporters who had an opportunity to demonstrate an ability to practise what they might otherwise preach. Such involvements conferred status and legitimated the right to enter claims about what might be done.

In their deliberations about the relevance of action research as an evaluaiton process, they rated highly the shared awareness of the problem and the need for change and development. They noted how it created dialogue, provided mutual support, and focused on the fact that assumptions can be wrong. Its main weaknesses were seen to be the time required to plan, implement, and review, including the liaison effort needed at senior management level.

In summary, interactive research and development involves considerable complexity in both roles and tasks. As can be seen, the tendencies towards marginal rather than structural change are marked unless steps are taken to strengthen the framework of organization to formalize action, provide liaison with policy makers, and ensure accountability.

Site Study

In some respects, a simpler alternative is to avoid professional researcher, support teacher or curriculum developer definitions of the consultant's role and focus on facilitating collaborative evaluation instead (Bell, 1987b).

This approach involves both individual and team contributions to a composite report which I refer to as a 'site study'. This jointly produced account of planned change is evaluated by the consultant by means of an issues analysis. The resulting draft evaluation document is then validated by participants using an agreed clearance procedure. This includes a 'case history' developed by a co-consultant from the available data so as to provide an independent check on interpretations (see Figure 11.5). Adopting this approach was to some extent distorted by the effects of one of the most prolonged periods of disruption in schools and served to emphasize the vulnerability of collaborative models of change which rely heavily on voluntary participation. Whatever means are used for consultancy crucially depend upon the willingness of participants to find time.

A constant dilemma for the consultant therefore is whether to intervene in order to save practitioner effort, or to stand back in order to preserve authenticity in the situation. The main aim must be to avoid data overload whilst maintaining the balance between inquiry and action. The constraints operating at this time helped to stimulate economies of effort and whilst opportunities were lost, a certain sharpness did result. What emerged as the main form of action learning were group and individual self-evaluation studies using nominal group techniques

Figure 11.5   Procedures for site study

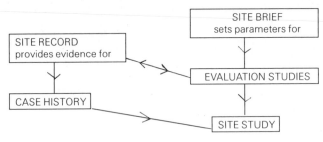

(O'Neil, 1981; Lomax and Mcleman, 1984) and conversations with the consultant in a structured series of interviews designed to encourage policy analysis.

The vehicle provided by site study for single-school collaborative consultancy also proved to be economical within the framework of a national project where several schools participated. It supplied a means of mediating the potential threat posed to developing practical professional knowledge from descriptions asserted 'on authority' — whether this be the perceived authority of the teacher as insider or the assumed authority of the consultant evaluator as outsider. This process of mediation resulted from combining two main means of inquiry: investigative method using techniques designed to illuminate and resolve practical problems, e.g. action research, case study, self-evaluation; and critical method using techniques to encourage appraisal of the knowledge and experience of partners in the change process.

The outcomes provided five types of record which were validated one against another: site studies developed by practitioner researchers; reports of cross-site group evaluation meetings; evaluation reports arising from an issues analysis of the site studies; case histories developed from the archive of data; and the judgments of the consultant based upon the unique experience of acting as go-between amongst all the participants. In summary, the idea of site study injects three main elements into a policy for collaborative consultancy: advice to help schools evaluate their own performance; efforts to facilitate research-based teaching; and initiatives to encourage systematic recording of the evaluated experience of participants.

School Development Projects

Stimulating the adoption of these elements in a development programme is, I suggest, best achieved by means of collaborative projects. The role of the action inquiry consultant then becomes one of coordinating the processes of take-up so as to provide a secure framework for cooperation. For our purposes, a distinction can be drawn between whole-school and team-based projects. In the former, practitioner research appears to be the logically appropriate method of collaboration. In the latter, school-focused study may more accurately describe the form of action inquiry involved.

The point here is not to be pedantic, but to draw attention to the need to match resources to the scale of ambition. Losing sight of differences between types of collaboration not only impoverishes possibilities, it also encourages the view that distinctions do not matter. The evidence discussed above points to the opposite (see also Rudduck, 1982; Webb, 1988). Whilst prevailing attitudes assume that drawing boundaries creates unnecessary divisions, the sovereignty of individual interests is not threatened in circumstances where sound principles of federal management are applied. Gestures of abandonment whilst indicating trust cannot safeguard the maintenance of cooperative attitudes, especially amongst the shifting fortunes of professional careers.

The concept of a 'whole-school' project prompts the thought that teachers are not the sole agents of educational processes although the majority of studies of school-based collaborative research implicitly assumes that they are. Teacher-based research is commonly talked about whilst the notion of practitioner research is less well used. The arguments for a more participatory approach to include inter-professional contributions and extended opportunities for pupils and adults other than teachers to take part cannot be entered into here (Kassam and Mustafa, 1982). I shall assume the connection and briefly consider the problem of method. I suggest that whole-school approaches are best suited to tackle policy issues, e.g. integration, gender, multi-cultural education. The extent to which collaboration already exists amongst partners in such policies is a precondition of their effectiveness. The aim therefore of practitioner research is to strengthen cooperation by systematic forms of reflection on the practices which flow from them.

The problem of part-ownership therefore needs to be recognized in the mode of inquiry. This indicates the need for an eclectic but coherent range of research involvements sufficiently broad to facilitate contributions yet sufficiently focused to enable coordination. This can be accomplished in five main ways:

1 *small-scale experimental studies* — where a hypothesis is tested through measurement of samples;
2 *evaluation* — where a variety of techniques mainly checklists, questionnaires, interviews, and observations are used either to judge pupil and teacher performance (self-evaluation) or performance in the wider context of the syllabus (curriculum evaluation);
3 *case study* — where a situation is studied through collecting evidence with a view to providing a critical portrayal;
4 *action research* — where a practical problem is systematically acted upon, monitored, evaluated and reported;
5 *review* — where a policy, practice or issue is studied through existing texts, reports or testimony, designed to provide an account of what is already known about the subject of investigation.

Practitioner research whilst being centred on either the study of samples (1), the study of performance (2), the study of a situation (3), the study of change (4), or the study of texts (5) is linked with a practical issue involving action learning through the organization of the project. The consultant's role is to establish an action inquiry framework and ensure that it works.

In attempting this in a primary school over one school year (Bell and Colbeck, 1984 and 1989), we concluded that there were certain main influences on success. Firstly, the school was clearly ready to evaluate its policy and practice. There had been a continuing programme of staff development, the time was ripe, and there was a willingness to commit resources. There was also sponsorship of key individuals amongst the collaborating partners with a history of professional cooperation and personal acquaintance to refer to. This led to active advocacy of roles and tasks with the result that barriers were at least recognized if not entirely overcome.

Not that this situation was easily achieved. On the contrary, problems of ownership and control needed careful negotiation so that the management of potentially sensitive data was agreed. This was resolved by observing a clear distinction between the content of the investigation (integration) and the process of the project (action inquiry). Data concerning the former was 'owned' by practitioners provisional upon clearance through the LEA. Data about the process of managing the project was 'owned' by the consultant with courtesy rights of clearance through the LEA. This distinction proved its worth on several occasions aiding role maintenance, clarity of discussion and task boundaries.

The main dilemmas arose when for the purposes of coordinating outcomes and seeking completion, the interface between process and content had to be bridged. This depended on judging an appropriate moment and issue for which to intervene. This was normally settled by being commissioned to undertake a specific task (e.g. editing minutes of meetings) on behalf of the project team which included all participants and which met regularly. Success therefore turned on effective management of project team meetings for which an active steering committee representing the main partners proved to be a key influence. The overriding priority for the steering committee was the organization of consent (Handy, 1977). In retrospect, Handy's six management principles of recognizing the right to disagree, controlling by planning not checking, managing by reciprocal trust, creating task groups, encouraging personal style, and husbanding energies could readily be observed when the team was operating at its peak. In team-based, as opposed to whole school projects, the same principles can apply whilst procedures may differ. In the example in Figure 11.6, organizing consent is made simpler but the emphasis on role clarity, task definition, schedules of activity, data control and resource accountability remain.

In one school's experience of adopting this approach (McKenna, op. cit.), the creation of a school development project was judged to be successful in terms of: project meetings encouraging professional dialogue; enhancing the responsiveness of the school to identified needs; stimulating the use of outside agencies, delegating authority so as to generate high levels of motivation amongst staff; providing an opportunity to re-evaluate dormant issues; and increasingly effective transfer of skills and knowledge as the project progressed. The problem areas

Figure 11.6   Outline project management strategy

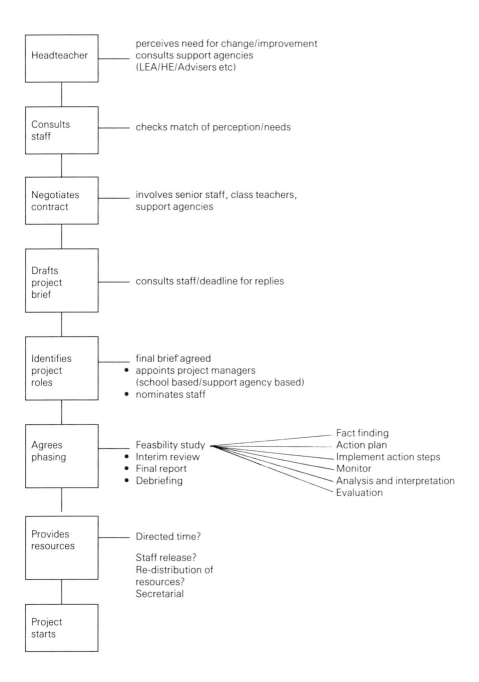

encountered included: the constraints of the timetable; unrealistic aims in relation to resources; staffing continuity; failure to involve a wider spectrum of participants including parents; difficulties in evolving effective criteria of evaluation; managing differing perceptions of priorities amongst the aims of the project; and inexperience leading to inadequate preparation.

Networking

So far, the examples selected have been limited to relatively small-scale collaboration but the goal of achieving more widespread types of professional cooperation will not be realized by these means alone. For instance, whilst school-based projects are good at diffusing ideas, they are notoriously bad at disseminating outcomes. Such considerations led to a pilot study which attempted to link research-based teaching and training with school development and to combine both of these to meet the challenges of diffusion and dissemination. The concept of school-centred action networks emerged as a result (Dennis, 1987).

A 'network' can be defined as a coupling of nodes or points in a systematic way. In the present usage, I refer to points of professional communication linked by means of a social network for social improvement. Networking in this sense implies communication and partnership with a view to disseminating ideas about 'good', i.e. tested, practice. In non-networked information systems, for example, traditional approaches to educational enquiry, collaboration is looked upon as merely being a contingent feature. As a consequence, knowledge is developed but not necessarily utilized. In a networked system, the cooperation necessary to link points requires active information transfer. In an extended 'action network' sense where the information transferred is also utilized, we move to the point where gaps between partners are minimal.

The professional communication characteristics of each type of activity are entirely distinct. In a non-networked system there are no agreed procedures for reflection, action or the free flow of information. In a networked action inquiry system, the presence of these factors necessarily brings about a qualitative change in the practice of participants. An example of an LEA sponsored network along these lines is outlined in Figure 11.7.

Improving the flow and quality of information can be attempted by harnessing information technology. Making a suite of databases available to participants further enhances the range and functions of professional communication. To date, the main types shown in Figure 11.8 have been distinguished.

Collaborative consultancy using this approach essentially means attempting to create an 'ideal speech community' (McCarthy, 1978). On this account, the extent to which gaps between partners are bridged will depend upon certain factors, namely: that participants enter dialogue under conditions of equal opportunity; that power relations are neutralized through an overriding aim to pursue truth; that participants have the same chance to raise issues, make proposals and call into question, sufficient to leave no assertions free from critical

Figure 11.7   Networking management model

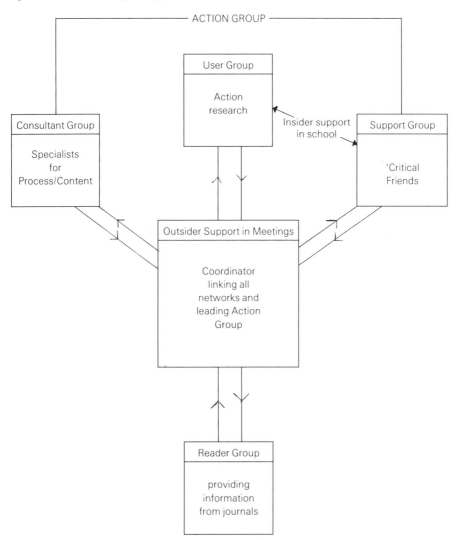

examination; and that discussion is sufficiently free from the distorting influences of group organization to enable a rational consensus to arise. The process consultant's role is to monitor the network to facilitate these key features.

The evaluated experience of two such networks (Hall, 1988) revealed their strengths and weaknesses. As to strengths, participants rated highly the network's influence in focusing on one problem and getting down to tackling it, the usefulness of a database and the resulting transfer of research information into other areas of professional activity, group discussions, enhancing pupil learning, developing valid forms of self appraisal and the professional development support

Figure 11.8   Knowledge base for practitioner research networks

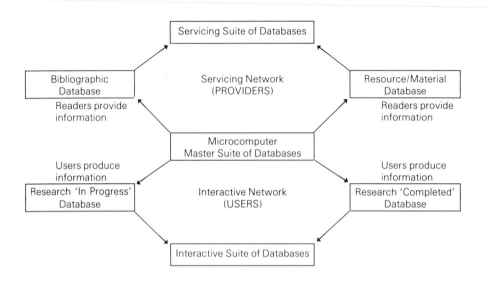

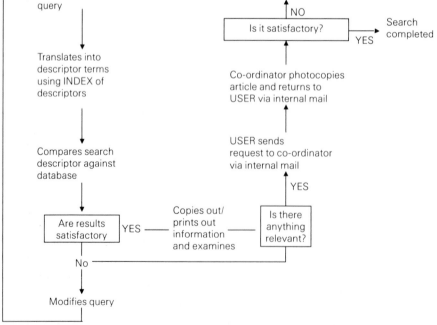

which arose from taking part. Concerning weaknesses, the partially developed state of the database, getting hold of material, delays in identifying a linked supporter, no examples of previous work of participants, and limited contact with consultants and supporters were highlighted.

The role of the network coordinator might well be occupied by the consultant, although in the pilot studies it was felt important to have a practising teacher seconded for this purpose. The main tasks which emerged were to provide a service to support research-based teaching, to disseminate knowledge and experience, to develop interaction amongst the partners, and to become a source of encouragement and understanding of the demands of researching practice.

The networks were organized on a termly cycle with a common structure of eight meetings to match the process of action research. This allowed the possibility of role change in the following network so that users become supporters, supporters become consultants, coordinators become evaluators, etc. In this way not only does the database of information accumulate, but there is an accumulation of skills which are deployed in support of other colleagues, which significantly strengthens subsequent networks.

The implications of this model of collaborative consultancy are far-reaching, especially in the opportunities presented for reducing the gap between award-bearing courses and theory and practice (e.g. all the supporters and consultants in Network 1 had been course members of an action inquiry-based Diploma). As the pool of available consultants in the future is likely to be drawn from institutions of higher education, the challenge of developing more responsive types of accreditation must clearly be a priority.

Accreditation

Award-bearing courses typically do not encourage collaborative consultancy. This is perhaps mainly due to an assumed conflict between the role of the tutor as judge of course standards and the tutor as co-partner in an enquiry. There is also the implication that the curriculum of courses is not negotiable because needs are known, whereas consultancy suggests a joint diagnosis of needs that cannot be assumed. This presumption of knowledge on authority is strongly embedded in the practices of institutions which favour the study of texts and the values of scholarship against the study of change and the development of practical professional knowledge.

Using action inquiry as a rationale for course design allows the possibility of accommodating these potentially conflicting demands. The opportunities for role change are extensive, for whilst there is a requirement to provide training in the skills of research-based teaching, there is also the invitation to participate in collaborative study of the management of change in course members' practice. In this way, the course process itself becomes a matter for joint improvement.

The question of matching course process with course content in the development of professionality is not a theme that can be fully explored here. I shall have to assume that educating the reflective practitioner is a matter of limiting dependency on knowledge on authority and enhancing opportunities for developing knowledge of practice through a 'reflective conversation with the situation' (Schon, 1983). Collaborative consultancy is one means of achieving this for it transforms the tutor as expert into the tutor as co-inquirer. The situation being studied also shifts from the problems of transmitting information (which machines are well suited to do) to the problems of transmitting a culture (which only teachers, trainers and educators can effectively achieve).

The role of the training institution in providing opportunities for collaborative consultancy through action inquiry will, therefore, need to focus on securing four main points of development: achieving better links between research and the improvement of schools; moving the location of support for the study of practice from college-based to school-based activities; paying closer attention to transferring practical knowledge from one practitioner to another; and giving greater scope for the supported self-study of practical problems in teaching (Bell and Pennington, 1988b).

The issue of judging course standards resolves itself to the extent that criteria are logically connected with the course process and in the degree to which course members fully participate in interpreting them. When there is a match of both, the course experience becomes self-checking and the tutor is then freed to engage fully in the problems and issues arising from the management of change. In considering appropriate criteria to ensure this effect, those developed by Lincoln and Guba (1985) were selected to meet these requirements, namely:

— *credibility* — the study must be believable by those who are competent to judge the subject of investigation;
— *transferability* — the study must be able to promote the exchange of experience from one practitioner to another, lessons must be capable of being learned from the evidence provided;
— *dependability* — the study must be trustworthy through having gathered evidence by reliable procedures;
— *confirmability* — the study must be capable of being scrutinized for absence of bias by making its evidence and the methods of analysis accessible.

Using such criteria as quality assurance standards for the change programme being pursued by course members encourages a transition in role from tutor to tutor-consultant. This is not a matter of mere word play. The culture of the course alters from skills training and information transfer to collaboratively developing knowledge of practice. The concept of a practitioner research group or 'critical community' (Ovens, 1988) becomes a more accurate description of participants' experience than a 'course'. The central issue then is one of maintaining rigour in both action and inquiry against tendencies for simple socializing to occur. Here, I suggest the broader concept of 'validation' as the more appropriate procedure to adopt than the narrower notion of 'objectivity'. The point of action inquiry is not to suppress subjectivity but to make its assumptions, implications and consequences explicit. The purpose of collaborative consultancy is not simply to adopt objective standards but to actively engage in a critical dialogue about a jointly experienced practical situation. The differences of emphasis may become more obvious when the four main types of validation are considered:

— *internal validation* — confirming categories arising from studying data collected on the basis of their frequency (saturation) and/or confirming interpretations by comparing categories arising in one data set with those from another (triangulation);

— *external validation* — referring analytic memos and interim reports to outsiders competent to judge the subject of investigation for comment and critique;

— *insider validation* — checking interpretations with participants in the practice being studied;

— *audience validation* — testing the credibility of final draft reports by seeking critical commentary from a review panel of persons representing the intended audience.

Unifying these interests can be accomplished by using the technique of 'audit evaluation' (Halpern, 1983) in which course members pair up to act as audit evaluators for each others' work. The step-wise sequence of acquiring a checklist of data held and related documents and materials, comparing procedures to problems addressed, comparing raw data to final product, noting whether influences flow logically from the data, and certifying in the final report the extent to which credibility, transferability, dependability and confirmability apply, substantially assists in building a critical community. The role of the tutor-consultant is to facilitate this process and/or to act as auditor.

The evaluated experience of adopting this approach to collaborative consultancy (Bell, 1988) indicates that course members valued highly resulting improvements in practice, in-depth study of a curricular area, the clarification of their own ideas, and the interaction between partners. The main weaknesses were to do with the question of timing in the school year for elements of the course process, the total demand on time, and the interference effects on routine teaching tasks. Hustler (1988) also comments on the ways in which time scales may not match, how course starting points may not fit the development of issues in the school, the risk factors involved in attempting change programmes, coordinating a research group when different directions, expectations and needs develop, problems of text and audience for the written work presented, and the potential for leaving participants isolated at the end of the course.

Conclusion

The themes I have tried to address relate to the task of mapping possibilities for collaboration and consultancy in circumstances where there is a joint intention to manage change. The proposal has been put that a significant guarantor of good intentions is a commitment to action inquiry. Approaches to both action and inquiry have been explored with a view to opening up some of the issues that emerged as a consequence of pursuing one or more of these routes. References to the need to develop practical professional knowledge as an outcome of collaboration is seen as a major determinant of success in raising standards. Examining the role of consultancy in the process of structuring partnership reveals a variety of ways of organizing consent. The scope of this endeavour indicates the need for more accounts of evaluated experience. In this respect, the present contribution is offered as a tentative and partial step in that direction.

References

ACSET, (1984) *Report on INSET for School Teachers*, Teacher Training Sub Committee, Advisory Committee on the Supply and Education of Teachers, 23 August.

BELL, G. H. (1982) 'Teacher research, microcomputers and primary education', *Computers and Education*, 16, pp. 235–42.

BELL, G. H. (1983) 'Computerised educational research information in Ontario, Canada; A case report of a study visit', *Collected Original Resources in Education*, (7.1), 1.

BELL, G. H. (1985a) 'Can schools develop knowledge of their practice?' *School Organization*, 5, pp. 175–84.

BELL, G. H. (1985b) 'INSET: five types of collaboration and consultancy', *School Organization*, 5, pp. 247–56.

BELL, G. H. (1987a) 'Innovation without change?'. In: Nixon, J. (Ed.) *Curriculum Change: The Sheffield Experience*, University of Sheffield.

BELL, G. H. (1987b) 'Site study as collaborative action inquiry'. In: Somekh, B. (Ed.) *Action Research in Development, Classroom Action Research Bulletin No. 8*, Cambridge Institute of Education.

BELL, G. H. (1988) 'Action Inquiry'. In: Nixon, J. and Groundwater-Smith, S. (Eds.) *The Enquiring Teacher: Supporting and Sustaining Teacher Research*, Lewes, The Falmer Press.

BELL, G. H. and COLBECK, B. (1984) 'Whole school practitioner research: The Sunnyside Action Inquiry Project', *Educational Research*, 26, pp. 88–94.

BELL, G. H. and COLBECK, B. (1989) *Experiencing Integration. The Sunnyside Action Inquiry Project*. Lewes, The Falmer Press.

BELL, G. H. and PENNINGTON, R. C. (1988a) 'Action learning and school focussed study, *Collected Original Resources in Education*, 12, 1.

BELL, G. H. and PENNINGTON, R. C. (1988b) 'The role of consultants/facilitators in school based enquiry', *Collected Original Resources in Education*, 12, 3.

DENNIS, S. (1987) 'Practitioner research and the microcomputer'. In: Smith D. (Ed.) *Electronic Media and Professional Communications in Education*, Council for Educational Technology (forthcoming).

ELLIOTT, J. (1978) 'What is action research in schools?', *Journal of Curriculum Studies*, 10, pp. 355–7.

FULLAN, M. G. (1986) 'Improving the implementation of educational change', *School Organization*, 6, pp. 321–6.

HALL, M. (1988) *Scunthorpe Action Research Network 2*, Trent Polytechnic, July (Mimeo).

HALPERN, E. S. (1983) 'Auditing naturalistic inquiries: the development and application of a model'. In: Lincoln, Y. S. and Guba, E. G. *Naturalistic Inquiry*, London, Sage Publications.

HAMPTON, H. (1988) 'Practitioner research: a methodology for cultural diversity', *Multi-Cultural Teaching*, **6**, Summer, pp. 8–13.

HANDY, C. (1977) 'The organizations of consent'. In: Boyd-Barrett, O. *et al.* (Eds.) *Approaches to Post School Management*, London, Harper and Row, 1983.

HOLLY, P. (1986) 'Soaring like turkeys? — the impossible dream', *School Organization*, **6**, pp. 346–64.

HUSTLER, D. (1988) 'Problems and opportunities in award bearing courses'. In: Bell, G. H. and Pennington, R. C. *The Role of Consultants/Facilitators in School Based Enquiry*, (*op. cit.*).

KASSAM, Y. and MUSTAFA, K. (1982) *Participatory Research*, Society for Participatory Research in Africa.

KENNY, R. W. and GROTELEUSCHEN, A. D. (1984) 'Making the case for case study', *Journal of Curriculum Studies*, **16**, pp. 37–51.

LETICHE, H. K. (1986) *From Europe to the Teaching Team*, Delft, Holland, Eburon.

LIEBERMAN, A. (1986) 'Collaborative research: working with, not working on', *Educational Leadership*, **43**, pp. 28–32.

LINCOLN, Y. S. and GUBA, E. G. (1985) *Naturalistic Inquiry*, London, Sage Publications.

LOMAX, P. and MCLEMAN, P. (1984) 'The uses and abuses of nominal group technique in polytechnic course evaluation', *Studies in Higher Education*, **9**, pp. 183–90.

MCCARTHY, T. (1978) *The Critical Theory of Jurgen Habermas*, Cambridge, Mass., MIT Press.

MCKENNA, M. (1988) 'Collaborative teaching and evaluation', In: Bell, G. H. and Pennington, R. C. *The Role of Consultants/Facilitators in School Based Enquiry*, (*op. cit.*).

MCLAUGHLIN, M. (1976) 'Implementation as mutual adaptation', *Teachers College Record*, **77**, pp. 339–51.

O'NEIL, M. (1981) 'Nominal group technique: an evaluation data collection process', *Evaluation Newsletter*, **5**, pp. 44–60.

OVENS, P. (1988) 'Certificate in educational action enquiry, *Progress Review*, Manchester Polytechnic.

REVANS, R. W. (1982) *Action Learning*, Bromley, Chartwell Bratt.

RUDDUCK, J. (Ed.) (1982) *Teachers in Partnership: Four Studies of In-service Collaboration*, London, Longman.

SCHEIN, E. H. (1969) *Process Consultation: It's Role in Organization Development*, Cambridge, Mass., Addison-Wesley.

SCHON, D. A. (1983) *The Reflective Practitioner: How Professionals Think in Action*, London, Temple Smith.

SIMONS, H. (Ed.) (1980) 'Towards a science of the singular', *Occasional Publication No. 10*, University of East Anglia.

STENHOUSE, L. (1975) *An Introduction to Curriculum Research and Development*, London, Heinemann.

STENHOUSE, L. (1978) 'Case study and case records: towards a contemporary history of education', *British Journal of Educational Research*, **4**, 2, 21–39

STENHOUSE, L. (1982) A Note on Case Study and Educational Practice. In R. Burgess (Ed.) *Field Methods in the Study of Education*. Lewes, The Falmer Press.

WALKER, R. (1974) 'The conduct of educational case studies'. In: Dockerell, W. B. and Hamilton, D. (Eds.) *Re-Thinking Educational Research*, London, Hodder and Stoughton, 1982.

WALLACE, M., BAILEY, J. and KIRK, P. (1988) *Action Learning: Practice and Potential in School Management Development*, National Development Centre for School Management Training.

WEBB, R. (1988) 'Outstation teams: a collaborative approach to research in schools', *British Educational Research Journal*, 14, pp. 51–64.

12
Conceptualizing Consultancy:
Towards a New Educational Practice

Michael Golby and Della Fish

This chapter considers the prospects for the development of consultancy as a wide range of practices which has grown over the past ten years yet still lacks a distinctive character and theoretical rationale. We are interested particularly in forms of consultancy with professionals which are educational and not coercive or managerial in nature. The education service has undergone much change over the decade, most of it associated with restriction and control of professional activity. Yet, paradoxically, there are new opportunities for creative initiatives towards more responsible, satisfying and productive educational consultancy. The closer audit of teachers' activities has included accountability to school governors, tighter management of schools with more hierarchically-defined roles for staff and a new emphasis on school-focused in-service education and training (INSET). The latter has produced grant-related in-service education and training (GRIST) conforming to politically identified priorities. It is INSET with a (sometimes severe) practical orientation and it is an example of the new urgency that has broken the mould of the traditional pattern of in-service courses. For that very reason, educational consultancy is on the brink of new possibilities.

We identify a new formation: a consultancy team comprising an external consultant and locally-based 'health visitor' (to adopt the originating medical metaphor). Such a combination we think particularly promising where teachers and schools come together, as they increasingly will, in the interests of concerted development. But practice without an established tradition to draw upon depends crucially upon the models of conduct held in the mind of practitioners. The medical metaphor is unsatisfactory for many reasons but perhaps most telling is the general disillusionment with the 'big science' it involves and new interest in self-help and preventive medicine. In any case, the relation of an educational practitioner to the consultant is clearly quite unlike that of the patient to the medical consultant. Principally, the educator and certainly those who commission INSET are much more likely to be looking for help at the level of continuing practice or principles than for remediation.

Given the specific nature of educational activity, consultancy for it will be *sui generis*. But how consultancy is practised and developed will depend fundamentally upon the connections made in the mind to other forms of social activity. Human conduct is controlled at root by the conception held of it by practitioners (Oakeshott, 1963; Langford, 1985). Those engaging in consultancy are bound to make use of metaphors for their work deriving from better established activities elsewhere. It is time to move on from medicine to consider more productive concepts. The education system is made up of an interlocking network of responsibilities and powers. Consultancy must locate itself securely within this system; it is not a personal service to a teacher or even a school but in an important sense a social service to a community administered through the machineries of local and national government. The rise of accountability and value for money as a key slogan makes this all the more necessary. It also makes consultancy something with potentially greater impact than heretofore since results will need increasingly to be demonstrated in terms of innovation and immediate impact.

While the 'Red Adair consultant' stands or falls by quick results in an emergency, his offering is technical and his effectiveness in 'capping the problem' unproblematically evaluated. Nor is there any ambiguity about ownership of his results; they belong to the management and ultimately to the shareholders. The outcome is all. He provides a service in a situation where professionals cannot cope for themselves. He does not teach the professionals anything, at least only incidentally and not as his main concern.

The inappropriateness of such a model for educational consultancy is clear. Not only are the values involved in educational action contestable, as for example in the TVEI context, but also more than an emergency service is required. In short, learning is looked for and power is to be passed to the practitioner in the form of more sophisticated practice and understandings. The consultant therefore will not come as 'expert' except in terms of the process of learning. It is not to the expert's advantage to pass on his specific skills. The medical metaphor has buttressed this 'technical' view of consultancy. But it is clearly inadequate where what is required is a learning profession not dependent 'patients'. Such considerations cast doubt on whether we should be considering troubleshooting as consultancy at all. If so, it will always be of limited scope even if essential as emergencies arise.

As something of a contrast, but still within a medical metaphor, a view of consultancy deriving from the practices of therapy might be developed. Here the emphasis is on rehabilitation through what the patient has to offer. Healing by means of self-knowledge and self-help may be sought in some therapies. This draws attention to the idea of proper or normal functioning. As applied to education, this view does some justice to the importance of process in learning (unlike the 'expert' view) but begs questions of value and principle. Towards what view of proper or normal education would an educational consultant be working? The therapeutic metaphor is silent in this area, which is inescapable for the educational consultant.

We shall have to come to values. But for the moment let us consider the fact that education is provided through institutions in socio-political contexts. Experts and therapists provide a service but do not normally pass on their professional knowledge. By contrast, much of what teachers learn is for onward transmission. Indeed, it is true to say that the 'real' clients for educational consultancy are the students who are the ultimate beneficiaries (or sufferers). But the good for students is not exclusively a matter for their choice nor even for their parents as 'consumers' of education. Despite recent political rhetorics to this effect, the developing, unrelenting and bipartisan moves towards the National Curriculum since James Callaghan's Ruskin College speech in 1976 provide ample evidence that the public interest in the work of schools is acknowledged in practice. This public interest is expressed institutionally in the interplay between local government, central government and the schools themselves, including teachers' associations and school governing bodies.

We must leave aside the red herring that the National Curriculum is not proposed as a universal curriculum since the public (private or 'independent') schools are exempt and City Technology Colleges and Grant Maintained schools not fully subject to it. So long as there remains a non-privatized education service, it will consist of broad groupings of interests formed around institutions and with varying degrees of power. For our present purposes what is important is that consultancy may be commissioned from any quarter, from individual teachers, departments, schools, consortia, local authorities or the various agencies of central government.

Within such socio-political realities the consultant must stake out a position. This will be a defined relationship to the interested parties, making clear the responsibilities and rights that go with each role. There is a considerable literature and case law in curriculum evaluation on bureaucratic and democratic evaluation. But most of this literature was made at a time when school and teacher self-evaluation was the mode. In the late 1980s we are faced not with the bootstraps operations of teachers, and enlightened teachers at that, but instead with the imperatives of the National Curriculum, testing at seven, eleven, fourteen and sixteen years of age and local financial management. The climate is quite different and the consultant is faced not merely with the task of establishing warm personal relationships and tasks. Instead the consultant must work in a power environment which will certainly require answers to the question 'whose side are you on?'. Nisbet (1979) puts the situation thus:

> For the evaluator, an accountability system is evaluation 'with teeth', armed with sanctions and charged with responsibility. Consequently, when evaluators are involved in accountability procedures they must declare their stance. Is their function to support the status quo in the distribution of power (among institutions as well as among persons); or are they to challenge the status quo, or — if that sounds extreme — to question it or open up the possibility of changing it?

The consultant will certainly receive the consultancy commission from one or another quarter, most likely from a responsible authority and in regard to the work of professionals in some way working for or employed by that authority.

Power is of little account where there is consensus at the level of values and procedures. But consensus is nearly always more apparent than real. People are often ready to please until circumstances drive them into conflict. We find as consultants that the more effective the consultancy the greater the need to deal with value conflicts, contradictions in outlook and view, and the effects of the imbalances in power which exacerbate these differences.

For such reasons, the idea of the consultant as ambassador has some value. Here, attention is drawn to the sovereignty and independence of the powers with which the consultant deals. The LEA or the Training Commission has the purse strings and the power to commission consultancy. But teachers individually and collectively have the power to resist and reject the overtures of those they may regard as representatives of foreign powers. Teachers also have professional rights in the matter, rights which have received very little analysis in the past decade of teacher-bashing.

The consultant as ambassador has need of both credentials and credibility. Credentials are symbols of legitimacy, authorizations to proceed. They derive from a formal position in a political hierarchy, independent of the personal qualities of their holder. Credibility by contrast relies upon personal qualities entirely contingent upon the conventional wisdom. Teachers, rejecting authority's right to intrude upon them, may fall back on the old defences: 'I'd like to see him with 4B on a wet Friday!'. Confronted with these varied perspectives, Nisbet (1979) recommends a 'pluralist solution':

> The evaluator cannot impose his own values in the choices he makes, and it has been argued that he cannot fall back on 'neutral scientific values'. But he is not therefore obliged to follow the lines prescribed for him by others. The solution lies in adopting a complex procedure to match the complexity of the situation he faces. The evaluator's choices should reflect the values of *a range of participants* in the process he is evaluating. Thus, in an accountability system in education, evaluation should aim to spread the responsibility and to spread the coverage. (p. 54)

The diplomatic metaphor breaks down when the consultant is seen not so much as a plenipotentiary of one power on the territory of another but as an independent professional mediating between a range of legitimate, or at least reckonable, interests. Diplomacy is not unusually accompanied by covert operations and here again the delicacy of the consultant's role within the power environment is underlined.

The foregoing metaphors provide a range of emphases possible in consultancy work. Individually they highlight particular aspects of consultancy activity. But we contend that none of them is adequate to a full characterization of the role. Teachers must be viewed as more than hosts to an emergency service. They must seek their own understanding of their own practical work and not rely upon 'medical' (or even 'surgical') intervention from time to time. Teachers must also recognize the legitimacy of the public interest in their work, as represented in the efforts of their employers to advise them and help develop their work. Those in authority must acknowledge the claims to professional dignity of teachers and the independence of judgment necessary in a consultant. Any proper characterization of consultancy then must do justice to the following features of the educational situation:

1 the limitations of 'bought-in' expertise;
2 the learned helplessness induced by dependence on outside authority;
3 the legitimacy of the public interest, at the very least in knowing about and influencing teachers' activities;
4 the independence of teachers and consultants in some central aspects of their professional work;
5 the importance of distinguishing a 'course' from a 'consultancy';
6 the significance of different perspectives and interests, all of which need to be taken into account;
7 the need to work with contending views of the consultancy process itself.

These are very generalized statements leaving much open to interpretation. It is our contention that the interpretations that are required are as much to be sought in practice and the analysis of practice as in purely armchair speculation. Accordingly, we proceed to a fictionalized case, all of whose features have occurred in our experience. The story may help shed some light on the characteristics of educational consultancy and argue for the deployment of more carefully constructed consultancy teams in the future.

GRIST came to Oakshire, in common with other LEAs, in April 1987. By May and June the advisory service was forming INSET arrangements and by July a decision had been taken to set up small working groups on particular curriculum problems identified by the authority and in line with the national criteria. Schools with known interests in each topic were identified and heads invited to select one teacher to work on the problem throughout the following academic year. Groups of teachers working on common problems, released from school to consult elsewhere, would meet regularly together. An external consultant would be hired to facilitate the work of these teachers. The external consultancy was commissioned after the slenderest of 'negotiations' as to the requirements of the assignment on either side. The brief was hazy and even in September the financial arrangements were still unclear. All of this was compounded by the promotion away from the scene of the adviser responsible for the original idea. In the ensuing vacuum the consultant had to negotiate new understandings with the head of the teachers' centre where the consultancy was based.

In October the consultant met the teacher group for the first time, when it emerged that supply cover had already been arranged for the whole year and decisions already taken about how it should be used and what the released teachers would do. The teachers were not at all sure why they had been selected and did not give evidence of strong interest in the subject in hand. Moreover, the consultancy had been portrayed to the teachers as straightforward INSET and the teachers were obviously in no state of preparedness to act as consultants in relation to their colleagues in schools. Crucially for the conduct of the group, it had been nearly doubled in size by the addition of a range of other LEA personnel and included one member who had originally been told she would be running the whole 'course'.

Much of this is at the level of practicality and reflects the haste of the transitional arrangements for GRIST. But hidden in the story lie the pitfalls and potential of consultancy in the new era. The following points are of the essence:

1   The consultant was hired on recommendation from a university academic who had worked previously but briefly in the LEA's INSET programme.

2   There was next to no specification of the intended mode of operation beyond the provision of 'support' to three groups of teachers. Thus, the relevant expertise was not well-defined. There was perhaps an implicit suggestion that the provision would be closer to our 'therapy' than 'expert' metaphor.

3   It was clear that there was no well-defined expectation of how the teachers and other LEA personnel would conduct themselves in relation to the consultant. Roles are mutually defined; unclarity in one begets unclarity in the other. This opens the way to adventurism and experiment (which may or may not be a good thing).

4   The possibility of local support, for example from the local higher education institution, had apparently not been investigated. This seems to be part of the old story that real knowledge comes from afar. Also that home truths can be the hardest to live with.

5   Innovative work is extremely vulnerable to contingencies which easily destabilize. The more innovative, the more easily destabilized.

In the Oakshire story the character of the initial brief and consequently of much of the early practice prevents a typification of the consultancy role under any one of our suggested metaphors. All the same, it is possible to describe the emergence of a local role within the practice of this consultancy which we believe has promise for elsewhere.

At the first INSET meeting a member of the local advisory network was introduced who would act 'as a kind of district nurse'. These words of the LEA adviser responsible for the consultancy seemed to come as a surprise to the 'district nurse', as they were to the external consultant. In practice this meant that the person would be present at all INSET sessions and make regular visits to the schools where the teachers were working. She came to refer to these visits to schools as 'interpreting the course' to the schools. Now, arguably, had the teachers been fully responsive to the ideas of the consultant there would have been little or nothing for the 'district nurse' to do. However, as it turned out this strategy proved very productive and might be a model worth testing elsewhere wherever a group of schools meets a consultant on neutral territory. A consideration of the 'district nurse' metaphor with its connotations of dressing wounds and attending the convalescent leads us to prefer that of the 'health visitor'. Health visitors work with clients not patients; they aim to educate as much as to treat; they interest themselves in environmental and community factors in their clients' situations not merely in their clinical condition.

In developing consultancy, then, we suggest the following be considered. Firstly, where outside consultancy is engaged, local interpretation should be sought. Such a local person would, like the good health visitor, have both local knowledge and credibility. He or she would seek signs of healthy response and identify and attend to impediments to good practice. Secondly the outside consultant should bring credibility and experience of the processes involved in educational deliberation. Schon (1987) has identified 'reflection-in-action' as a set of key professional processes. Schwab (1969) has suggested 'something for curriculum professors to do', namely 'chairmanship' of deliberating groups seeking to put practice on a reflective footing. Such a chairmanship involves far more than holding meetings. It means securing full discussion, active enquiry and well-conceived experiment in the consultancy group.

This combination of outsider and insider with complementary roles will of course come into effect in diverse ways and with mixed results. We cannot legislate for personal commitment, local traditions and the general slipperiness and contingency of the practical world. Where we do see promise is in the concept of the consultant as a stranger asking the searching questions and creating with a local partner an environment in which teachers can move towards release from the the tyranny of the obvious and the 'taken for granted' in their practice.

In an earlier paper (Golby and Fish, 1980) we discussed some of the rights and responsibilities of the consultant. In this chapter we have stressed the utmost importance of underlying concepts in giving any practice its distinctive character. In an emerging field such as consultancy it is all the more important that practitioners interrogate their assumptions since the future shape of their work is at stake. Expert, therapist, ambassador, chairman? These and other metaphors need exploration. Priest, counsellor, architect? These too have their attractions. It is probable that a diversity of practice will develop reflecting the general pluralism of ideas that marks modern educational debate. Pluralism, however, is also a feature of all those other practices with which we might compare educational consultancy. Medicine, technology, diplomacy are only *relatively* settled in their ways. This reminds us that each and every practice must find its own identity in its own setting. Metaphors are at their most interesting and most useful point precisely when they cease to be applicable.

References

GOLBY, M. and FISH, M. A. (1980) 'School-focused INSET: clients and consultants, *British Journal of Inservice Education*, 6, pp. 83–6.

LANGFORD, S. G. (1985) *Education, Persons and Society*, London, Macmillan.

MURPHY, R. and TORRANCE, H. (Eds.) (1987) *Evaluating Education: Issues and Methods*, London, Harper and Row.

NISBET, J. (1979) 'The role of evaluators in accountability systems'. In: Murphy, R. and Torrance, H. (Eds.) *Evaluating Education: Issues and Methods*, London, Harper and Row.

OAKESHOTT, M. (1963) 'Political Education. In: Laslett, P. (ed.) *Philosophy, Politics and Society*, Oxford, Blackwell.

SCHON, D. (1987) *Educating the Reflective Practitioner*, San Francisco, Jossey Bass.

SCHWAB, J. J. (1969) In: Westbury, I. and Wilkof, N. (Eds.) (1975) *Science, Curriculum and Liberal Education*, Chicago University Press.

Notes on Contributors

Carol Aubrey is Lecturer in Education at the School of Education, University of Durham. She has written extensively on special education, the relevance and application of behavioural techniques to social and academic problems, and school consultancy in relation to pupil behaviour. She has researched special education legislation, school psychology and methods of working with the handicapped in France.

Prior to taking up her present post at University of Durham, she was first engaged in a three-year research project in applied psychology at University of Aston in Birmingham, then worked as an educational psychologist in Shropshire before taking up a post as Lecturer at Department of Education, University College, Cardiff.

Les Bell is Senior Lecturer in Education at the University of Warwick. He is a primary trained teacher who taught in both primary and secondary schools before joining the staff of Coventry College of Education. When the college joined the University of Warwick to form its Faculty of Education he was given the task of developing managment courses for teachers. He is now responsible for educational management courses in the M.Ed., M.A. (Primary Education) and B.Phil., as well as for a range of shorter in-service courses.

He has written extensively on school organisation and educational management and is co-author with Peter Maher of *Managing Pastoral Teams* (1986), Oxford, Blackwell and *Appraising Teachers in Schools* (1988), London, Routledge.

Gordon H. Bell is Professor and Dean of Education, Trent Polytechnic, Nottingham. He taught in a variety of primary, secondary and residential schools before entering teacher education and training. His main interests have focused on methods of developing knowledge of practice through collaborative evaluation of action programmes. As Director of the EEC-funded 'Europe in the Primary School' project since 1982 he has lectured extensively on these themes in a European context. Most recent publications are: Bell, G.H. and Colbeck, B. (1989) *Experiencing Integration: The Sunnyside Action Enquiry Project*, Lewes,

The Falmer Press and Bell, G. H., Mines, A. G. and Ovens, P. (1989) *Europe in the Primary School in England: The UK Case Study*, Pavic Publications.

Christopher Day is Senior Lecturer and Head of the In-Service Unit in the School of Education, University of Nottingham where he is responsible for the management of an extensive regional programme of professional development activities for teachers. Before moving to his present post he worked in primary and secondary schools, initial teacher training and as a local education authority adviser. He has worked extensively in in-service teacher education both in the UK and abroad with particular reference to staff and curriculum development and school-based consultancy. As part of his in-service commitments he directs regional and national management courses for heads and staff with management responsibilities, and his particular interests focus on the ways in which external consultants can support professional learning and change.

His recent publications include *Managing Primary Schools: a Professional Development Approach* (1985), London, Harper and Row, *Staff Development in the Secondary School: Management Perspectives* (1986), London, Croom Helm, *Appraisal and Professional Development in Primary Schools* (1987), Milton Keynes, Open University Press, and *Partnership in Education Management*, (1988), London, Routledge.

Della Fish is Principal Lecturer in Education, West London Institute of Higher Education, and Director of Studies for B.Ed. Primary course. Her areas of special interest are consultancy (the topic of her M.Ed. study (1980) at the University of Exeter was the theory and practice of consultancy), initial training and course design and consultancy to teams in para-medical professions.

Her publications have included an article co-authored with Michael Golby, entitled *School-focused Inset: Clients and Consultants* (1980), *Turning Teaching into Learning: TRIST and the Professional Development of Teachers* (1988) West London Press, which she edited, and *Learning through Practice in Initial Teacher Training: A Challenge for the Partners* (1989), London, Kogan Page.

Joan Figg is a Senior Educational Psychologist now working in North Cleveland, having previously worked in Lincolnshire, Nottinghamshire and for the ILEA. Her post graduate professional training was at University of Exeter, followed by an advanced course in consultation at the Tavistock clinic.

Her main professional interest is the application of consultation to education.

Michael Golby is Senior Lecturer in Education in the School of Education, University of Exeter. He has taught in primary schools, a College of Education and as a full-time member of the Open University staff. His research interests centre on school governance and he directed the Leverhulme project, *Parents as School Governors*, which reported in 1989.

Harry Gray is Lecturer in School Organisation and Management in the

Department of Educational Research at the University of Lancaster. He has practised as a management consultant in the private sector and is currently working with a number of secondary schools as a process consultant. His particular interests are management consultancy, experiential learning and gender issues in education. He has written widely on educational management and including *Change and Management in Schools* (1985), Deanhouse, editing *The Management of Educational Institutions* (1982), Lewes, The Falmer Press, co-authoring with Andrea Freeman, *Teaching without Stress* (1987), London, Harper and Row and editing *Management Consultancy in Schools* (1987), London, Cassell. Since writing this chapter, Harry Gray has joined the Training Agency as a Higher Education Adviser.

David Hopkins lives with his wife Marloes and son Jeroen in Cambridge. He is the tutor in Curriculum Studies at the Cambridge Institute of Education and has previously worked as an Outward Bound Instructor, school teacher and University and College lecturer. He has a PhD in teacher education from Simon Fraser University, Canada and was a consultant to the OECD/CERI on their International School Improvement Project. His recent publications include *A Teachers Guide to Classroom Research* (1985), Milton Keynes, Open University Press, *In-service Training and Educational Development* (1986), London, Croom Helm, *Improving the Quality of Schooling* (1987), Lewes, The Falmer Press and *Evaluation for School Development* (1989), Milton Keynes, Open University Press. He is also a mountain guide and has climbed in many of the world's great mountain ranges.

Howard Lewis teaches in the Faculty of Education, Humanities and Social Science at Derbyshire College of Higer Education. He has taught in primary and secondary schools and is interested in teacher education and the educational system of France. He has published in both areas including a work entitled *The French Education System* (1985).

Colin Turner is Staff Tutor at the Further Education Staff College, who works widely round the post-16 education system and occasionally in industry as a management trainer and consultant. His special interests are organisational behaviour, organisational development and interpersonal relations. He is author of a number of papers on organisation theory as applied to education institutions, including Open University texts with Colin Morgan, *Role, the Education Manager and the Individual in the Organisation* (E321.14) (1977) and *The Colleges and Schools: Provision for the 16-19 Year Old* (E222.12) (1979). He has written a book entitled *Developing Interpersonal Skills* (1983) Coombe Lodge and the following monographs, *The Netherlands: 16-19 Education* (1979) with Pippa Andrews and Russ Russell, Coombe Lodge, *Vocational Education and Training in Sweden* (1982) with Penny Rawlings, Coombe Lodge and *Vocational Education and Training in Finland* (1986), Coombe Lodge. Research publications have been

Preparing for Change (1986) and *Curriculum-led Institutional Development: Resource Material* (1987) both London, Longmans for FEU.

His professional appointments include External Examiner for M.Sc. in Education Management at Anglia College of Higher Education and Consultant to Aga Khan Education Service.

Rob Stoker works as an Educational Psychologist in North Yorkshire and until recently (May, 1989) worked in North Cleveland. His first degree was at University College, London with further professional training at the Institute of Education and the Tavistock clinic.

He has a particular interest in the area of human relations in organizations and 'irrational' aspects of management decision-making. His articles include *Systems interventions in schools – the ripple effect* (1987) for the Association of Educational Psychologists. He is an Associate Fellow of the British Psychological Society.

Index